# FOUNDATIONS OF THEOLOGY

FOUNDATIONS OF MUSIC

# Foundations of Theology

Papers from the
International Lonergan Congress 1970

*Edited by*
*Philip McShane S.J.*

University of Notre Dame Press

American edition, 1972


UNIVERSITY OF NOTRE DAME PRESS
Notre Dame, Indiana 46556


First published by
GILL AND MACMILLAN LTD
2 BELVEDERE PLACE
DUBLIN I
and in London through association with the
MACMILLAN
Group of Publishing Companies

*Jacket design by Des Fitzgerald*

Library of Congress Catalog Card Number: 76-167705

PRINTED AND BOUND IN THE REPUBLIC OF IRELAND BY THE
BOOK PRINTING DIVISION OF SMURFIT PRINT AND PACKAGING,
LIMITED, DUBLIN

# Contents

# List of Contributors

B. C. BUTLER is Auxiliary Bishop in Westminster. He has written several books of New Testament studies and on Ecclesiology, such as *The Originality of St Matthew*, *The Church and the Bible*, and *In the Light of the Council*.

JOSEPH D. COLLINS is a student of American social and religious history as a doctoral candidate at Columbia University and Union Theological Seminary, co-produces radical political feature films and is co-authoring a critical examination of the U.S. Government's *Latin American Alliance for Progress*.

FR FREDERICK E. CROWE S.J. is President of Regis College, Toronto, where he has been Professor of Theology for many years. He has edited a considerable number of Fr Lonergan's works and is author of *A Time of Change: Guidelines for the Perplexed Catholic*.

FR CHARLES E. CURRAN is Associate Professor of Moral Theology in the Catholic University of America. He is author and editor of a number of books in the area of moral theology, the latest of which is *Contemporary Problems in Moral Theology*.

CHARLES DAVIS is Professor of Religion at Sir George Williams University, Montreal, and is author of many books including *God's Grace in History* and *Christ and the World Religions*.

LANGDON GILKEY is Professor of Theology at the Divinity School of the University of Chicago. He has written a number of books including *Naming the Whirlwind: the Renewal of God-Language*, and *Religion and the Scientific Future*.

FR ALOYS GRILLMEIER S.J., Professor of Dogma and History of Dogma in the Jesuit Theological Faculty at Frankfurt, is author of such works as *Der Logos am Kreuz* and *Christ in Christian Tradition*.

GEORGE A. LINDBECK, Professor of Theology at Yale University, is an expert in both medieval thought and contemporary Roman Catholic theology. He is co-author of *The Papal Council and the Gospel* and was an official Lutheran observer at Vatican II.

FR BERNARD LONERGAN S.J., author of *Insight* as well as various treatises in theology and many articles, at present completing *Method in Theology* at Regis College, has been appointed Stillman Professor for Roman Catholic Studies at Harvard University for the year 1971–72.

FR PHILIP MCSHANE S.J. lectures in Methodology in the Milltown Institute of Theology and Philosophy, Dublin, and is author of several books including *Randomness, Statistics and Emergence* and *Music that is Soundless: An Introduction to God for the Graduate*.

FR JOHN NAVONE S.J. is Professor of Theology at the Gregorian University in Rome. His writings include *Personal Witness: A Biblical Spirituality* and *Themes from St Luke*.

HEINRICH OTT is Ordinary Professor of Systematic Theology at Basle University. He has recently published *Wirklichkeit und Glaube, I–Zum theologischen Erbe Dietrich Bonhoeffers*, 1966; and *II–Der personale Glaube*, 1969.

FR QUENTIN QUESNELL S.J., Chairman of the Department of Theology and Religious Studies and Professor of New Testament, Marquette University, Milwaukee, includes among his works *The Gospel of Christian Freedom* and *The Mind of Mark*.

FR KARL RAHNER S.J. is Professor of Dogma and History of Dogma in the theological faculty of the University of Munster. Among his many works are the volumes *Theological Investigations* and the philosophic work, recently translated, *Spirit in the World*.

FR DAVID TRACY is Assistant Professor at the University of Chicago Divinity School and writes extensively on problems of contemporary theology. His most recent work is *The Achievement of Bernard Lonergan*.

# Editorial Note

I FIND little need for elaborate editorial comment on this first volume of papers delivered at the International Lonergan Congress. The volume is most closely related to Fr Lonergan's present preoccupation with the task of providing a basic structuring and orientation of the entire theological enterprise. This volume, then, serves as a partial context for Fr Lonergan's forthcoming work, *Method in Theology*. But the possible succeeding volumes of this series will serve to keep this work in the wider relevant context of all Fr Lonergan's writings and interests.[1]

Some indication of the contents of the next two volumes may conveniently be given here:

I would like to thank the editorial committee who advised me on the selection of papers: Mr G. Barden, Mr J. Collins, Rev. F. Crowe S.J., Rev. M. Lamb, Rev. J. Navone S.J., Rev. D. Tracy, and Rev. B. Tyrrell S.J. Particular thanks are due to Mr Garrett Barden who helped me more directly as assistant editor. And of course my thanks to Michael Gill and his staff.

PHILIP McSHANE S.J.

*Footnote:*
[1]My general comment on the significance of the various works of Fr Lonergan is in fact already available in a version of the two papers I delivered at the Congress: *Plants and Pianos: Two Essays in Advanced Methodology*, Milltown Institute, Dublin 1970.

# ABBREVIATIONS USED FOR SOME OF THE WORKS OF BERNARD LONERGAN

*Insight*    *Insight: A Study of Human Understanding*, London: Longman Green and Co. 1957; revised edition 1958.

*Collection*    *Collection*, New York: Herder and Herder 1967.

*Th.N.C.*    'Theology in its New Context', *Theology of Renewal* I, ed. L. K. Shook, C.S.B., New York: Herder and Herder 1968.

*D.D.T.* I    *De Deo Trino* I, Rome: Gregorian University Press 1964.

*D.D.T.* II    *De Deo Trino* II, Rome: Greg. Univ. Press 1964. These two volumes of *De Deo Trino* constitute the last revision of *De Deo Trino Pars Analytica et Pars Synthetica*, Rome 1961, and of *Conceptio Analogica Divinarum Personarum*, Rome 1959.

*D.V.I.*    *De Verbo Incarnato (ad usum auditorum)*, Rome: Greg. Univ. Press 1964, 2nd edition.

*Func. Sp.*    'Functional Specialties in Theology', *Gregorianum* 50 (1969).[1]

*Fut. Chr.*    'The Future of Christianity', *The Holy Cross Quarterly* 2 (1969).

*Th. M.F.*    'Theology and Man's Future', *Cross Currents* 19 (1969).

*Footnote:*    1. In the first footnote to this paper Fr Lonergan mentions that it is to be the second chapter of his book *Method in Theology* (cf. below pp 162, 194). In an interview at the Florida Congress (published in *Clergy Review,* June 1971) he indicated that when the book appears, this paper will in fact be chapter five.

# Foreword

*Foundations of Theology* is the first volume of papers written for Ongoing Collaboration: The International Lonergan Congress. In this Foreword I am not going to launch into an exposition or critique of the thought of Bernard J. F. Lonergan. That was the role, in part, of the seventy-odd participants in the Congress whose papers constitute these volumes. Still others, although not in every case different persons, have written in popular and scholarly periodicals around the world of the Congress regarded as an already happened happening. Nor is it my task to introduce the contributions in these volumes. Such is the function of the Editor, Philip McShane. The most fitting role, then, for me, as the Congress Committee Chairman and as the Congress sponsor, might be to write a few words, but not a blow-by-blow chronicle, of the origins and intentions of Ongoing Collaboration.

Over two years ago, Bernard Tyrrell, a close friend and for some years my mentor in Lonergan's thought, hit upon the idea of providing the opportunity for an international group of a dozen or so Lonergan specialists to come together and share their own work and Lonergan's own recent and as yet largely unpublished developments. I at once agreed to help organise and to finance such an endeavour. David Tracy, then of Catholic University and now of the University of Chicago, joined us to become the third Congress Director. Our earliest planning sessions soon led us to feel strongly that the original idea of a group of Lonergan specialists should be expanded to include individuals who, though conversant in varying degrees with Lonergan's thought, were quite critical of it. In this way, such a gathering would not look like, nor indeed be, a school of disciples at the feet of the Unquestionable Master. Clearly anything like such worship would not be sanctioned by Lonergan himself, for when Tracy, Tyrrell and I informed Lonergan of the Congress, he made a suggestion characteristic of his modesty: call the congress 'Ongoing Collaboration' and not the 'Lonergan Congress'. The Committee compromised with 'Ongoing Collaboration: The International Lonergan Congress.' Neither Lonergan nor we wanted any form of ongoing adoration but only ongoing collaboration, and that as critical as possible.

With these non-institutional origins began what Plato, as Bernie Tyrrell continually reminded me, would have called a beautiful risk. The Congress, as we intended it, was to be an attempt at something innovative. In the course of human history there have been men of exceptional reflective abilities who develop a body of relatively systematic thought having profound and usually barely realised implications. Each such rare thinker has tended to attract and radically influence a group of students who, especially during their teacher's lifetime, are often mesmerised by his thought. Consequently these remarkably creative minds are more or less isolated and parochialised. Certainly we cannot deny their influence but we can wonder what might be the state of human ideas today if each such thinker had been criticised by persons of penetrating intellectual capabilities but who were working out of different traditions, perspectives and, not least importantly, involvements. In other words, the progress of thinking in large measure rests upon critically influencing the most notable thinkers. Most critiques of these thinkers have come only as post-mortems, even though criticism, full and fertile, must be grounded in structures of living response. At least the contemporary ease of long-distance travel should facilitate, although by itself not guarantee, creative critical collaboration.

Parallel to the lack of critical response to living seminal thinkers has been the dearth of opportunity for men and women in diverse fields to come together in serious collaboration, especially in areas of humanistic concerns. And when there have been attempts, usually a central focus has been lacking. Similarly, even in the field of philosophy in recent years 'conventions' have tended to become more and more tribal—that is, limited to a single tradition—and, therefore, perhaps rather trivial. While some of these gatherings are doubtlessly of some value for each 'in-group', basically they are without intercourse and consequently both self-starving and indigestible by more vital organisms. Certainly they seem utterly anachronistic in this self-styled ecumenical age.

The essential idea of Ongoing Collaboration: The International Lonergan Congress lay in bringing a group of men and women of diverse traditions, perspectives and involvements into a critical dialogue with a living seminal thinker, precisely thereby focusing the collaboration.

In the opinion of the conveners of Ongoing Collaboration, Bernard Lonergan offered all the prerequisite qualifications for providing the focus for such an attempt at collaboration. His extraordinary thinking is in the main so fundamental (attempting to understand human understanding in all its diverse modes and manifestations: 'Thoroughly understand what it is to understand, and not only will you understand the broad lines of all there is to be understood but also you will possess a fixed base, an invariant pattern, opening upon all further developments of understanding.'), so fundamental in fact that as a focus of collaboration his thought invited the reckoning of specialists in an unlimited variety of fields. Lonergan himself formally stated this invitation years ago in the closing paragraphs of his Introduction to *Insight*:

If I may be sanguine enough to believe that I have hit upon a set of ideas of fundamental importance, I cannot but acknowledge that I do not possess the resources to give a faultless display of their implications in the wide variety of fields in which they are relevant. I can but make the contribution of a single man and then hope that others, sensitive to the same problems, will find that my efforts shorten their own labour and that my conclusions provide a base for further developments.

Still another reason for selecting Lonergan was that his thought culminates in (and he tells us it has always been the propelling heuristic) the problematic of method—a foundational concern of any collaborative effort. Lastly, Ongoing Collaboration's focusing on Lonergan meant focusing on a thinker still alive and, most importantly, still creative and productive.

But no one should think that choosing Lonergan as focus was tantamount to an ideational mummification of Lonergan. For the focus need not be the aim. Our focus was Lonergan but our aim was 'beyond Lonergan' in the sense that hopefully Lonergan himself always has the potential of going beyond himself, as indeed has every participant in our Congress, through critical collaborative exchange. It was, therefore, the ceaseless effort of the Committee to seek out those who could and would be most critical of Lonergan—point out his personal, intellectual and cultural blindspots (Lonergan has superbly analysed the dysfunctions of blindspots and biases), undermine his assumptions, develop what he only suggests, demonstrate his thought's relevance or lack of relevance in fields little known to him, or even bring the value of his whole enterprise into question.

Our efforts were not, of course, entirely innovative. Some thirty years ago, Paul A. Schilpp, of Northwestern University, questioned 'the curious etiquette which apparently taboos the asking of questions about a philosopher's meaning while he is alive.' Accordingly, Professor Schilpp compiled in a volume the critiques of various contemporaries of Dewey's philosophy along with Dewey's own responses. Since then there have been a number of other such volumes. As much as Schilpp's efforts have improved on the traditional *Festschrift* approach (whereby a thinker was honoured by a number of his peers who contributed articles quite often only vaguely related to the thought of the subject of the *Festschrift*), Ongoing Collaboration attempted to go beyond Schilpp in making their central aim *collaboration* between a seminal thinker and those whose own work might influence his thinking or be influenced by it, through, in addition to critical papers and the focus thinker's written responses, bringing the collaborators together *in vivo*.

Early in our planning many 'sceptics' advised us that we could expect a large number of polite refusals from among our distinguished international group of invitees. We were pleasantly surprised, therefore, by the overwhelming favourable response evidencing, perhaps, a felt need for such a project. Counting on more decliners, our originally planned group of 'twenty or so' soon expanded to over seventy. With such an expansion in the number of participants I began to be concerned whether they really would be able to discuss anything in depth. During those early days my nightmares' *leitmotiv* was a crowded cocktail party of faceless people discussing the weather in six languages. Getting a large group of people together, even so-called brilliant people, guarantees nothing in itself of the quality of the interaction. For help I turned to Fr Eric O'Connor, long experienced in group cognitive endeavours, and now President of the Thomas More Institute in Montreal where over twenty years ago Lonergan was involved in adult education courses on insight. After serious consultation with his staff, Eric O'Connor advised us that the Congress was viable as long as we carefully planned our sessions into several small group discussions (never more than eleven participants per group) with experienced, stimulating discussion moderators. During the course of the following year the Thomas More Institute staff contributed many hours of consultation with us in developing a most varied and lively four-day schedule for the Congress. The success of Ongoing Collaboration was in no small measure due to this cooperation.

Another ingredient in the planning derived largely from my firm conviction that lecture presentations constitute an unbeatable means for destroying dialogue and indeed for simultaneously putting large numbers of minds into a comatose condition. The plan of the Congress, therefore, was that each participant would finish six weeks in advance his written response to some aspect of Lonergan's thought, which in turn could be xeroxed and distributed to all the other participants for advance reading. Eric O'Connor and Cathleen Going, also of the Thomas More Institute, organised the writing of excerpts of the seventy-odd papers in order to further facilitate discussions. Still another organisational ingredient, unique to Ongoing Collaboration, I believe, was possible through the generous donation by Sister de la Croix of the facilities of Marymount College in Boca Raton, Florida. Congress participants had the opportunity of spending a few informal days together before the actual Congress, which greatly helped make for relaxed interaction at the actual Congress. A similarly hospitable and verdant ambience for the Congress was provided by St Leo College, Florida. We are grateful to the College President, Anthony Zaitz, and to Fr Robert Fucheck and the other monks of the nearby St Leo Abbey for much practical assistance in addition to their generous hospitality. Here allow me also to publicly communicate my personal thanks and that of all the participants to William Dodd, Walter Conn, Peter Elly, Brian Grogan and my indefatigable secretary Marguerite (Meg) McKenna for their dedicated assistance with many details of the forming and directing of the Congress.

The actual event of the Congress more than fulfilled the expectations of the Congress conveners. Lonergan himself was in excellent spirits and showed himself to be remarkably ahead of a number of critiques and open to further development. I, who had been so sceptical about the possibility of real exchange in discussions, found myself witnessing surprisingly non-defensive discussions of theoretical questions, even by persons long identified with particular positions. Kenneth Rexroth perhaps best captures in words what was the experience of authentic collaboration on the part of all the participants. I would like to quote his description from an article in the *Antioch Review* especially since he came to the Congress sceptically and reluctantly (I had to persuade him during two eleventh-hour cross-country phone calls not to cancel his earlier agreement to come):

It was a realisation of the spirit of Pope John, an infra- and inter-subjective noumenous happening, ultimately unanalysable into any taxonomy. This was the big event, the important thing . . . set up modes of discussion which created an atmosphere not unlike that of an ideal Quaker ashram or Benedictine retreat . . . The all-pervasive atmosphere of a creative community of agapé, of affection, respect, the meetings turned into conversations 'unprogrammed' as Quakers say. The conversations were lively enough, but their foundations were no longer contention but contemplation . . . The atmosphere of comradeship and joy was an outward sign of an inner spiritual reality. It was a meeting in interiority. It was not necessary finally to argue about 'infra- and inter-subjectivity.' The meeting of persons was apparent. If the Conference was the most important thing since Vatican II, this is why it was.

The publishing of these volumes of the papers of Ongoing Collaboration constitutes part of the collaboration. In Lonergan's responses to the papers included in each volume he shows in part how he has been affected by the other Congress participants. The papers should be of particular interest to all students of Lonergan's thought. The publishing of the papers and Lonergan's responses should make possible continued collaboration in ever wider circles. Without the creative and painstaking work of Philip McShane, the Editor of these volumes, and the assistance of all the advisory editors, as well as the genuine interest in the project shown by the publisher Michael Gill, this aspect of Ongoing Collaboration might never have become a reality.

Many times since the Congress I have been asked in one form or another: 'What did the Congress all amount to? What were the results?' Such questions inevitably remind me of a journalist, famed for his coverage of Vatican II, who observed Ongoing Collaboration. On the last day of the Congress this somewhat frustrated man nearly pleaded with some of the group to 'come up with a blueprint for the future'. 'Can't you give us something of a new Constitution for the Church in the modern world?'

This journalist reflected the mentality of the many consensus-seeking theologians at the recent Concilium Conference in Brussels who apparently believe that the raising of a question is fruitful only if it leads to a formula on which all can agree. Such a mentality was hardly that of Ongoing Collaboration. Carl Braaten, one of the participants, makes a similar point in an article in *The Lutheran World:* 'One could not help but contrast (Ongoing Collaboration) with the ecumenical wastelands where delegates picked for long and loyal service to the establishment gather to whack away at a tired agenda prepared by bureaucrats with an eye to tangible dividends for their shaky institutions.' Ongoing Collaboration was neither institution-conceived nor institution-minded. Ongoing Collaboration was more in the spirit of Lonergan's own emphasis on ceaseless questioning. Yes, radical openness to the new, eros for truth, mutual influences felt by all the participants and perhaps a new paradigm for future gatherings, but there were no 'answers'.

Certainly there is something good and beautiful in the happening of this Congress. That should be more than clear from Kenneth Rexroth's description. Yet in all sincerity I find a large part of my spirit still questioning the meaning of it all. The meaning of it all beyond an unconditioned gift to my rare friend Bernie Tyrrell. The meaning of it all beyond a richly deserved tribute to a man who in years-long labour with little worldly recognition, has never hesitated to open any door of the mind, even when such inquiry meant that he must walk through and out of many a comfortable dwelling. The meaning of it all beyond some possible revisions in the thinking of this man or of some of the other participants. And assuredly the meaning of it all beyond the creation of more volumes for our libraries. Maybe because I am post-World War II, a member of the 'Now Generation', I am too impatient with myself and others, intellectuals and academics who treat ideas as ends in themselves or as *objets d'art* and who, pampered (or better, made harmless) by the powerful and affluent few, continue to play with ourselves while the majority of men are brutally deprived of basic human dignities and are individually and institutionally victimised by their 'fellow men'. Do we intellectuals do our intellectual thing simply to distract ourselves from the dizzying emptiness of not knowing what to do and yet knowing all too well that something ought to be done?

One of the Congress participants, Daniel Berrigan, S.J., was prevented from being with us during the Congress because his resistance to imperialist wars and his assaults on American social amnesia made him an outlaw, passionately and vengefully sought after by the F.B.I. and the Federal Prison which at this moment imprisons his body but not his spirit. Berrigan's paper was delayed until after the Congress, ironically by a Post Office workers' strike. I shared xeroxed copies of this paper with F.B.I. agents who several times burst in upon me in my Manhattan home hoping to capture this dangerous criminal. In his paper Dan Berrigan questioned whether the Congress be 'the spirit of inquiry cut loose from the actual fate to which most men today are condemned'. Addressing himself directly to the participants, he declared,

It is not only intellectuals who question one another in the course of such a congress as yours. It is man himself, assailed in his very power of survival, victimised and without recourse, who questions you. Between a federal prison and the scene of your Congress a great gulf is opened. The press of the world will dutifully report your insights; the forces of government, if given the opportunity, will applaud them. In the measure that your inquiries remain platonic and abstract, you will threaten no power or domination . . . Intellectuals, it must be said, are often skilled in tolerating the intolerable. They go along with the public drift of things, as long as their personal immunities and privileges remain intact.

The significance in Ongoing Collaboration I ask for, then, is simply this: Has this Congress made us any less tolerant of the intolerable?

JOSEPH D. COLLINS

Columbia University
*2 November 1970*

# Lonergan and Ecclesiology

## B. C. BUTLER.

THE difficulty of the task before me is not to be underestimated. I am asked to consider what light the thought of Lonergan throws, or may be expected to throw, on the Church; the actual or possible connection between that thought and ecclesiology. And the first difficulty is: understanding Lonergan. Lonergan has spoken of this difficulty in relation to the task of interpreting Aquinas.

The temptation of the manual writer is to yield to the conceptualist illusion; to think that to interpret Aquinas he has merely to quote and then argue; to forget that there does exist an initial and enormous problem of developing one's understanding; to overlook the fact that, if he is content with the understanding he has and the concepts it utters, then all he can do is express his own incomprehension in the words but without the meaning uttered by the understanding of Aquinas.[1]

I cannot claim with confidence that I have understood Lonergan. I know not how many times I have read *Insight*. I think I understand to some extent the main lines of his argument. I feel sure that I can recognise gross deformations of his thought when they are propounded by others. I am not so sure of the correctness of my own interpretation. But I am personally comforted by some remarks which I have translated from Lonergan's *Conceptio Analogica Divinarum Personarum* (p. 13):

We should not underestimate or despise the benefit obtained by one who makes a real effort of theological understanding without actually attaining his goal. His effort will lead him to attend to everything that can bring him to such understanding, i.e. to divine revelation and the faith-teaching of the Church. And there is much fruit to be gained from a serious, prolonged and accurate consideration of revelation and

I

its consequences. So it is wrong to suppose that such a man is wasting his time unless he reaches the goal of an understanding of the revealed mysteries.

Something analogous can obviously be said of the man who tries, without success, to understand the thought of Lonergan himself. He himself speaks of the benefit of his long years of study of Aquinas: 'After spending years reaching up to the mind of Aquinas, I came to a twofold conclusion. On the one hand, that reaching had changed me profoundly. On the other hand, that change was the essential benefit.'[2] Lonergan can claim not only to have tried, but to have succeeded in his effort, to understand Aquinas, and I do not claim to have understood Lonergan. But I can state that the effort to do so has changed me profoundly, and I can affirm the benefit of that change.

A second difficulty is that my chief attraction to Lonergan is at the level of philosophy, not of theology. It is *Insight* that has changed me and benefited me so profoundly. And *Insight* is a work of philosophy, not of theology. Only in the chapter on Special Transcendent Knowledge, if we omit the Epilogue, does *Insight* come to the brink of theology. And even there Lonergan merely affirms the existence of the 'solution' to the problem of evil, which solution, in the Epilogue, is by implication identified with the Catholic religion.

Indeed, and it is my third difficulty, I know no very significant part of his published work in which Lonergan explicitly takes ecclesiology as his subject. One cannot therefore expound his teaching on the Church; one can only suggest something of what it might be. Ecclesiology can be approached from several starting-points. You can study the Bible, to find in it the doctrine of the People of God. You can move on to find Jesus speaking of the little flock to whom it is God's good pleasure to give the Kingdom. You can examine the two gospel texts which actually use the word Church. You can move on to the Acts of the Apostles, to the Pauline corpus with its notion of the faithful as comprising the body of Christ, and so to the rest of the New Testament. Then you can turn your attention to Church history, hoping to discern within the traditions which it contains the golden vein of the sacred tradition which is the gospel transmitted. In this way you can build up a heuristic structure, indeed can to some extent fill it in with a concept of the Church. And at length you can turn to the contemporary scene and, using your structure and your concept as clues, you can identify the Church with the Catholic communion centred in the see of Rome. This point reached, it is of course likely that you will have to go back to revise your understanding of Christian history and even your exegesis of Scripture in the light of the present Church's self-knowledge and self-presentation. Secondly, you can begin not with the Bible and past history but with the Church as she 'subsists in the Catholic Church' today, seeking to understand her and only then going back to read the Bible and Chrisian history in the light of that understanding. To some extent, this is what Newman did in his *Essay on Development*. Contemporary Christianity had its own shape, palpable and undeniable. When one turns back to the Bible, one is bound to conclude that either original Christianity has ceased to exist, or else there must be allowed the possibility of a development of the original gospel. This notion of development gives Newman a clue to the understanding of Christian history, and the clue leads him irresistibly to the Catholic communion as the contemporary embodiment of the Church Christ founded. Both these starting-points assume the truth of the Christian gospel. It can be argued that a more comprehensive ecclesiology could take its start not from this assumption but from the philosophic view of reality which can be reached without appeal *a priori* to revelation. You can, in other words, seek to determine the structure, conditions and implications of human knowing. You can reflect that, since *quicquid recipitur secundum modum recipientis recipitur*, the structure of the real must be isomorphic with the structure of human knowing—it being certain that knowing is knowing being and so transcending subjectivity in the objectivity of the judgement. You can, within these general conclusions, build up with the help of modern science and its twin systems of classical and statistical laws an immensely strong case for the hypothesis that we live in a universe of emergent propability. At this point, after a necessary excursion into the field of ethics, you can move on from the metaphysics of proportionate being to general transcendent knowledge and, at length, affirm the existence of God, the unrestricted act of understanding and self-understanding. Arrived at this point, you find yourself faced with the problem of evil and, according to Lonergan, with the certainty that God, in his goodness, will have provided a solution.

I need not give a detailed account of the heuristic structure whereby Lonergan holds that the solution can be identified. It is, however, sufficiently obvious that anyone who has followed and accepted his argumentation will, at the end of it, face an obligation—if he is not already a Catholic—to make contact with a Catholic priest and seek admission to the Church.

What I wish to do here is, firstly, to mention a necessary limitation involved in this method of discovering the Church. The solution sought is that which corresponds to the problem posed. That problem is the problem of evil. The solution will therefore be a scheme of redemption. It does not, however, follow that the solution will, in its concrete nature, be exclusively or even primarily a scheme of redemption. In a detective story the culprit to be discovered must satisfy the clues that have been provided. But, when discovered, he may be found to have also all sorts of characteristics which are not foreseen by the clues. The clues may direct one to a man who is left-handed, endowed with a subtle sense of the comic, and suffering from acute financial difficulties. But the culprit, when identified, besides satisfying these requirements, may prove to be also a man with a taste for Chinese antiques and a strong love of children. So too, that which is the solution of the problem of evil may in fact be also, in itself and prescinding from the problem of evil, the culmination of the whole cosmic process, related indeed to sin but even more profoundly related to the whole finality of the universe.

Secondly, let us underline some of the elements of the heuristic structure which may be specially relevant to an ecclesiology.
(1) 'The solution will be universally accessible and permanent.'[3] After the fall of our first parents God 'ceaselessly kept the human race in his care, in order to give eternal life to those who perseveringly do good in search of salvation.'[4] 'At all times and among every people, God has given welcome to whosoever fears him and does what is right.'[5] 'Those also can attain to everlasting salvation who through no fault of their own do not know the gospel of Christ or his Church . . . Nor does divine Providence deny the help necessary for salvation to those who, without blame on their part, have not yet arrived at an explicit knowledge of God.'[6] If, then, we are to maintain the principle that *extra*

*ecclesiam nulla salus*, we shall have to broaden out the traditional concept of the Church beyond the limits of the Catholic communion. And, since the solution has 'to come to men through their apprehension and with their consent'[7] we appear to require some theology of death on the lines of *The Moment of Truth* by L. Boros (London 1965).

(2) 'The solution will be a harmonious continuation of the actual order of the universe. For there are no divine afterthoughts.'[8]

(3) Since the problem arises 'because man's living is prior to learning and being persuaded', therefore the solution must 'reverse this priority' by providing intellect, will and sensitivity with forms or habits that are 'operative throughout living', and these forms or habits will be at least relatively supernatural.[9] They will constitute a new and higher integration of human activity, and they will pertain to 'system on the move'.

(4) The emergence of the solution will 'be in accord with the probabilities' in a universe of emergent probability. But, in view of the unpreparedness of men in various stages of history and development for the full solution, we need to suppose 'an emergent trend in which the full solution becomes effectively probable'. (I take it that this refers, in the concrete, to the Old Dispensation as paving the way for the New, and finding its apogee in Mary in whom the two dispensations overlap. There is a problem here of *causae inter se*, or to put it another way, the problem of generation in general: a new form presupposes a disposition to receive it, but the *ultima dispositio* is logically posterior, in at least one aspect, to the new form itself.)

(5) 'The solution, in its cognitional aspect, will consist in a new and higher collaboration of men in the pursuit of truth' and 'because the solution meets a problem of error, the new and higher collaboration in the pursuit of truth will provide an antidote to the errors to which man is inclined.'[10] If one reflects on this, it is likely that one will conclude that the higher collaboration in question will include some teaching authority, guaranteed by divine assistance against the proneness of man to error; it being observed that the solution takes root in a single act of assent by the believer, but grows by degrees in a mentality which has been and remains subject to the general context of human error. As is pointed out later, the act of faith is an assent of intellect to truths transmitted through the collaboration.

(6) The believer will collaborate with the solution, and since the solution is for all men and is universally accessible, there will be 'a collaboration that consists in making known to others the good news of the solution and its nature'.[12]

(7) The solution 'must penetrate to the sensitive level and envelop it'[13] and this because man remains not only intelligent but also both dramatic and practical, as also because man's intellectual life needs the support and cooperation of his sensitive and imaginative life. We need both the sign of intelligible contents and the symbol of man's orientation into the known unknown. The solution, then, will be 'a mystery that is at once symbol of the uncomprehended and sign of what is grasped', and this mystery must be embodied in a true history.

(8) The solution need not be, but it may be, 'absolutely supernatural', taking man up into a dispensation which, while it satisfies the requirements for the solution of the problem, takes him further to a destined end which is strictly incommensurate with his nature, though not of course in contradiction to it. If this hypothesis is realised, as of course it is and as Lonergan believes it to be, then 'to be just a man is what man cannot be'.[14] In consequence, there is bound to be tension between the solution and a humanism in revolt against it.

(9) In view of the probability of heresies and schisms, the preservation of the solution, certain because it is God's solution, but to be realised 'through human channels and in accord with the probabilities', will be effected through some appropriate institutional organisation of the new and higher collaboration.[15]

(10) The new collaboration will not be merely at the cognitional level, but will 'link in charity' actual human beings in their full concreteness, 'living human bodies' says Lonergan, to the performance of the task set by the actual world order.[16]

From all this it seems clear that, once the identification of the solution indicated by the heuristic structure has been carried out, the solution will be seen to be 'Christ' in the Augustinian sense of that term, i.e. Jesus Christ together with his members; or to put the matter the reverse way, the solution is the Church as including Jesus Christ its first member. But the solution as it exists at the present moment of history will be the Church in the more ordinary sense of that term, excluding not only its deceased members but also those not yet born into it. The

Church, taken in this latter restricted sense, cannot of course be understood without reference to its past history (including Christ its origin) and to its future as that future can be prospectively foreseen in history; nor must we forget the eschatological consummation introducing the 'new heavens and the new earth'.

I wish to suggest that the kind of ecclesiology that will arise naturally out of this Lonerganian scheme of thought must be profoundly empirical in its starting-point. Theology is a systematised set of understandings, acts of understanding, and readers of *Insight* will remember that the text for the whole book is a quotation from the *De Anima* (III, 7) of Aristotle: 'Understanding understands the forms in the phantasms'; and every philosopher will know that, for Aristotle, the phantasms depend on sense data. With such a starting-point we are bound to arrive at an ecclesiology far removed from the 'non-historical orthodoxy' of which Michael Novak speaks in his *The Open Church*, or the 'anti-historical immobilism' of which Lonergan prefers to speak.[17] And since it will be an ecclesiology not of some ideal Platonic Church 'in the heavens', but of the actual Church in its historical reality, and since that Church, embodying for each period of history and for every human context a solution which is in continuity with the order of an emergent probability, is a system on the move, therefore the ecclesiology will have a great flexibility and an openness which can allow for surprising changes and unpredictable novelty. An order of emergent probability rests on the reality of non-systematic process, and non-systematic process 'can be the womb of novelty'.[18] 'Within a large non-systematic process there can be built a pyramid of schemes resting on schemes in a splendid ascent of novelty and creativeness.'[19] And this is more manifestly true when we have reached, in the ascending order of schemes, the human level, since in man intelligibility has risen to the level of intelligence and 'inquiry and insight are not so much a higher system as a perennial source of higher systems . . . Sensation supposes sense organs; but understanding is not another type of sensation with another sense organ; it operates with respect to the content of sensation and imagination; it represents a still further degree of freedom'.[20] This higher freedom of man is not only presupposed by the solution, i.e. by Christ and the Church, but—since the order introduced by the solution is in continuation with the order

which created the problem, and development is in the direction
of ever greater freedom—will be enhanced by the advent of the
solution. The gospel comes not to destroy life but to bring life
more abundant.

The element of unpredictable novelty in Christian history for
which our ecclesiology will have to make room not only means
that *les portes de l'avenir sont toujours grand-ouvertes*; it means that
we can look back with a critical eye on the past history of the
Church. If you combine Newman's theory of development with
a deterministic attitude to law, you may easily conclude that
since a certain development has taken place in the Church, not
only is it to be accepted as valid but all theoretical alternatives
to it are to be excluded as contradictory of the gospel. You may
find yourself saying that, because in fact the Church moved
away from its Jewish matrix to the culture of the Roman-
Hellenic empire, therefore Christian theology could only have
developed on Greek lines. I would wish to say that, if there is
any element of truth in this assertion, it derives not from the
historical and contingent fact that the Church moved on the
whole westwards and not eastwards from Palestine, but from the
fact that Hellenic philosophy had in principle started man off on
the journey to a fully critical epistemology and metaphysics; the
inevitability arose, in other words, not from Christian history
but from philosophic necessity. On the other hand, the growing
papalism of the Church from Damasus onwards is a historical
development which can be looked upon as wholly explicable by
external and contingent factors operating on Christian history;
things could have worked out otherwise, and perhaps better.
And this critical attitude to past history was in fact, if unthemati-
cally, sanctioned by the procedures of Vatican II, looking back
behind scholasticism and the Fathers to the Bible, and through
the Bible to Jesus Christ, for the source and criterion of the
Church's renewal.

I say 'source and criterion'. For if it is right to affirm the gospel
as a womb of novelty, it has also to be remembered that there
are limits within which freedom can effectively and properly
operate. In the general case of emergent probability, development
can only take place within the limits of the concrete idea of being
—broad enough limits no doubt, but sufficient to save us from
the notion of a world of sheer irrationality. These limits will of

course hold also for development within the Church. But since the Church is a particular and universal solution to a universal and particular problem, the problem of evil, her development must be subject to the further and more specific limits of the solution as incarnate in Jesus Christ. As we have seen, the mystery which is the inner heart of the solution must have its sensible component, and this component must be not myth but history.[21] Jesus Christ, according to the Christian tradition, is himself the 'word' of God, the divine answer to a human question which was humanly unanswerable. Our heuristic structure could not by itself assure us that the solution would be God personally involved as man in human history; that we learn after we have identified the solution. But having learnt it, and having realised that as man Jesus had a historical beginning and a historical end, we can see at once that the Jesus of history is permanently normative for the Christian religion.

Here again, however, the principle intervenes: *quicquid recipitur secundum modum recipientis recipitur.* While Jesus Christ in himself is the *hapax*, the once-and-for-all, our understanding of him will develop; and it will be the corporate understanding of the human collaboration in which the solution takes on substance and remains for ever contemporary. And at once we are faced with those problems of interpretation, translation, or hermeneutics about which *Insight* has much to say in another context.[22] Lonergan dismisses one theory of interpretation with the sardonic comment that, pushed to its logical conclusion, it would make interpretation's goal the production of a fully scientific critical text of, for instance, Plato's works—whereupon, of course, the task of interpretation would be not at its end but in fact only at its starting-point. There is a warning here for the biblical theologians. To take one example: biblical theology can work out the biblical notion of collective personality, which finds its apogee in the biblical figures of the first and the second Adams. But, after all, at the end of this process of reconstruction, we are only at the beginning of the necessary effort to understand what these figures and this notion can mean for us—and what they must mean when we attempt to reach a universal view-point. I think that Lonergan has, by implication, made his point that the Church cannot get on without a metaphysic which, while not itself derived from revelation necessarily, is yet critically established and irrefutable—whether this metaphysic be implicit or, as is ideally required, also explicit. This thesis will be unwelcome to many at this time of prejudice against all metaphysics and especially against a metaphysically based theology. But welcome or not, it must stand.

The need of interpretation, coupled with the certain fact that divine assistance has provided the Church with an institutional safeguard for its essential message, has led in the course of time to the formulation of definitions of faith which, if emanating from the pope, satisfy the conditions laid down by Vatican I, and if from an ecumenical council, satisfy analogous conditions. In an article, 'The Assumption and Theology', first published in 1948 and reprinted in 1967 in *Collection*, Lonergan by implication accepts the classical theological view that such definitions are both certainly true and irreformable. So far as I know he nowhere gives his reason for this view. I suggest that an argument can be worked out on the following lines: the solution is something that the world of proportionate being needs but is incapable of providing from its own resources. It is therefore a two-sided thing. It comes from 'beyond' and its preservation is implicitly guaranteed by the fact that it is the divine response to an abiding problem. But it is only a solution because it can be, and is, incorporated into human experience and is freely accepted by responsible men; from being transcendent, and without ceasing to be transcendent, it becomes also 'immanent' in the responsible freedom of human living. Statistically, it is inevitable that heresies and schisms will be born of this interaction between a divine intervention and human freedom. But philosophy, anticipating the verdict of faith, gives us certainty that nevertheless the solution will survive in its fullness and in its permanent availability. This permanence and permanent availability, granting the continuity between human life under the problem and human life with the solution, entail the existence of an institutionalised collaboration of believers.

If, now, the institutional organisation were liable to mis-state the fundamental requirements of full participation in the collaboration, the solution in its fullness would cease to be available to man's reasonable and reflective acceptance; and it would thus be incapable of fulfilling its role as the divine solution of the basic human problem. It follows that, when the institutional organisation imposes the acceptance of a dogma as a condition *sine qua non* of full membership of the collaboration, that dogma carries the full authority of the solution itself.

Two reflections may be in order here. It is obvious that infallibility, as above justified, is restricted to matters that either form part of the permanent solution itself (or, to transpose into Christian language, are part and parcel of the original Christian revelation) or are so profoundly entailed by the truth of the solution that they cannot be denied without undermining the revelation itself.

Secondly, there is a question of recognising in any given case the commitment of the organisation to a particular dogma or alleged dogma. Theologians may be called upon, in view of our present understanding of the Church's self-transcendence in the non-Catholic Christian bodies, to justify the affirmation that, for instance (and it is a crucial instance) the definition of papal infallibility by Vatican I was in fact the commitment of the Church as a whole, and not merely of the Roman Catholic communion. I myself think that the answer to this question is already given when it is realised that the fullness of the solution is necessarily bound up with the permanence of a full collaboration, or in Christian language of a 'perfect communion'. But it is an issue which will have to be fully argued out in ecumenical circles.

I want now to pass on to another aspect of ecclesiology where it is possible that Lonergan's thought may be of help to us. We have seen that, since the solution must 'penetrate to the sensitive level and envelop it', the solution will take shape as a sign and symbol. This appears to me to mean that the Church must be essentially sacramental, with a sacramentality of efficacious sign. This sacramentality will be pervasive of every aspect of the solution. It will be remembered that the solution is one, universal and permanent. It is also, in its inner core, something resident in the will and intellect of men. In order that it may remain one, it must be transmitted from man to man and from generation to generation. But, in the order of things, such transmission or communication involves language or, more generally, signs. It is through signs that the collaboration is itself constituted, and by them it is maintained.

A problem left over by Vatican II is the more accurate

determination of the relations obtaining between the juridical and the sacramental aspects of the Church; and in particular the relations between the papacy and the aspect of the Church as sacramental. I suggest that, if we take the implicit ecclesiology of Lonergan seriously, it is necessary to subsume the papacy under the general notion of the Church's sacramentality. This sacramentality is assured, at key points in the Church's structure, by the seven sacraments. There is, however, no sacramental rite by which the papal office is conferred on one who is already a bishop; and in the case of a non-bishop elected to the papacy, the rite by which he becomes bishop of Rome is identical with the rite by which a man becomes bishop of any other see. I cannot understand how the papacy can be kept within the sacramental order of the Church except on the supposition that episcopal consecration, of its nature, incorporates a man into the episcopal college as that college is structured with the papacy at its head. Thus there is no need for a special 'papal sacrament' since the papacy is already part of that to which episcopal consecration incorporates a man. On the other hand, there will then be no papal powers which are not already implicit in the idea of the episcopal college. As is maintained, for instance, by Rahner, the pope, even when he acts *seorsim* (*Nota praevia*) is still acting as head of the college.

The fact that the collaboration, the Church, is constituted and maintained by signs may serve as an introduction to some thoughts of Lonergan which go beyond the limits which he set himself in *Insight*. In that work he was constructing an epistemology and a metaphysic which prescinded from particular human viewpoints. The book, if true, is true for man in every age and of every culture. In some more recent work Lonergan has taken his stand with us at the particular stage of human historical development in which we are all involved, and he has moved more explicitly from the notion of man as a substance to that of man as a subject, man as he makes his own environment and as he makes himself. This distinction, between man the substance and man the subject is worked out in 'Existenz and Aggiornamento'[23] and in *The Subject*, 1968. The importance of this work in the general development of Lonergan's thought need not here be emphasised. What I would wish to do is to suggest some of its relevance for post-Vatican II ecclesiology.

That council was more concerned with the historical Church than with improving the classical definition of the Church, above all in the 'Constitution on the Church in the Modern World' in which it sought to locate the Church in its contemporary milieu. What is emphasised in this Constitution is the accelerated change that marks the present age of world history. This process of change is not dictated by rapid changes in man's material environment. It is the result of man's own growing impact on that environment and on his growing control of it and of his own life processes. A very simple example of this might be the improvements in medicine with their effect upon the growth of the world population and the innumerable problems which stem from this. More and more man is becoming the artificer of his own world, and the man-induced changes in the environment, in social structures and in the sphere of culture are having their reaction upon man himself:

These changes recoil upon him [man himself], upon his decisions and desires, both individual and collective, and upon his manner of thinking and acting with respect to things and to people. Hence we can already speak of a true social and cultural transformation, one which has repercussions on man's religious life as well.[24]

Drawing out his distinction between man as substance and man as subject, Lonergan says that, as substance, man is 'always the same'. But he is also subject, and 'the being of the subject is becoming. One becomes oneself'. And in this developing process, 'the subject has more and more to do with his own development', until he reaches the point at which he realises that it is 'up to himself to decide what he is to make of himself'. He has in effect been making himself all along; but now the time has come when, open-eyed and deliberate, he decides what he is to be: autonomy decides what autonomy is to be. And 'this critical point is never transcended . . . Today's resolutions do not predetermine the free choice of tomorrow'.

The process of deliberate self-making is set within not only 'a first world of immediacy', that of immediate sense-experience of the world of which through one's body one is a part, but also within a second world 'mediated by meaning'—the world which transcends our immediate experience and is communicated to us by meaningful signs in the total language of humanity. This is

3

a world which we know 'intelligently and rationally, and it is
not ideal but real', though it includes a great deal that is to be
classified as fiction or myth. It is only in this second world that
we can be (in the full sense realisable in this life) 'free self-
constituting' subjects in a freely constituted world; but this only
in so far as the world 'mediated by meaning' is being transformed
into 'the world constituted by meaning, the properly human
world, the world of community', which is 'the product of
self-constituting subjects'. 'John XXIII affirmed that freedom is
constitutive of human nature.'[25]

If you ask me what all this has to do with ecclesiology, I would
point to the word 'community' in my penultimate quotation,
and then remind you that for Lonergan the Church is a
'collaboration', and that for Vatican II it is a 'communion'
subsisting in the 'complete communion' of the Catholic Church.
If now we turn our attention to the Catholic Church as a
historical datum, it is clear that it is largely composed of members
who have not yet effectively become subjects. A large proportion
of them are infants; a large proportion form the student population of our primary parochial schools. And of those who are
adults in age, how many are covered by Lonergan's description
of 'the drifter':

The drifter has not yet found himself; he has not yet discovered his
own deed and so is content to do what everyone else is doing; . . . he
has not yet discovered his own mind and so he is content to think and
say what everyone else is thinking and saying; and the others too are
apt to be drifters . . .[26]

And, so far as one is a drifter, one is 'unauthentic'. What I am is
one thing, what a genuine Catholic happens to be is another,
'and I am unaware of the difference'. Are not drifting and
unauthenticity the reason why, when large numbers of Catholics
migrate from a Catholic culture like that of Ireland to a non-
Catholic culture, there is a high fall-out of lapsers? Is not drifting
partly the explanation of the number of Catholics who are
losing contact with the Church at the present time?

Yet by definition the Church is a *societas fidelium*, a community
of believers. And the faith which makes one a believer is
essentially a free and responsible act and habit, an 'obedience by
which man entrusts his whole self freely to God, offering "the

full submission of intellect and will to God who reveals," and freely assenting to the truth revealed by him'.[27] If freedom is constitutive of human nature, it is not less true that responsible freedom in its members is of the essence of the Church.

These considerations lead one to reflect that the Church's true mind cannot be equated with the sum-total of the opinions held by her members. From the point of view of evidential value there must be a vast difference between the passively received opinions of the immature, together with the irresponsible fancies of drifters, and the tenets of those who have faced and responded positively to the challenge of the critical point 'when the subject finds out for himself that it is up to himself to decide what he is to make of himself'. And we must not forget that 'the critical point is never transcended . . . What is to be achieved can be ever expanding, deepening. To meet one challenge is to effect a development that reveals a further and graver challenge'.[28]

While therefore it is true that there is an infallibility *in credendo* that takes shape in the *sensus fidelium*, it is manifest that there is no straightforward way to determine what the real *sensus fidelium* is. All one can say is that the mind of the Church will usually disclose itself only very slowly; and of course its ultimate articulation will remain the task of the episcopal college. As a rider to these reflections it may be added that the conditions for the development of a healthy *sensus fidelium* will be an atmosphere of responsible freedom which the Church has not always fostered very vigorously. The challenge of Vatican II is a call to allow us to grow up and a call to us all to grow up ourselves. This challenge is urgent in a world where education is spreading with unexampled rapidity and extension.

Man has always been a subject. But our 'new conceptual apparatus' is an effect and a cause of our new reflective realisation of this fact: 'Without repudiating the analysis of man into body and soul', without denying that man is a substance, 'it adds the richer and more concrete apprehension of man as incarnate subject'.[29] And when man is apprehended as incarnate subject, the study of history moves into its own place at the centre of the stage, and ecclesiology, for its part, has to move from a study of eternal essences and an unchanging divine law to the study of the Church in its actual duration.

That these considerations are relevant to the present day is one of the lessons that can be learnt from Lonergan's paper, 'Dimensions of Meaning'.[30] The world constituted by meaning can be 'controlled',[31] and by a change of control a whole culture can be affected, and in the end destroyed or created. We are living in an epoch in which the classical culture that finds its roots in Greek philosophy has 'broken down'.[32] The new culture which is still coming to birth, or rather, already born, is still extending its conquest of the field of human meaning, 'makes thematic . . . the vertical liberty by which we may emerge out of . . . prepersonal response to become freely and responsibly, resolutely yet precariously, the persons we choose to be. . .' The effort to understand, at the root of this cultural transition, is not enough. There is needed judgement, and the effort to judge meaning still lags behind. 'Judging and deciding', in our modern world, 'are left to the individual, and he finds his plight desperate. There is far too much to be learnt before he could begin to judge. Yet judge he must and decide he must if he is to exist, if he is to be a man.' Catholic philosophy and Catholic theology are matters, 'not of revelation only but of culture also.' Hence they are faced today with 'the gravest problems, mountainous tasks', and are invited to 'herculean labours'. Some will attempt to evade these problems, others will be tempted to wild and erroneous solutions of them. 'But what will count is a perhaps not numerous centre, big enough to be at home in both the old and the new, painstaking enough to work out one by one the transitions to be made, strong enough to refuse half-measures and insist on complete solutions even though it has to wait.'[33]

Such a 'centre' can hardly be found outside the ranks of those who have accepted the responsibility of making themselves in freedom and in obedience to reason. 'If our renewed theology is not to be the dupe of every fashion, it needs a firm basis and a critical stance.' The new foundation will have to be 'the subject', not indeed 'as scientist' but as theologian. And one becomes a subject—such is the message of 'Theology in its New Context'— by a 'conversion' which is in principle radical: 'The convert apprehends differently, values differently, relates differently because he has become different. The new apprehension is . . . not new values so much as a transvaluation of values.' Conversion is personal, but 'it can happen to many and they can form a community to sustain one another in self-transformation, and to help one another in working out the implications, and in fulfilling the promise of their new life. Finally, what can become communal can become historical. It can pass from generation to generation. It can spread from one cultural milieu to another. It can adapt to changing circumstances, confront new situations, survive into a different age, flourish in another period or epoch.'[34] What Lonergan is here describing, in a passage that reminds one of a famous passage in Newman's *Essay on Development*, is the origin and development of the Church. 'Religion', he says, 'is conversion in its preparation, in its occurrence, in its development, in its consequents, and alas in its incompleteness, its failures, its breakdowns, its disintegration.' And he goes on to infer that theology should be reflection upon conversion, and it is in such reflection that we can hope to reach a foundation for a renewed theology.

But, if conversion is the foundation of religion and reflection on conversion the foundation of theology, we are brought back to the fact that the Church is, materially speaking, much more than a community of the converted. As already indicated, it contains a large number of the immature, and a large number of drifters. It has been one of its historical characteristics that it has baptised infants and has refused to turn itself into a sect of saints. It follows that theology has to apply its own dialectic to the data for a renewed ecclesiology. It also seems to me to follow that the theology that will matter for the future will be the reflection of men who are themselves 'authentic' and 'converted'.

What has all this to do with ecclesiology? Have I not been talking about ecclesiologists rather than their science? But such considerations can lead one on to the question of the place of the theologian in the Church. This place can be overlooked in an ecclesiology of ideal essences, for there is no divinely established *ordo theologorum*. Theologians are rather to be looked for among the 'charismatics' of whom *Lumen Gentium* speaks in the chapter on the People of God. As I have elsewhere tried to explain, if the sacramental structure of the Church, within which falls the teaching office of the episcopal college and its head, is 'the static element in the Church, as it were the supernatural skeleton of the mystical body',[35] the dynamic element comes from the Church's charismatic life. It is for a new dynamism in our thinking that we look today to the theologians, and one of the tasks of theology itself will be to examine more closely the relations between the charismatic activities of the theologians and the teaching authority of the Church. My experience of Vatican II taught me the immense importance of theology. The needs of the Church in this age of transition in culture make this importance of supreme moment to us. We have to thank Lonergan for his own magnificent contribution in this field.

## SOME ILLUSTRATIONS

*Insight, page 225*: 'The dominant groups may be reactionary or progressive or any mixture of the two. In so far as they are reactionary, they are out to block any correction of the effects of group bias and they employ for this purpose whatever power they possess in whatever manner they deem appropriate and effective. On the other hand, in so far as they are progressive, they make it their aim both to correct existing distortions and to find the means that will prevent their future recurrence. Now to a great extent the attitude of the dominant groups determines the attitude of the depressed groups. Reactionaries are opposed by revolutionaries. Progressives are met by liberals. In the former case, the situation heads towards violence. In the latter case, there is a general agreement about ends with disagreement about the pace of change and the mode and measure of its execution.' One thinks of Sulla.

*Insight, page 227*: 'The specific difference of human history is that among the probable possibilities is a sequence of operative insights by which men grasp possible schemes of recurrence and take the initiative in bringing about the material and social conditions that make these schemes concretely possible, probable and actual. In this fashion man becomes for man the executor of the emergent probability of human affairs. Instead of being developed by his environment, man turns to transforming his environment in his own self-development.'

This of course does not mean that man can solve his own 'problem'; it is insoluble without divine intervention. On the other hand, once the solution is provided, and bearing in mind that the solution is permanent and that it is in continuation with the scheme of emergent probability, it seems clear that redeemed man will have not fewer but more possibilities open to him;

that creative novelty should be more, and not less, a feature of resultant human history. One is reminded of a thesis of Christopher Dawson, that Christianity has proved to be a constant source of new human initiatives; and of Leeuwen's contention that technological progress is itself a by-product of the gospel. The view that modern science has its intellectual roots in the Christian world-view is well known.

*Insight, page 230*: 'The function of human intelligence, it is claimed'—under the influence of the general bias of common sense—'is not to set up independent norms that make thought irrelevant to fact but to study the data as they are, to grasp the intelligibility that is immanent in them, to acknowledge as principle or norm only what can be reached by generalisation from the data. There follow the need and the development of a new culture, a new religion, a new philosophy; and the new differs radically from the old. The new is not apriorist, wishful thinking. It is empirical, scientific, realistic. It takes its stand on things as they are. In brief, its many excellencies cover its single defect. For its rejection of the normative significance of detached and disinterested intelligence makes it radically uncritical.' Thus one might wrongly take the Kinsey Report as setting norms of sexual behaviour.

*Insight, page 231*: Cosmopolis: '. . . If ideas are not to be merely a façade, if the reality is not to be merely a balance of power, then the use of force can be no more than residual and incidental. But cosmopolis is not concerned with the residual and incidental. It is concerned with the fundamental issue of the historical process. Its business is to prevent practicality from being short-sightedly practical and so destroying itself . . . Cosmopolis is above all politics. So far from being rendered superfluous by a successful World Government it would be all the more obviously needed to offset the tendencies of that and any other government to be short-sightedly practical . . . Its business is to break the vicious circle of an illusion: men will not venture on ideas they grant to be correct because they hold that such ideas will not work unless sustained by desires and fears; and, inversely, men hold that such ideas will not work, because they will not venture on them and so have no empirical evidence that such ideas can

work and would work . . . While shifts of power in themselves
are incidental, they commonly are accompanied by another
phenomenon of quite a different character. There is the creation
of myths. The old régime is depicted as monstrous; the new
envisages itself as the immaculate embodiment of ideal human
aspirations . . . It is the business of cosmopolis to prevent the
formation of the screening memories by which an ascent to
power hides its own nastiness . . . it is its business to encourage
and support those that would speak the simple truth though
simple truth has gone out of fashion. Unless cosmopolis undertakes this essential task, it fails in its mission . . . It itself must be
purged of the rationalisations and myths that became part of the
human heritage before it came on the scene . . . There is needed,
then, a critique of history before there can be any intelligent
direction of history . . . The liberal believer in automatic progress
could praise all that survives; the Marxist could denounce all that
was and praise all that would be; but anyone that recognises the
existence both of intelligence and of bias . . . has to be critical . . .
cosmopolis . . . is a withdrawal from practicality to save practicality . . . It is not easy . . .'
     Could not theology perform some of the functions of
cosmopolis?

*The Subject, page 26*: 'Just as the existential subject freely and
responsibly makes himself what he is, so too he makes himself
good or evil and his actions right or wrong. The good subject,
the good choice, or the good action are not found in isolation.
For the subject is good by his good choices and good actions.
Universally prior to any choice or action there is just the transcendental principle of all appraisal and criticism, the intention of
the good. That principle gives rise to instances of the good, but
those instances are good choices and actions. However, do not
ask me to determine them, for their determination in each case
is the work of the free and responsible subject producing the first
and only edition of himself. It is because the determination of
the good is the work of freedom that ethical systems can catalogue
sins in almost endless genera and species yet always remain rather
vague about the good . . . We come to know the good from the
example of those about us, from the stories people tell of the
good and evil men and women of old, from the incessant flow

of praise and blame that makes up the great part of human conversation, from the elation and from the shame that fill us when our own choices and deeds are our own determination of ourselves as good or evil, praiseworthy or blameworthy.'

# Dogma versus the Self-Correcting Process of Learning

## FREDERICK E. CROWE

THE problem I am attacking began to emerge about two centuries ago, and has been with us in fairly clear formulation most of our own century. Thus, Maurice Blondel in 1904 and Van Austin Harvey in 1966 were able to state it in approximately the same terms. Blondel defines his problem as that 'of the relation of dogma and history, and of the critical method and the necessary authority of doctrinal formulae.'[1] He tells us his task is 'to achieve the synthesis of history and dogma while respecting their independence and solidarity.'[2] The execution of the task has a twofold danger: '. . . some tend to behave as though history had to depend absolutely on dogma, others as though dogma had to proceed exclusively from history and be subordinate to it.'[3] Harvey's approach is different but fundamentally he deals with the same question. Over and over he charges that 'orthodox belief corrodes the delicate machinery of sound historical judgment.'[4] He examines the three greats of the passing era, Bultmann, Tillich, and Barth, and concludes: 'None of the three theologians makes clear how it is possible to be both a critical historian and a believer.'[5] The new quest for the historical Jesus and various other efforts to solve the problem also fail in greater or lesser degree to achieve their goal.

The mention of Blondel and Harvey will help those who move in other thought-worlds than mine to locate the problem. But it also serves to bring out the tenacity of a question that has changed so little in sixty years and is so much the same for such different writers. Blondel and Harvey differ widely in approach and in solution. Blondel was a philosopher by trade; he worked in the context of Catholic modernism; his solution was given in terms of a Catholic tradition that is 'not a limitative and retrograde force, but a power of development and expansion';[6]

his explanatory principle was a philosophy of action: '"To keep" the word of God means in the first place to do it . . . ; and the deposit of Tradition . . . cannot be transmitted in its entirety . . . unless it is confided to the practical obedience of love.'[7] Harvey works in the context of Protestant thought determined by Troeltsch; his explanatory categories are strongly historical; he postulates a perspectival image of Jesus, a memory-impression which controlled the views and beliefs recorded in the gospels; he reconciles the conflict between doctrine and history by a theory of 'soft perspectivism': 'This difference in perspective may be such that the two descriptions of the same event also differ, but the two descriptions are not logically incompatible . . .'[8] The contrasts then between Blondel and Harvey are obvious, but so is the similarity in conceiving the problem: the difficulty of holding fast to absolute beliefs on historical events, when scientific research repudiates traditional 'history' and itself attempts to reach no more than probabilities subject to perpetual correction.

I am not going to follow the direction taken by either Blondel or Harvey, profitable though that might be. I am led, rather, to attack the problem in the context of Fr Lonergan's thought— 'in the context of'—there is a handy phrase that enables me to avoid the claim that I speak for Lonergan and allows me to think in the way that is now second-nature to me without always distinguishing original elements from the form they may have taken in my mind.

There is a preliminary, historical question in regard to change or development in Lonergan's own thought. I have stated my topic in terms of dogma and the self-correcting process of learning; I have done so deliberately in order to make the opposition sharp between the absolute of faith and the continual revision implied in a process that gradually eliminates misconceptions, mistakes, and plain errors. The preliminary question, however, our own little historical problem, is whether Lonergan's thinking has so changed that these terms can be said any longer to be pertinent. The self-correcting process of learning is still pertinent; in fact, one of Lonergan's latest writings applies it to the area of religious doctrines in a way hardly seen so explicitly before.[9] But does the concept of dogma any longer apply? There are good reasons for asking the question, and I really have to delay on it a moment.

There is no doubt that Lonergan's thinking has undergone a profound reorientation in the last five years, and that in a way which bears directly on the present question. If we take his *De Deo Trino* to mark a kind of term in the prior phase and compare it with some of his later work, we find extremely significant differences. In the trinitarian treatise we read the assertion, like a kind of refrain, that theology rests on truths, not on data: '. . . non a datis sed a veris incipit.'[10] And this is expressly set in contrast to the sciences, both the natural and the human. But, when you come to his article on the functional specialties of theology, you are struck by the fact that through several pages of what he seems to regard as his definitive statement, he is able to list and describe all eight functions, to assign the ground for their division and to state its need, all without once using the word 'truth'. You read fourteen pages in that article before the word occurs, and then it does so rather innocuously.[11] Or you might compare the faculty psychology of the 1964 treatise where Lonergan can still speak of the intellect's influence on the will,[12] with the disappearance of such language from the work of the last two or three years. His present cast of mind is much better represented by statements like this one: '. . . man exists authentically in the measure that he succeeds in self-transcendence, and . . . self-transcendence has both its fulfilment and its enduring ground in holiness, in God's gift of his love to us.'[13]

The differences are striking and I think it important to advert to them. At the same time their exaggeration would be as wrong as their neglect. The article on functional specialties may not use the word 'truth' but it uses the idea under other names, such as: what is reasonably affirmed, judgements of fact, elimination of contradictions and fallacies, the refutation of error, the distinction between correct and incorrect understanding, etc.[14] Furthermore, *De Deo Trino* had already distinguished between the truth on which theology rests and the truth towards which it strives; the latter deals with an object that grows and changes, it begins with hypotheses, it may reach no more than probability.[15] True, this is stated of the truth of theological understanding, not of the truth of revelation, but it does provide for the self-correcting process of religious learning already in 1964, just as the role of truth is still maintained in 1969.

There is a development but it is not a revolution. To get an

accurate view of the transition we should examine *The Subject*,
which was the Aquinas Lecture for 1968. Here the new orientation seems to be emerging clearly. Truth is objective, yes, but
do not be fascinated by objectivity, for there is the subject also
to consider.[16] The new attitude is spelled out, the faults of the
old orientation are exposed, there is an admission of today's
alienation from dogma. Still, that alienation is regarded as a
reaction against the previous one-sided insistence on objectivity;[17]
we are nowhere exhorted to abandon all attachment to dogma.
A similar point is made in 'The Absence of God in Modern
Culture'; here there is reference to the 'softening, if not weaken-
ing, of the dogmatic component once so prominent in Catholic
theology,'[18] but this is attributed to the theologians' inability to
ground their objective statements; I see no reason to think
Lonergan accepts it as an optimum state of affairs or that he has
abandoned his own great labour to overcome that inability.
When he says, in the latest article to appear, '. . . faith claims
truth and certainty,'[19] I do not think he regards the claim as
false. What has happened between 1964 and 1969, I would judge,
is that a new understanding of values and their role has been
added. This does not eliminate the role of truth; it supplies it
with a better dynamism, especially in the religious sphere.

In any case the problem is real for many of us; it exists in our
minds in terms derived from Lonergan's earlier work, and I will
set it forth in those terms as well as I can, with the nuances that
distinguish our concept of the problem from those of Blondel
and Harvey. There are such nuances, and to advert to them may
forestall possible misunderstandings. Where Blondel's concern
was apologetics, and Harvey's the morality of historical knowledge, Lonergan's concern has been cognitional process; he has
worked on a level so fundamental that it should be relevant both
to Blondel's interest and to Harvey's but he himself has made
few forays into either of their fields. Again, his work on dogma
was naturally done in the context of theology, much of it in the
narrower context of dogmatic treatises, whereas his work on the
self-correcting process of learning was confined largely to his
philosophical work, *Insight*; we have, therefore, to put the two
together.

Our problem, then, can be set up as follows. The relevant
aspect of dogma, which it shares with all truth, is the absolute

character of its positing: 'Caesar's crossing of the Rubicon was a contingent event occurring at a particular place and time. But a true affirmation of that event is an eternal, immutable, definitive validity.'[20] The absolute character of dogma can be the more strongly affirmed in that it rests on the infallible knowledge of God: 'Sed qui in verbo Dei invenitur sensus, a divina scientia eaque infallibili procedit.'[21] But the self-correcting process of learning seems to suppose just the opposite of this absolute character; it seems to suppose mistakes and errors, in our beliefs as well as in our independent affirmations: 'Mistaken beliefs exist, and the function of an analysis of belief is overlooked if it fails to explain how mistaken beliefs arise and how they are to be eliminated.'[22] As mistaken beliefs have the same roots as error in general, so their correction has the same general remedy; there is no radically new element in 'the problem of eliminating from one's own mind the rubbish that may have settled there in a lifelong symbiosis of personal inquiry and of believing. For learning one's errors is but a particular case of learning.'[23] That general case of learning is thus described: '. . . the spontaneous and self-correcting process of learning is a circuit in which insights reveal their shortcomings by putting forth deeds or words or thoughts and, through that revelation, prompt the further questions that lead to complementary insights.'[24] Lastly, though the role of learning in historical studies is not stressed (Lonergan's category of 'history' was not at all fully developed at the time of *Insight*), still it is sufficiently acknowledged: 'As the data assembled by historical research accumulate, insights are revised continuously in accord with the concrete process of learning.'[25] Our problem, then, is this: does the self-correcting process of learning apply to dogma? if it does, how can dogma remain dogma? if it does not, how can dogma and historical inquiry deal with the same historical event? How bring them into confrontation? it seems as if they must be kept in quite separate and watertight compartments, the modern version of the double truth.

To meet this problem I will adopt tactics something like those the agnostic has used against proofs of the existence of God; he forces his opponents to qualify and to qualify until, he says, the thesis has died the death of a thousand qualifications. I think the method is legitimate for me, simply because the present problem rests on a thousand misconceptions and clearing them up eliminates the problem. My first step then is to ask about our starting-point: is it the present, or is it the past? I will affirm it is the present, and will point out the particular cognitional stance involved in such an affirmation. Secondly, I will go on to ask about the fixed dogmas our present has inherited from the past and about their relation to human thinking and future progress. Finding that dogmas already given leave us considerable freedom to go on learning in a human process, I will ask, thirdly, how those dogmas themselves arose, and whether the learning process that was then involved required the reversal of the believer's former world. My fourth step will take us to that former world of our beginnings; I will ask whether there are dogmas in Scripture, and in what way they may exist there. My last step will be to ask how a theologian and believer can live at peace with his dogmatic foundations in the Scriptures despite the perpetual revisions that may result from critical work on the gospels and the other writings that record our historical origin.

My answer to the first question is that our starting-point is the present, and since this is going to result in a difference of stance between Roman Catholic and Protestant, where the latter may appear to be left floundering with the problem while the former escapes, I would like to assure our Protestant brothers from the outset that I am not abandoning them—I may even adduce principles that will help them remain Protestant! But my concern now is analysis of the data.

In some sense surely all of us who were born into Christian homes have the present as our starting-point; it is from parents, pastors, teachers, that we learn our faith and through their witness that we adhere to Christ. But the Roman Catholic continues throughout life, or may so continue, to take as his proximate rule of faith the dogma of the Church, presented to him by those who are authorised to speak for the Church. The Protestant, I suppose, somewhere along the line is taught that the Scriptures, not the institutional and present Church, are his only rule of faith; and so, as soon as he begins to read scriptural criticism, he is involved in the problem of the historicity of the records. The difference is that the Catholic postulates continuity of the present doctrine of the Church with that of the past, and can do so according to his dogmatic principles, whereas the

Protestant, in order to be a Protestant and remain consistent with his Protestant position, must postulate discontinuity.[26] I am not sure that Luther, in order to be a protestant, a reformer, needed to postulate discontinuity; but to be a Protestant, to belong to a separated Church and to justify that separation, one must, it seems, postulate discontinuity.

I certainly do not mean to affirm that the proximate rule of faith, the magisterium of the Church, which sufficed for us when we were children and is still operative for us in adulthood, can be made an excuse for intellectual complacency and laziness. The proximate rule has to derive from the original rule. Our beliefs are not independent of certain historical events said to have occurred many centuries ago, and we cannot be indifferent to what historical research discovers in regard to those events. We must put our dogmas into confrontation with what the historians say actually happened, and achieve a symbiosis of what we believe with what we can rationally assert by means of historical science. However, I do mean to affirm that the problem loses some of its urgency for us; we can postpone it, or, if we do attack it, we can live in relative peace of mind while investigation goes on. We have what Lonergan calls our existential history, prior to narrated history, to critical history, to methodical history,[27] to support us in the meantime.

However, that is a denominational difference in faith-attitude; theologically it is not the main thing. The basic difference here is one of general cognitional stance, what might be called today the mind-set, and this seems to me much more important for sorting out the various misconceptions that lie behind our problem. The instructive parallel is the difference between Newman and Descartes.[28] Descartes would begin with a universal doubt and go on to establish all knowledge on the secure basis he discovered by this method; but what in fact happened was that many accepted his starting-point but could not follow his footsteps and so ended in scepticism. Newman, on the contrary, would prefer to begin from a universal credulity, with the prospect of eliminating error in due course as the truth developed and occupied the mind. This he regarded as 'the true way of learning'[29] and the very terms he used shows how relevant his cognitional stance will be to our problem of dogma and the self-correcting process of learning.

In our second step, therefore, we assume the cognitional stance of a Newman rather than of a Descartes; we take the dogmas that are the rule of faith for the Catholic child as they are for the Catholic theologian, and we ask about their relationship to human thinking and learning, especially to the historian's progress in the study of the gospels and to the modernist's attempt at a contemporaneous doctrine. Now, without making an exhaustive inventory but confining myself to the dozen or so dogmas that enter the theological work I have done (really there are hardly more than that), I would say that they are not likely to be directly touched by gospel criticism. My favourite dogmas are the conciliar definitions of the fourth and fifth centuries which, Lonergan says, are couched in 'catholic' language. That is, the movement of thought in patristic times was away from the particularities of the Hebrew mind, or of the Pauline or the Johannine mind, towards what is universal.[30] 'What the Father is, the Son is too'—that is the gist of the Nicene dogma.[30a] But such a statement is a long way from direct conflict with statements on the human consciousness of Jesus. Even the dogma of Chalcedon, where it deals with the human and historical as in the statement, 'Whatever man is, the Son is too,' does so in a way that leaves our faith free from the vicissitudes of gospel criticism.

Similarly, if we go in the other direction, towards development of a theology based on the dogmas, there is little restriction on the learning process. The dogmas are not a continent but a beachhead, not the sea of infinity but little islands scattered on the sea; they are not boundaries (at least, not *just* boundaries), they are also openings to further investigation; not a *summa theologiae*, but fragmentary items of knowledge. As Fr Rahner says of Chalcedon, it is not an end but a beginning.[31] Once we realise the extremely narrow strip of infinity occupied by the dogmas and, as well, the general heuristic character of their formulation, many of the difficulties vanish which arose from a false perspective in which dogmas loomed as the horizon itself of religious thought. On the side or the object there is room for infinite advance; on the side of our concepts we are not bound by any supposed determinateness of our categories.

I said that dogmas are not likely to conflict directly with the results of gospel criticism, which suggests that there may be an ultimate confrontation. In fact, there is a relationship. The dogmas claim to be true; their truth may be largely heuristic in conception, but it does refer to a concrete, historical figure who lived at a certain place in a certain time. So we have to take a third step and ask about the emergence of the dogmas. I am not yet dealing with the Scriptures, but heading in that direction. I am concerned here with the process of formulation and acceptance of dogmas, and the relation of that process to the total consciousness of the believer.

We need now a concept of the total object of that consciousness in its conglomerate aspect. Lonergan uses the neat little phrase, 'the subject and his world'.[32] It is that 'world' that I am interested in, but under a particular aspect. The original concept is Heideggerian, I think, but Palmer makes Heidegger's world 'a structural whole of interrelated meanings and intentions'.[33] I would qualify that statement somewhat; I think much of this world is unstructured, many of its elements are not related to the rest in any specific way. It is a conglomerate world, more like the contents of a wastepaper-basket, or the collection of treasures a boy carries around in his pockets, or the odds and ends of furniture stored away in the attic of an old homestead. It is the total intentional object, then, of consciousness, the aggregate, the summation from beginning to end of the stream of consciousness, the integral of an extended lifetime, the deposit of long-continued experience. It consists of images, memories, mental schemata and associations, links vaguely made and half forgotten, things loved or feared, old ideas and new worries, questions and puzzles, answers half glimpsed, poems learned long ago by heart, words concrete and abstract, 'if only . . .' for-mulations, suspicions, guesses, opinions, beliefs, assumptions, judgements and prejudgements, information and misinformation, commandments and precepts, graces accepted and rejected, causes to which one is committed or projects for which one is responsible—the whole precipitate of a lifetime but, like the patrimony of a community, quite undifferentiated, a hodge-podge, a conglomerate object that stands to mind-set as materials to their meaningful arrangement. Biologically stored in brain-cells and nervous system, consciously it is vaguely objectified as the one vast world within the horizon of the mind, only partially explored and largely unorganised.

I think we need this concept, this view of one's world, for it is within such a total object that small and fragmentary bits of truth emerge, and it is within the religious counterpart of this 'natural' world that small and fragmentary bits of dogma emerge into religious consciousness. The truth may have a fundamental role, linking us to the real as gravity links us to mother earth, but like gravity it need not figure largely in our consciousness or in our 'world'. No, it is the world itself in its totality that makes us what we are existentially, not the truth that is embedded within it, not even the truth that happens from time to time to emerge into a differentiated object. When some special experience occurs, like hearing the good news of salvation, or feeling the twinge of conscience, or conceiving a great idea, or realising at long last and accepting some fundamental truth, the experience occurs against the background of the former totality and settles into its more or less modest place in the new totality.

In the context provided by this totality we can set the self-correcting process in general and achieve those increments of truth which pertain to learning, even religious learning, without magnifying the step to the cataclysmic proportions of a complete overthrow of our world. We can do this as individuals, and we can do it as a Church, for the whole Church is a learning Church. What makes the learning process a traumatic experience, not to say disaster, for many of us, is our misapprehension of what is going on. We make truth *the* object of mind, looming up in solitary splendour. Not only that, but we take elements to belong to the level of truth when in fact they are mere suppositions or assumptions or plain picture-thinking. Or, when we actually have a dogma, we take it to be the comprehensive statement of the matter instead of just a glimpse of the total truth. Then, surely, learning becomes a traumatic experience. Instead of a modification in the arrangement of the furniture in our world, the world itself is overturned. The truth we have learned now looms as a totality set in direct opposition to a 'truth' (translate: supposition) that we held before as if it too had been a totality. But, in fact, it was previously there as part of the furniture of the mind, undifferentiated, imprecise. In Lonergan's phrase, it had not been 'promoted'[34] to the status of truth.

What is the process of this promotion?[35] The immediate factor in most dogmas was the question for reflection, the 'yes or no' question. But generally a long period of clarification precedes such a question. Thus at Nicea the question was: Is the Son God in the same sense as the Father is God? The question is limpidly clear in those terms, which I borrow from Prestige,[36] but even at Nicea it was clear enough. My point, however, is that that question could hardly have been asked without the labour of clarification implicit in New Testament writings and beginning in earnest 150 years before Nicea. During that period of mental effort the Church was in the position we are in today with regard to collegiality; that is, they did not even know what question to put in a 'yes or no' form. So the ideas have to occur, they have to occur in all their variety and opposition. What we call subordinationist ideas of the Son had to appear on the scene for the consubstantiality of the Son to be clearly conceived. Similarly today a one-sided view of the papal role, a tendency towards absolute monarchy in isolation from its subjects, such an idea had to appear and have its vogue before we could begin to conceive the situation properly.

Still the conciliar way is not the only way. There is a variety of methods by which cognitional elements in general are promoted to the level of truth. There is the formal, authoritative way in which the scientist works, striving to concoct a crucial experiment that will settle the matter definitively. There is the opposite extreme of a question too rudimentary to require more than an understanding of everyday language and a set of sensing apparatus: 'Is it raining out?'—the matter is settled by looking out of the window.[37] But in between there is the type of community judgement illustrated by Newman's example: Great Britain is an island. It is not settled by taking a look, and I doubt whether anyone ever performed a crucial experiment on the question. How is it promoted to the level of truth? By something, I should say, that is parallel to what Lonergan calls 'indirect verification' in the field of science: '. . . the law of falling bodies was verified directly by Galileo, but it also has been verified indirectly every time in the last four centuries that that law was among the presuppositions of a successful experiment or a successful application.'[38] In a similar way a long history of wars and commerce and adventure testifies indirectly to the Briton's supposition that he lives on an island. I am not saying that community beliefs cannot be wrong; they can indeed be wrong, and for a very long time, but not when the belief comes, through the very process of living, under daily verification of this indirect kind, not at least among rational men—the fanatics we have always with us (that Flat-Earth Society!).

You see where I am heading: towards the real area of controversy, the gospels. We have dogmas in the Church, religious cognitional elements that have been promoted to the level of truth by a formal process parallel to that of science: there are ideas, then there are opposed ideas, there is debate, even violence, there is a long process of clarification, there is the settlement of the matter by conciliar action. But the question is whether there are other truths promoted to the level of truth by a more informal process; the question is especially about other truth before the dogmas appeared; the classic instance of dogma occurred three centuries after Christ—how did the truth exist during that period? how was it contained in the scriptural accounts of Christ? We have come to the fourth step of our investigation.

Let us first recognise that for the believer of New Testament times his religious 'world' was an object as conglomerate as that I described for the man in the street: it was filled with assumptions, guesses, memories, pictures from the Old Testament, images of Jesus—a 'perspectival' image, if you like—images too of the apostles and holy places, of saint and sinner, with commitments and hostilities, beliefs, suspicions—the whole lot. His way of looking at the structure of the universe, his view of what we call the three-storey universe, can be located without trouble in the conglomerate, at a level far below that of belief. It had not yet been promoted to truth; it had not been tested; it had not even been questioned. If the question on the structure of the universe had been put, and the answer given, 'The universe is a three-storey job,' you might say that here at last we have a good solid error, but this would be, I think, to distort somewhat the mind of the primitive Christian, who would hardly conceive the question in the way you ask it.

What then in this conglomerate world has been promoted, at least informally, to the level of truth? The detailed answer can be given only to individually specified questions, which must be answered each on its own merits. But I would list a few categories of 'truth' that can be found in the Scriptures. The first is one that in fact everyone of us tacitly accepts and affirms by his conduct even while he may be denying it by his theological dissertations: it is the truth of the original kerygma, much as it is found in 1 Corinthians 15:3–4. This is so obviously foundational to the whole enterprise of sacred science that to regard it as mere imagination, the expression of mere subjective experience, a mere idea, would eliminate all truth from the Christian religion and invalidate the whole quest from the beginning (see Paul in 1 *Cor.* 15:12–19 and *Gal.* 1). I do not say that this proves the truth of the kerygma; I say it proves that we tacitly accept its truth in making our commitment and engaging in our enterprise. I do not say either that the kerygma has reached the carefully defined stage of the Nicene definition; I do say that it is sufficiently well defined for us to build our religious lives and our theological pursuits on it as a basis. Finally, I would make a parallel with Newman's 'Great Britain is an island.' In each case you have something so foundational that to reverse it would be almost literally to overturn one's world. It may be too that, where Newman's proposition is indirectly verified by a good many centuries of history, the kerygma is verified in its own way by Blondel's 'faith in action'. But that is not really germane to my purpose; I am not at the moment verifying our Christian faith for anyone, I am trying to locate the element of truth where it belongs.

There is a second set of cognitional elements in the New Testament that I would regard as promoted to the level of truth, those on which there has been something like particular reflection, express argument, and duly formed judgement by those whose charismatic qualities equip them to speak for the Church. This set is not well defined in my thinking yet, but a step towards clarification would be to compare two candidates for inclusion and ask why I would accept one and reject the other. I would wish them to include Paul's position on the law-gospel question; I would *not* wish to include his theological treatise on the head-dress of women in church. Why do I spontaneously make this difference when Paul argued both questions so explicitly? There is less difficulty perhaps about including the law-gospel doctrine, for this was so closely linked with the foundational truth of Christianity, was so widely debated within the Church and settled (at least in practice, with dogmatic implications) by something like a general council. But why would I not include Paul's position on women's headdress? I suppose the marginal character of the question is relevant in helping us determine how thoroughly Paul formed his faith-judgement but if that judgement were really formed I would wish to include even marginal items. I suppose too the moral field in which the question rises is relevant, for a moral question may be settled one way today and another way tomorrow when the situation is different. But there are dogmatic elements involved, so we must look further. The narrow extent of participation in the Church is relevant, again as a clue to how well and duly formed Paul's judgement may have been, but those who hold that the apostles were prophets and more than prophets would not regard this as decisive if Paul as an apostle were really operating on the level of truth. This is, I think, the fundamental point. So what I am really saying is that Paul had not quite fully promoted this matter to the level of a truth of faith, that he was really only 'arguing' for what seemed to him to be proper Christian conduct. My view gains antecedent probability from the context as I described it, but is also half-expressed in Paul's very conclusion: 'However, if you insist on arguing, let me tell you, there is no such custom among us' (I *Cor.* 11:16). That seems to mean, 'Well, even if my arguments are not convincing, do as I say anyway,' and would put this cognitional element in the conglomerate somewhere beyond a mere idea, but somewhere short of truth, would locate it perhaps where we would locate a probability in a developing science.

All this means that we cannot escape our responsibility for judging in the twentieth century simply because the Church of our fathers spoke in the first century. We have not only to form our judgement on new questions as the early Church did, we have also to form our judgement on whether the early Church had duly made up its mind. It is not a matter of judging whether the early Church was right; we are not today going to judge the objective question all over again; if that has already been done the decision is normative. But we are judging the *stance* of the early Church: have we or have we not a duly formed faith-judgement of Paul or another apostle or the Church as a whole?

We have to exercise our own judgement, then; we cannot shirk that responsibility. This applies to the third set of elements in the New Testament which I think have been promoted to the level of truth: certain reflected statements where the existential sense of the word 'is' can be determined. The word 'is' does not always mean such a statement; it can occur in a question, or in a supposition, or in argument on the way to truth, or in a simple piece of fiction where the real affirmation is never articulated at all.[39] But when John says at the end of his gospel that he had written it in order that his readers might believe 'that Jesus is the Christ, the Son of God,' (20:31) it is clear enough not only that this is the existential use of 'is' but that the statement is the reflected and utterly central core of his faith about Jesus. If the evangelist's charism means anything at all, or, if you wish, if the early Church's acceptance of his gospel as her faith means anything at all, then we have here a cognitional element promoted to the level of truth and normative for the later Church. I would go further and say the same about the other evangelists in so far as their 'theses' can be determined, for each of them has a thesis too, though it may not be articulated as neatly at the end of the gospel as it is in John's. There is no need to demand from them an elaborate conceptualisation of their message, any more than it was necessary to do so in regard to the kerygma itself; there is no need to suppose that any of them, or all of them together, wrote the definitive Christology; even if they are just like the blind men around the elephant (and I think the most trenchant critics would grant that much) they have said something true and normative.

I come now to my fifth and last question, which is perhaps the step you have been waiting for. All that I have said might be admitted by the believer familiar with the problem of Blondel or Harvey; he might still say that I have not met the historians where they take their stand, on the question of the *ipsissima verba* and the *ipsissima facta* of the historical Jesus. I have discussed the gospels; I have not discussed Jesus of Nazareth. Do not expect too much from me at this point; I am neither an exegete nor a historian. What I promised to do was to examine the way a dogmatic theologian (and a believer) can live at peace with his dogma on Jesus and even relate it to work on the historical Jesus, allowing for the perpetual revisions that advancing historical science may require. I will illustrate this rather briefly and in one example only; however, that example is taken from a crucial area, that of the knowledge Jesus had.

There is a dogmatic thesis that Jesus had what we call the

beatific vision. It is commonly regarded as a 'truth' that is *proxima fidei*, that is, an element of doctrine that is just short of having been promoted to the level of an article of faith. The authorities would certainly take a dim view of its denial, and so would I, on independent theological grounds. It has a history: I have not traced it through the New Testament but the scriptural basis is growing clear in John's conception of the Saviour. The Fathers took very difficult and important steps in distinguishing human operations from divine; the scholastics elaborated distinct elements in the human knowledge. But I would say it is possible for a naïve realist to read all this long history and be utterly incapable of handling the problem of the 'beatific vision' and the 'ignorance' of the last day, a problem that would seem to put dogma and history in direct conflict but that really loses its urgency in the Lonergan view of Christ's human knowledge.

No one seriously thinks of the beatific vision as resulting from a special pair of binoculars enabling one to see an old man with a long white beard. The beatific vision is understanding; it is understanding of God; God is comprehensively conceived as *ipsum Esse*, in the rolling Latin into which they translated John Damascene: 'totum enim in seipso comprehendens, habet ipsum esse velut quoddam pelagus substantiae infinitum et indeterminatum.'[40] Now Lonergan's thesis of 1964 on the knowledge of Christ (I believe it was his last piece of work as a 'scholastic' theologian) struggles with the relationship of this *scientia ineffabilis*, which is that of a vision of God that cannot be uttered, to a *scientia effabilis* that characterises Jesus' historical life and can be communicated to his fellow man.[41]

I will not go into this; if it is familiar I need not; if it is not familiar, a few minutes of explanation would not help much. But let us remind ourselves that *scientia ineffabilis* does not mean simply that human words are lacking; it means more fundamentally that human ideas and concepts are lacking. The illuminating parallel is that of the mystics—illuminating because they talked much more about their psychological experiences than Jesus did. They simply could not express what they had 'seen' (translate: understood), they had to resort to 'pictures' of a garden being watered or of a castle that has rooms within rooms, the interior mansions.

The point is that Jesus did not look at a series of 'objects' of knowledge lined up on the shelves of the divine mind, and then turn to communicate to his disciples the secrets of that vast warehouse, perhaps making a mistake as he did so. The point is that there is an infinity between the object of his vision and particular items of the created world and human history. What was given to Jesus was not an encyclopedia of the divine ideas, all conveniently arranged in alphabetical order (Aramaic language). There just is not and cannot be any such direct transfer as naïve realism would conceive from beatific vision to daily life. The one is so remote from the other as an 'item' of knowledge that in the course of a long lifetime, or even in the course of an era of human history, men might never bring them into relationship; much less then is this going to occur in the short span of thirty years. I say it is remote as an item of knowledge; I do not mean that it does not guide and guarantee particular items, but it does not do so in the way a premise guides a conclusion, or a yardstick guarantees my estimate of length. It is more like our notion of being. That is only a notion, where Jesus had understanding; our notion is empty, only an anticipation, where the understanding of Jesus was full and actual. But there is a similarity of role; just as our notion of being is remote from our judgement on today's weather as an item, while guiding and guaranteeing it in a fundamental way, so the vision Jesus had can be related both remotely and immediately to his judgements in the human and historical sphere. As our notion of being hardly comes to our attention, though it is so basic in human consciousness, so the vision of Jesus could guide his judgements without having the alerting character of an alarm bell or compass needle.

I would go further then than Blondel. Where he explained the early Church's expectation of an imminent Parousia in terms of what the disciples could absorb of the Master's message,[42] I would explain it more basically in terms of what the Master could himself conceive in a human way. I would say that, side by side with the vision of God, in a relationship that was both remote and immediate, there was the conglomerate that is the world of every man. Within this conglomerate, guided and guaranteed by the vision, but in such a way that the relationship could perhaps remain unattended to, a vision of man and his world slowly emerged. This emergence would be quite compatible with the normal biological and psychological stages of human growth. There is nothing in the vision of God that prevents a boy of twelve who is just coming to puberty from reflecting in a way he never did before on the meaning of life, on coming to a sense of his vocation and realising that he must devote himself untrammelled to the Father's business. As the years go on, this understanding of the destiny of man, of man's responsibility for conducting himself in such a way as to remain open to communion with the All, of the awful possibility of closing himself to such communion, of the terrible consequences of the daily *kairos*, this understanding may grow sharper and sharper and express itself in the parables of crisis. Along with this there may begin to emerge the understanding of a need for a fundamental option between the 'merely human' and the divinely human, of the need to die to the human in order to set it in proper proportion and to begin to live the divinely human life. But this whole process is compatible with, indeed supposes, no formed judgement whatever on a variety of questions (which may include the date of the last day) that are not immediately related to the task in hand. Thus I am satisfied in my own mind with having seen how one might proceed in reconciling the human experience of Jesus which the historian investigates with a particular doctrine, a quasi dogma, that is of some importance in theology.

To recapitulate now the last four steps of my argument: There is dogma; it is normative, the core of our faith and the basis of our theology; but it is of a sort that leaves the historian singularly free to pursue his investigations. The dogma arose in a learning process, but the effect of its emergence was not to overturn one's religious world, it was merely to bring some elements in the conglomerate object of consciousness into clear relief. There is basis for dogma in Scripture, but we have hardly begun yet to work out in any systematic way the catalogue of such unformulated dogmas, or the conditions under which we might affirm them to be contained in Scripture. Further, the elements that seem the most likely candidates for inclusion in the catalogue are not such as to corrode 'the delicate machinery of sound historical judgement.' This is tested, sketchily, in the particular case of the knowledge Jesus had. I consider that the supposed opposition between dogma and the self-correcting process of learning has died the death of a thousand qualifications. Maybe, if it enjoys a resurrection in the minds of my readers, my laziness will be pushed to a more accurate account of my position or, if that proves impossible, to an abandonment of what is untenable.[43]

# Christian Conversion in the Writings of Bernard Lonergan

## CHARLES E. CURRAN

LONERGAN'S recent writing emphasises the importance of conversion as the transformation of the subject, which thus constitutes the basic horizon of the individual.[1] Horizon is the maximum field of vision from a determined viewpoint and embraces both relative horizon which describes one's field of vision relative to one's development—e.g., psychological, sociological, cultural—and basic horizon which describes the human subject as related to the four basic or transcendental conversions: intellectual, moral, religious and Christian.[2] This paper will attempt to study Lonergan's understanding of Christian conversion and its relationship to the other three transcendental conversions.

### I

Lonergan asserts that conversion as a theological topic receives very little attention in traditional theology[3]—an assertion which holds quite true in Catholic theology although some Protestant theology has paid more attention to the concept. Leading French theological dictionaries such as *Dictionnaire de Théologie Catholique*, *Dictionnaire de la Bible*, and *Catholicisme* do not even contain articles on conversion as such. The manuals of Catholic moral theology do not even mention the term in their quite narrow treatment of moral theology. In the past few years, however, Catholic theology has begun to discuss the reality of conversion. Bernard Häring has insisted on the centrality of conversion in the moral life of the Christian.[4] A 1958 article by Yves Congar develops the concept of conversion with emphasis on the bibical understanding of conversion and the psychological experience of those who are converted, but the article still to a great extent

41

views conversion in terms of confessional conversion to a particular Christian denomination, specifically conversion to Roman Catholicism.[5]

Why has conversion emerged as an important concern in Roman Catholic theology only in the last few years? Lonergan himself suggests one significant reason: 'It is a topic little studied in traditional theology since there remains very little of it when one reaches the universal, the abstract and the static.'[6] Lonergan thus sees the neglect of conversion in traditional theology as stemming from an approach that has not appreciated the importance of interiority, historicity, and the individual. Conversion tends to be a very existential and individual phenomenon which escapes the categories of what Lonergan has described as the classicist approach to theology.[7]

Lonergan has mentioned an important factor, but there seem to be other factors which also explain the neglect of conversion in Roman Catholic theology in the past. An investigation of these reasons will be useful later in evaluating and criticising Lonergan's own notion of conversion. Catholic theology, when it did mention conversion in the past, generally limited it to the phenomenon of a non-Catholic's joining the Roman Catholic Church. Unlike the *Dictionnaire de Théologie Catholique*, the *Catholic Encyclopedia* published in the United States in 1911 does contain an article on conversion, but the entire article considers conversion only as entry into the Roman Catholic Church.[8] Dogmatic theology could not avoid a consideration of the reality contained in the concept of conversion, but the discussion generally took place under the heading of grace and justification. Christian conversion became a more important topic in contemporary theology precisely because of the renewed emphasis on biblical theology. The centrality and importance of conversion in the Scriptures and in the life of the early Church ensure that a biblically oriented theology must develop such a concept. The terminology of the theology manuals of the past reflected the scholastic philosophical categories and the language of the hierarchical magisterial pronouncements about Christian faith. The current shift to biblical categories and to contemporary philosophical categories, including the existentialist categories, has influenced the greater attention given to conversion in the more recent theological literature. A comparison of the article on conversion in the *New Catholic Encyclopedia* published in 1967 with the article in the 1911 encyclopedia well illustrates the centrality of the biblical foundation in the theological consideration of conversion.[9]

Moral theology in the Roman Catholic tradition has also neglected the concept of conversion. The reasons for such a neglect obviously include some of the factors already mentioned such as the lack of a biblical orientation and the stress on objective universal norms which did not give enough importance to the existential involvement of the subject in freely responding to the loving call of God in Christ. A legalist approach and the separation of moral theology from dogmatic theology favoured a view of man's moral actions considered as individual acts in relationship to a norm and not as actions expressing the heart of the person who has received the gift of divine sonship. In fairness to the Roman Catholic tradition in moral theology, the discussion of the virtues, as found, for example, in the approach of Thomas Aquinas, did discuss the moral self and the attitudes that should characterise the Christian self, but the manualist tradition failed to develop or even continue the Thomistic emphasis on the virtues. These manuals likewise failed to develop any other considerations of the person or the moral subject in keeping with more contemporary approaches in philosophy which stress the shift to interiority and subjectivity.

There is another important theological reason explaining the failure of Catholic moral theology to develop a consideration of conversion. Conversion presupposes the existence of human sinfulness, for the call to conversion remains an invitation to change one's heart, to be transformed, to pass from death to life, from darkness to light, from sin to love union with God and neighbour. Catholic theology with a poor understanding of the nature-grace relationship did not really appreciate the way in which sin does affect the person. Human nature remains the same in all possible stages of the history of salvation and is apparently not greatly affected by human sinfulness. Moral theology continued to consider sin as an individual action which is not in conformity with an objective law rather than viewing sin as affecting the subject in his intimate relationships with God, neighbour and the world. In general, human sinfulness is interpreted as depriving man of sanctifying grace but leaving his human nature intact.

Even the more widely acclaimed statements of Catholic teaching and philosophy seem to me to suffer from a failure to take seriously sin and its effects on human existence. *Pacem in Terris*, the famous encyclical of Pope John on peace, reveals a naïve and over-optimistic approach precisely because it fails to give sufficient importance to the reality of human sinfulness as it affects man today. In the concluding paragraph of the Introduction of the encyclical, Pope John claims that by those laws found in his nature men are taught about their relationships with their fellow citizens and with their states, the relationships that should exist among states and the urgent need to act for a world community of peoples. Unfortunately no discussion of the unconcern, lack of responsibility, selfishness, pride, etc. of men and nations ensues in this encyclical.[10] The too optimistic tone of the encyclical comes from a rationalism which does not take cognisance of the reality of human sinfulness. Paul Ramsey has pointed out the lack of realism in other aspects of *Pacem in Terris* precisely because the encyclical fails to acknowledge the reality and power of human sinfulness.[11] Elsewhere, I have developed a theology of compromise to deal with difficult human decisions in which the sin of the world is present, forcing one to act in a way that one would not choose if there were no sinfulness present in our world.[12]

Bernard Häring, who more than any other Catholic theologian has developed the concept of conversion, realised the need to change the concept of sin as it was generally understood in the manuals of moral theology. Sin does not primarily describe an individual, external act but rather an orientation of the person which involves the relationship of an individual with God, neighbour, self and the world.[13] Conversion is the biblical call to a change of heart. Even for the person who has now accepted the loving gift of God in Christ Jesus, Häring emphasises the need for continual conversion which comes from the fact that man never totally responds to the call of God but always falls short. In his consideration of continual conversion Häring tries to give an acceptable interpretation of the traditional Lutheran formula of man as *simul justus et peccator*. The Christian through the love of God dwelling in him by the gift of the Spirit constantly struggles to overcome the sinfulness which still remains a part of his existence. Häring's notion of continual conversion explains in a dynamic way the reality generally referred to as venial sin.[14]

Protestant theology generally has been more open to the concept of conversion or metanoia, for Protestant theology has been more biblical in its orientation, more conscious of the reality of human sinfulness, more aware of the importance of the conscious subject, and more open to expressing the Christian message in the categories of contemporary philosophical understandings of man. Liberal theology in the Protestant tradition tends to play down the reality of sin and conversion, but the more fundamentalist approaches in Protestantism have emphasised conversion as the central event in religious experience. The famous revivals, which in some form are still with us today, attempt to bring about this conversion in the hearer of the good news. The evangelistic movement in Protestantism with its stress on preaching the word of God aims ultimately at conversion. 'Conversion is a revolution of the life of the individual. The old forces of sin, self-centredness and evil are overthrown from their place of supreme power. Jesus Christ is put on the throne.'[15]

The emphasis in evangelical approaches on the individual—to the apparent exclusion of the need for the Christian and the Church to become involved in the social issues of the day—evoked criticism from other Protestant theologians. Reinhold Niebuhr objected to the approach of Billy Graham for its failure to show the social and cosmic dimensions of Christianity.[16] Somewhat the same criticism together with a more optimistic view of man underlies Gibson Winter's rejection of confessional proclamation in favour of prophetic proclamation:

By contrast the confessional assembly proclaims a present relationship of forgiveness wrought in the past but effective now and to eternity. The emphasis in the confessional assembly is upon the present acceptance of a relationship to God established in the saving history; the principal moment is the meaning of the present in the light of the past. Hence the crucial work of proclamation is preaching, for the principal issue is to acknowledge this relationship which God has initiated.[17]

Recent defences of the proclamation of conversion have responded to such criticism by emphasising the social and cosmic dimension of conversion,[18] but the evangelical proclamation of conversion generally tends towards individualism and does not appreciate the vocation of the Christian to cooperate in the work of bringing about the new heaven and the new earth. The place of conversion in theology, the reasons for its meagre development in Roman Catholic theology, and the criticisms of conversion in Protestantism furnish a helpful perspective in an attempt to analyse the concept of Christian conversion in Bernard Lonergan.

## II

Lonergan has not developed a systematic explanation of his concept of Christian conversion and its relationship to the other transcendental conversions—intellectual, moral and religious; but he has stressed that theology today needs to develop an understanding of conversion as a new type of foundation. 'What is normative and foundational for subjects stating theology is to be found, I have suggested, in reflection on conversion, where conversion is taken as an ongoing process, concrete and dynamic, personal, communal, and historical.'[19] Lonergan points out the philosophical reasons for his insistence on conversion; but, as is more evident in his treatment in *De Verbo Incarnato*, he is more than familiar with the scriptural data which stress the reality of sin and consequently also of conversion. Speaking of conversion in general, Lonergan maintains:

It is not really a change or even a development, rather it is a radical transformation on which follows, on all levels of living, an interlocked series of changes and developments. What hitherto was unnoticed becomes vivid and present. What has been of no concern becomes a matter of high import. So great a change in one's apprehensions and one's values accompanies no less a change in oneself, in one's relations to other persons and in one's relations to God.[20]

Lonergan specifically considers questions connected with Christian conversion in two different places, in the last chapter in *Insight* and in the concluding theses of his treatise *De Verbo Incarnato* in which he develops his theology of redemption.[21] Both considerations, although developed in terms of different starting points and perspectives, consider the question of Christian conversion in connection with the problem of sin and evil.

Lonergan, unlike some in Catholic theology in the past, does struggle with the problems related to sin. The development of the theme of redemption in *De Verbo Incarnato* commences by enunciating the fact that redemption means not only the end but the mediation or process to the end; namely, the paying of the price, the vicarious passion and death of Christ the mediator because of sins and for sinners, the sacrifice offered by our high priest in his own blood, meritorious obedience, the power of the resurrected Lord and the intercession of the eternal high priest. The second step explains the scriptural data in terms of the vicarious satisfaction of Jesus, whereas the third thesis (Lonergan was still employing at this time a thesis approach in theology) tries to give intelligibility to these scriptural and theological data in terms of the just and mysterious 'law of the cross'. 'The Son of God was made man, suffered, was raised, because divine wisdom ordered and divine goodness willed not to take away the evils of the human race through power but according to the just and mysterious law of the cross to convert (change) the same evils into a certain supreme good.'[22]

This thesis does not attempt a demonstration but rather seeks intelligibility. Redemption involves a transformation in which evil is transformed into good, and death is transformed into life. The death of Jesus results from the sin of those who put him to death, which action is the *malum culpae*. Out of loving obedience Jesus accepts this death (*malum poenae*) and thus transforms it into a good because of which the Father raised him from the dead and made him Lord and Messias. In itself death is the penalty of sin, but Jesus transformed death into a means of redemption and life. (Lonergan rightly points out that the death of Jesus does not result from the vindictive justice of the Father who would have to require the death of Jesus to satisfy for the punishment due to sin.)

The principle of transformation or conversion thus becomes the law of the cross for all those who are united with Christ Jesus through faith and baptism. Evil in the world results from sin, and man overcomes this evil not by succumbing to the temptation of using evil to overcome evil but by a daily carrying of his cross with a love that transforms evil into good. The law of redemption or transformation of evil into good through love thus becomes the law of life for the Christian.

At first sight Lonergan's understanding of Christian conversion seems to echo the conversion themes proposed in some Protestant literature, but a closer examination reveals significant differences. Take as an example a comparison of Lonergan's concept with that proposed by Dietrich Bonhoeffer who, while strongly influenced by Barth and also appreciative of Lutheran emphasis, nevertheless also argued for a place for the 'natural' in his ethics. Thus Bonhoeffer avoids both the extreme Barthian and extreme Lutheran positions which would be even more divergent from the proposals of Lonergan. Bonhoeffer develops an ethic of formation which describes the way in which the form of Jesus Christ becomes present in our lives and in our world. Bonhoeffer's fragmentary *Ethics* begins by showing the inadequacy and futility of ethical approaches based on reason, conscience, duty, free responsibility or noble humanity.[23] 'It is only as one who is sentenced by God that man can live before God. Only the crucified man is at peace with God. It is in the figure of the Crucified that man recognises and discovers himself. To be taken up by God, to be executed on the Cross and reconciled, that is the reality of manhood.'[24]

The transformation or conversion proposed by Lonergan, despite his insistence on its totality in his later, generic considerations of conversion and despite the transformation motif of the law of the cross, remains much less radical than the conversion implied in the formation ethics of Bonhoeffer, which in turn is less radical than the concept of conversion implied in Luther and Barth on theology. There are indications of Lonergan's less radical approach to conversion even in his explicit treatment of redemption in *De Verbo Incarnato*; whereas *Insight* both in its general heuristic structure and in its specific treatment of sin and the problem of evil emphasises Christian conversion within a wider context of integration and not radical transformation.

In *De Verbo Incarnato* the thesis on satisfaction in the redemption discusses at great length the concept of God's judgement which consists in the fact that the divine will chooses the order of the divine wisdom. There are four possible orderings within the divine justice—good comes forth from good, evil comes forth from evil, evil comes forth from good and good comes forth from evil. All four of these orderings are found in human and Christian life so that the entire Christian life cannot be reduced to any one of these models; thus the law of the cross does not adequately and totally explain the Christian life. God directly wills good; God indirectly wills natural defects and the *malum poenae*, but God only permits and does not will the *malum culpae*. Redemption involves the reintegration or reparation of the order of divine wisdom which is the eternal law existing in the mind of God. Such an understanding of redemption does not imply the existence of a wiser and more powerful being who corrects the order laid down by God, but rather the present order contains not only the good that God wills but also the *malum culpae* which God in no way wills but only permits and the evil of natural defects and the *malum poenae* which God only indirectly wills. In so far as evil men sin, their evil violates the order of divine justice; but in so far as all things are subject to divine providence and governance, the violated order is repaired or reintegrated. Thus the mystery of sin and redemption shows forth the multifaceted wisdom and justice of God. The law of the cross based on the ordering by which God brings forth good from evil represents one of the many orderings all of which together comprise the divine justice. The bringing forth of good from evil represents only one aspect or one part of the totality of the divine wisdom and justice so that the law of the cross is not the complete explanation of the justice and ordering of God.[25]

The general structure of *Insight* indicates that sin does not involve a completely radical break and destruction of everything that is human; and thus conversion is not a radical transformation which completely negates the existing human structure. *Insight* employs a moving perspective which develops and builds upon the detached, disinterested, unrestricted desire to know. Sin is viewed as a hindrance to this full development of the self but not as the destruction of this human structure. In fact, Lonergan only poses the problem of evil and an attempted solution in the last chapter of *Insight*, but the solution remains in total harmony with the basic self-transcendence of man the knower and decider which forms the heuristic structure for the entire argument of *Insight*. In man one can observe openness as a fact—'the pure desire to know'. This openness belongs to the very structure of man and continually urges him to expand his basic horizon in terms of what Lonergan later describes as the four transcendent and fundamental conversions.[26]

This primordial fact of openness is 'no more than a principle of possible achievement, a definition of the ultimate horizon that is to be reached only through successive enlargements of the actual horizon.'[27] Notice that Lonergan here employs the term 'enlargement', a term which is less radical than 'conversion'. Such successive enlargements in man cannot be achieved precisely because of his sinful state which thus needs to receive openness as a loving gift from the self-communication of God. This gift is not only grace as *sanans* (i.e. healing the basic powers that man has but cannot develop because of the bias, prejudice, etc. which Lonergan describes in *Insight*) but the gift of openness is grace as *elevans* because this ultimate enlargement is beyond the resources of every finite consciousness although it alone approximates to the possibility of openness defined by the pure, disinterested, unrestricted desire to know. The fact that Lonergan introduces his solution to the problem of evil only in the last chapter of *Insight* indicates that evil or sin does not totally destroy the human reality. Lonergan thus philosophises within the Catholic tradition which has generally upheld the fact that one can go from man to God through one's reasoning, whereas elements in the Protestant tradition, either because of an insistence on a more total and radical disruptiveness of sin or because of the neo-Orthodox tenet that one cannot go from man to God, see no possibility of such sustained development in our understanding of man and his relationship to God. Lonergan's concept of conversion, precisely because of his view of man, cannot be as radical as that proposed by some thinkers in the Protestant tradition.

Lonergan's explicit treatment of the problem of evil and sin in *Insight* again does not regard sin in as radical a way as do some other theological views. Sin obviously does not destroy everything human for Lonergan. Sin affects man's will, intellect and sense faculties but does not destroy these. The solution to the problem of evil as a harmonious continuation of the subject's self-transcendence calls for the introduction of cognate forms that will allow man to sustain the development that is impeded because of his bias and prejudice. Lonergan stresses that the solution to the problem of evil will always be a harmonious continuation of the order of the universe, and that man will not only acknowledge and accept the solution but also collaborate with it. The problem of evil exists precisely because God takes seriously man's freedom, and thus the solution to the problem of evil must also take seriously the freedom and cooperation of man. Lonergan posits three possible solutions to the problem of evil—natural, relatively supernatural and absolutely supernatural solutions. The solution offered for the Christian is the absolutely supernatural solution whose sole ground and measure is the divine nature itself. Even the absolutely supernatural solution involves higher integration in emergent consciousness, but it heightens the tensions which arise whenever the lower levels are transcended and integrated into a higher level.[28]

The emphasis on conversion in general and Christian conversion in particular seems to vary somewhat in Lonergan's different considerations. His latest article speaks of conversion as a 'radical transformation which is neither just a change or development'. In the theological consideration of redemption the law of the cross involves a seemingly radical transformation of evil into good or of death into life, but the law of the cross exemplifies only one aspect and not the totality of the divine wisdom and the divine justice. *Insight*, with its moving viewpoint and harmonious development based on the pure, detached, disinterested, unrestricted desire to know, only introduces a solution to the problem of evil in the last chapter, thus indicating that the disruption of sin and evil is far from being total and radical. The absolutely supernatural solution to the problem of evil is still characterised as an integration on a higher level or an enlargement.

The radicality of Christian conversion ultimately depends upon the radicality of sin. Lonergan here follows the Roman Catholic tradition which views sin in a less radical way than approaches in non-liberal Protestant theology. In *Insight* sin does not destroy the development of man but rather constitutes an obstacle that can be overcome in terms of a higher integration. In his treatment of sin in *De Verbo Incarnato* Lonergan curiously accepts and proposes a very inadequate definition of sin. In both theses in which sin appears as one of the terms, sin is defined as a bad human act in which the malice is considered primarily from a theological viewpoint and consists in an offence to God.[29] Even in developing these two theses Lonergan generally ascribes the death of Jesus, primarily at least, to the sin of the Jews or of

Pilate or of those who actually put Jesus to death. A more appropriate theological understanding of sin would challenge Lonergan's understanding of sin especially as found in *De Verbo Incarnato*. Sin describes the multiple relationships of the individual with God, neighbour, self and the world. There also remains a cosmic aspect of sin, somewhat similar to the personified notion of sin found in St Paul. Sin as this personified force is obviously the primary factor in the death of Jesus; in fact the death of Jesus in one aspect seems to be the hour of the triumph of the power of darkness, but the resurrection marks that transforming victory of Jesus over sin and death.

I would generally agree with the approach that views sin as not destroying the basic structure of man, the self-transcending subject; but Lonergan too often views sin merely as an act or as a reality primarily affecting the subject. The approach to sin in *Insight* in terms of a lack of the cognate forms of faith, hope and charity could be expanded to see sin ultimately in terms of the lack of relationships of love with God, neighbour, self and the world. Sin is not primarily an act but a condition affecting or even severing man's multiple relationships. In this view sin, and consequently conversion, would be more radical without denying the continuity between sinful man who remains a self-transcending subject and the man who has experienced a Christian conversion which is an absolutely supernatural solution to the problem of evil. Lonergan must realise that he has employed different and even conflicting terminology in describing Christian conversion as a radical transformation, conversion, development and enlargement, and integration. Logically, it seems Lonergan should adopt a more radical understanding of sin in terms of relationships or of a condition of separation from God, neighbour, self and the world—which, however, still sees the sinful man as a self-transcending subject who finds his own fulfilment in the supernatural solution to the problem of evil which is aptly described as Christian conversion.

For most Christians continual conversion remains the most important problem of daily Christian existence, for normally the true Christian should already have overcome the alienation of sin and entered into the basic relationship of love with God, neighbour, self and the world. In this world no one ever completely overcomes the reality of sin, but the law of Christian growth and existence shows forth the rhythm of the paschal mystery in the need to constantly die to ourselves in order to rise in newness of life. Lonergan mentions this aspect of conversion in both *De Verbo Incarnato* and *Insight*, but continual conversion, precisely because of its importance and centrality, calls for a more extensive development and consideration.

Lonergan's notion of conversion, like that proposed by some in Protestant theology, remains open to the charge of individualism for failure to pay sufficient attention to the social, ecclesial and cosmic aspects of redemption. In *De Verbo Incarnato* sin was explained merely in terms of an act and the malice was seen in relationship to God; whereas sin involves man in the core of his being and affects his multiple relationships with God, neighbour and the world. Redemption, at least in *De Verbo Incarnato*, emphasised the personal or individual aspect without developing the cosmic and social aspect. One would not expect this work to include a full-scale development of the ecclesial understanding of redemption for the Christian but at least some mention of this dimension is necessary. In *Insight* Lonergan does acknowledge a social and cosmic dimension to the reality of sin by showing how bias and prejudice bring about the social surd. This could serve as a basis for developing a social and cosmic understanding of Christian conversion which seems to be implicit in some of Lonergan's thinking, but one would have to conclude that this aspect of conversion needs further development. The complaint among some Protestant scholars that conversion theology has been too individualistic finds something of a parallel in Johannes B. Metz's criticism that the transcendental method employed by Karl Rahner does not give enough importance to the world and history.[30] At the very least, Lonergan needs to develop the social and cosmic aspects of Christian conversion.

### III

The Lonergan of *Insight*, according to David W. Tracy, sees basic horizon as expanded by the higher viewpoints which involve intellectual, moral, religious and Christian conversion.[31] Having considered the concept of Christian conversion in Lonergan, one must logically consider the relationship which exists among the various conversions. The four conversions do not constitute the central discussion in *Insight*. The major consideration centres on intellectual conversion as the self-transcending subject moves to the higher viewpoints of empirical consciousness, intellectual consciousness, and rational consciousness, which correspond to the actions of experience, understanding and judgement. Chapter XVIII treats of moral conversion and ethics in terms of rational self-consciousness; chapter XIX develops religious conversion in terms of general transcendence although most of the chapter explicitates Lonergan's argument for the existence of God. Chapter XX poses the problem of evil and proposes a possible heuristic solution in terms of special transcendence.

Problems arise from a number of sources. In his later writings, Lonergan stresses the conversion that involves a radical transformation which is not merely a change or even a development, but *Insight* speaks of integration, enlargement and development rather than radical transformation or even conversion, for Lonergan cannot be as radical as others might be precisely because of his understanding of the subject's self-transcendence and the reality of sin. Lonergan himself in his later writings seems to indicate that there is little difference between religious and Christian conversion. In an essay entitled 'The Future of Christianity' Lonergan develops under the heading of religious conversion many of the same points that he considered earlier in *Insight* and *De Verbo Incarnato* in relation to Christian conversion.[32] The problem of evil and the law of the cross seem to be included under religious conversion which calls for renunciation and sacrifice, but Lonergan does not explicitly develop the problem of sin and evil in this very abbreviated context. Obviously Lonergan's understanding of conversion and of the relationship among the various conversions raises a number of perplexing questions. I will venture suggestions which explain some of the apparent inconsistencies, call for some revisions and raise further questions.

There are definite indications that Lonergan's treatment of the four conversions in *Insight* does not correspond with his later writings on conversion. Although chapter XIX of *Insight* discusses general transcendence and the existence of God, the discussion remains in the realm of a rational argument for the existence of God. Belief comes into the discussion only in the last chapter when the problem of evil is raised. Lonergan in *Insight* does not really consider religious conversion as involving an orientation to a personal God who is both Other and Redeemer. Although Lonergan mentions the problem of evil at the end of chapter XVIII on Ethics, he does not propose a solution to the problem of evil until he arrives at his consideration of special transcendence which seems to correspond with his understanding of Christian conversion. All would have to agree that the problem of evil and its solution cannot be ignored on the level of moral and religious conversion and just left to the level of Christian conversion.

My proposed solution to the understanding of the relationship among the conversions and of Lonergan's insistence on the somewhat radical and total nature of conversion (realising how he tempers such language because of his whole understanding of man and of sin) would be to combine the moral, religious and Christian conversions into one generic concept of conversion which retains the somewhat radical character that Lonergan seems to demand of conversion and which calls for a much closer relationship between the moral, religious and Christian aspects of conversion.

A theological perspective would tend to see the moral, religious and Christian conversions as more intimately united and together embracing the total phenomenon of conversion. Lonergan himself in his later writings obviously sees a close similarity between religious and Christian conversion, even to such an extent that many people would wonder what is the real difference between them. Catholic theology has insisted upon the universal salvific will of God by which God offers all men the saving gift of his love. The radical conversion of saving belief does not depend upon an explicit acceptance of Jesus as Lord, for all men, whether they have heard of Christ Jesus or not, in the mysterious providence of God receive his loving invitation. Catholic theology has avoided the danger of a narrow Christology which would exclude people from the family of God who did not explicitly acknowledge Jesus as Lord.

On the level of moral conversion, one of the fundamental considerations in the manualistic treatment of grace was the fact that man without the gift of grace could not for long observe the substance of the natural law.[33] Christian theology sees the problem of evil existing on the moral level and bringing about a moral impotence even with regard to the fundamental substance of the natural law. Thus moral, religious and Christian conversion do not constitute three totally different conversions but rather they are intimately joined in the one total theological conversion. So intimately are they joined that Catholic theology has been willing to admit that where one of these is present the others are present, at least implicitly. One of the three cannot exist in the individual person without at least the implicit existence of the other two. Such a theological understanding corresponds to the biblical notion of conversion as the change of heart which intimately affects man in his relationships with God, neighbour, self and the world.

Does this theological understanding bringing together the moral, religious and Christian aspects of conversion contradict the approach of *Insight* which seems to distinguish four conversions—the intellectual, moral, religious and Christian? Perhaps not. *Insight* with its moving viewpoint considers the self-transcending subject with the exigencies of the pure, detached disinterested, unrestricted desire to know. Lonergan heuristically develops his argument in *Insight* in terms of the basic openness of the subject who gradually moves to a higher level of integration. In a later article, Lonergan distinguishes openness as fact or capacity from openness as achievement and openness as gift.[34] Lonergan describes openness as fact as man's capacity for self-transcendence. *Insight* develops precisely in terms of describing the various levels involved in this capacity for openness, but even in *Insight* Lonergan emphasises that man can never totally achieve this openness, and that total openness is ultimately pure gift on the part of God. The moving viewpoint of *Insight* does not intend to give a total picture, but views man merely in terms of this fact of openness or this capacity for self-transcendence.

In the real, existential order, man can only receive this openness as gift—a gift that far transcends him but still fulfils the capacity for openness which is his. *Insight* purposely abstracts from the fact of openness as gift which in the existential order remains a most important fact, if not the most important fact about man and his relationship to God and others in this existence. A consideration of man merely from the viewpoint of openness as fact or as capacity for self-transcendence can more easily make

distinctions between the moral, religious and Christian conversions; but in the existential order the three are more intimately
united because the problem raised by each of these conversions
remains the same problem of evil and the solution for one is also
the solution for the other. In the real order openness as gift brings
with it the radical conversion which is at one and the same time
moral, religious and Christian even if all these levels are not
explicitated in the one reality of this conversion.

This joining together of the three conversions into the one
conversion in the existential order does not seem to contradict
the different viewpoint of *Insight*. Even according to *Insight* these
three conversions all occur on the same level of rational self-
consciousness or existential consciousness. Here in the existential
order these three conversions are better interpreted as three
aspects of that profound (but not totally radical) transformation
which the Scriptures refer to as the change of heart.

Obviously the question arises of the fidelity of the above
explanation to Lonergan's own thought. At the same time such
an understanding also raises further questions of its own. What
are the exact relationships between and among these three
aspects of conversion? Lonergan has been dealing lately, even if
only in an indirect manner, with the relationship between the
religious and the Christian aspects of conversion. On at least two
different occasions Lonergan has cited the work of Friedrich
Heiler who lists the characteristics common to all religious belief.
These characteristics include some of the items which Lonergan
incorporated in his study of Christian redemption and these
abbreviated expositions include in an implicit way the factors
underlying the law of the cross in the life of the Christian.
Lonergan realised the problem and the need to show what is
distinctive about Christianity, but he has not managed as yet to
develop this aspect.[35]

The danger seems to be that Lonergan will not give enough
importance to the historical person of Jesus Christ and the way
in which he revealed the love of the Father. The absence of any
explicit eschatology in Lonergan's writings also could indicate
that he is not giving enough importance to the historical aspect
of God's revelation. Certainly Lonergan, who emphasises the
need for historical consciousness, cannot overlook the historical
reality of Jesus Christ and his revelation of the Father's word and

work. On the other hand, this is not a problem peculiar to Lonergan, for every Christian theologian must come to grips with this question. Recent writings on anonymous Christians or implicit Christians or Christ and his Church as the extraordinary means of salvation are all different attempts at dealing with the same problem.

What is the exact relationship between the moral aspect of conversion and the religious-Christian aspects? Lonergan has not given public attention to this relationship although in *Insight* he raises the problem of evil in connection with ethics and moral conversion. The moral impotence of man's effective freedom ultimately raises a problem that man himself cannot solve. Lonergan in the chapter on ethics merely poses the problem and suggests that 'the solution has to be a still higher integration of human living. For the problem is radical and permanent; it is independent of the underlying physical, chemical, organic, and psychic manifolds; it is not met by revolutionary change, nor by human discovery, nor by the enforced implementation of discovery; it is as large as human living and human history.'[36] The higher integration and solution to the problem of moral impotence can only be the conversion on the level of rational self-consciousness which results from the loving gift of God, openness as gift.

What then is the relationship between this moral-religious-Christian conversion and the intellectual conversion which is developed at great length in *Insight*? Intellectual conversion involves the self-structuring process of the human intellect, 'the self appropriation of one's rational self-consciousness'. Moral conversion in *Insight* involves the movement from the level of judgement to the level of decision. The rational self-consciousness which self-affirmation confirms must expand itself into the domain of doing, acting and making. For this reason there is a close relationship between intellectual conversion and the moral aspect of existential conversion. Ultimately in the real order the problem of sin enters here, and the ultimate solution requires a solution to the problem of evil. The rationally conscious subject demands that his actions correspond to his knowledge. Decision seen as an individual act certainly follows judgement as a form of higher integration. However, one cannot merely view decision as an individual act, but rather one must consider the rationally self-conscious subject and his moral impotency with regard to effective freedom.

How is intellectual conversion related to the other existential conversion in human existence with its moral, religious and Christian aspects? All would have to agree that one of these conversions could exist without the other, so that there is no necessary link between them. One could ask Lonergan if his moving viewpoint of *Insight* does correspond with human experience and to what degree the intellectual conversion in the transcendent self calls for a more existential conversion. Lonergan's own willingness to grapple with the problem of evil and sin indicates that the relationship between the two conversions cannot be as continuous as Lonergan would maintain in *Insight*. Sin brings in the character of discontinuity, although I would agree that this does not destroy all continuity in the development of self-transcendence. But sin and the real order do involve more discontinuity than Lonergan is willing to admit in *Insight*, and for that same reason the solution to the problem of evil in the real order cannot involve a harmonious and continual development from moral conversion to religious conversion to Christian conversion but rather the existing discontinuity does call for a more radical solution which embraces at one and the same time the three aspects of moral, religious and Christian conversion.

If Lonergan continues to emphasise the somewhat radical character of conversion and continues to bring religious and Christian conversion closer together, then it seems he must admit that in the real order there are only two conversions—the intellectual conversion and what we have called the existential conversion with its moral-religious-Christian aspects. Since *Insight* was written merely from the viewpoint of self-transcendence as capacity, the fact that there are only these two conversions would not necessarily be contradictory to the development in *Insight*. Perhaps Lonergan can even use *Insight's* development to explain the difference between the moral, religious and Christian aspects of the one reality of existential conversion; but this difference cannot be in terms of the problem of evil, since this problem and its solution are intimately linked with all three aspects of existential conversion.

# Lonergan and the Teaching Church

## CHARLES DAVIS

THE writings of Bernard Lonergan have exerted and continue to exert a powerful influence upon me. Indeed, when I read them, they do more than influence me; they temporarily overwhelm me. I find myself caught up in the onward drive of his powerful mind as he moves methodically from point to point, clarifying confused issues, shedding light on a wealth of material and bringing widely diverse areas of thought into relationship. When I start reading him, it is difficult for me to break off and do anything else. I finally emerge in a state of intellectual euphoria —or should I say drunkenness? I have learned more from Lonergan's writings than I can easily recount. I must, however, mention my chief debts.

It would be too great a claim to say that under his guidance I have fully succeeded in appropriating my own rational self-consciousness. But this much is true. He has enabled me to become sufficiently familiar with the dynamic structure of my consciousness for me to experience the process of discovery, differentiation and appropriation of my conscious activities as an intellectual and moral transformation. To the study of Lonergan I owe the greatest change I have undergone in my self-understanding.

Because of my background, it was Lonergan the Scholastic who was able to help me as no other thinker could have done. Despite a preliminary perusal of *Insight*, I first grasped Lonergan's meaning through the *Verbum* articles. They led me to an understanding of the book. This indicates the nature of the help he chiefly gave me. It was not so much that he gave me a new awareness of the problems raised by modern thought, set me thinking personally about a variety of issues and made me grasp what much modern thought was about. Other thinkers could have done the same for me. Where his role was indispensable for my development was in his clarification of what had become the confused jumble of the scholastic tradition. His Latin theological treatises and lecture notes are, I suppose, inaccessible to those who have not been through the grind of a scholastic training. For me, believe it or not, they were exhilarating in their deployment of powerful and clear thinking. Lonergan leavened with understanding the dead conceptual dough of the scholastic tradition as I had received it. This was for me an immense liberation. It meant that I was able to assimilate the scholastic tradition in which I had been educated and bring order and clarity into the elements of my past formation. Scholastic philosophy and theology became a mental inheritance from which I could start, not a block preventing my further development. I did not have to destroy my past: I could grow out of it.

In my own search for truth I now need to look to other thinkers than Lonergan. Apart from my reservations about his thought, which I shall be briefly indicating, I find that so comprehensive and so powerfully systematic a thinker as Lonergan tends to imprison lesser minds. In a similar fashion Hegel captured several generations. But even though I turn now to listen to others, I doubt whether I shall meet with any writer who will exert the same impact upon me as Lonergan. When the tradition in which one has been born and educated produces a major thinker, he inevitably retains a privileged place in one's personal development. I come now, however, to the paradox which suggested the theme of this paper to me.

The impact of the inexorable onward drive of Lonergan's thinking is not felt only by those from within the scholastic tradition. John Wren-Lewis, scientist and Anglican lay theologian, was the reader chosen by Longmans, the publisher, to report upon *Insight*. He told the publisher that the book was a major work by any standards. In an article he has described the effect the reading of the book had upon him in these words:

When I had finished it I found I had been forced, by a process of iron logic, to conclude that I ought to make my submission to Rome forthwith. I found the conclusion utterly unacceptable, not just because the Roman communion seems to me unlikely ever to be reformed from its totalitarian attitudes, but also because I could not bring myself to believe that a total personal commitment could possibly be forced by a neat piece of logical argument. So I set out to go through the book with a fine tooth-comb to see if Professor Lonergan had put something over on me somewhere—and my resulting discovery formed the basis for a very great deal of my subsequent thinking.

I am not at the moment concerned with Wren-Lewis' discovery of what he considered the flaw in Lonergan's argument, but simply with the impact the book made upon him as a most persuasive presentation of the case for joining the Roman Catholic Church.

The paradox is this. I am convinced that I myself should never have been able to leave the Roman Catholic Church, had it not been for my reading of Lonergan. Let me say that I am dealing here, not with the reasons which immediately led up to my decision and which I set forth in *A Question of Conscience*,[1] but with the influences which, in Lonerganian terms, established the horizon within which I did my thinking and took my decision. These influences were many, and it is difficult to be sure of the relative part each played. Nevertheless, as far as my present self-knowledge goes, the reading of Lonergan freed the spiritual dynamic within me from the heteronomy that had severely circumscribed and oppressed it and, in doing so, liberated me to pursue the truth as I saw it and to make a radical decision when this was demanded of me.

But why did I not find considerations in Lonergan strong enough to counteract the reasons that led me to reject the Roman Catholic Church? After all, Lonergan himself has made no secret of the purpose of his work as the support and strengthening of the faith and the Church to which he has devoted the service of his own life. That purpose comes across clearly at the end of *Insight*. I have just mentioned Wren-Lewis' vivid perception of where Lonergan would lead him. Lonergan has gone to modern thought with the intention of 'despoiling the Egyptians'.[2] He has worked for the adaptation of the Roman Catholic Church, religion, faith and theology to the new context of modern culture while, however, regarding that Church, religion, faith and even that theology as remaining substantially the same through the required cultural transition. How, then, could Lonergan have such a powerful impact upon me and yet fail to convince me of the validity of the chief purpose of all his work?

The simple answer is that Lonergan assumes what I questioned. He therefore provided nothing to meet my particular difficulties. This personal experience has led me to suspect that like other powerful systems Lonergan's rests upon unquestioned assumptions. It is my purpose here to suggest this line of criticism.

In his *De Deo Trino* Lonergan refers to the infallible magisterium of the Church as alone capable of making judgements concerning revealed doctrine with complete certitude:

... neque alia sapientia de doctrina divinitus revelata tuto iudicet nisi quae divinitus adiuta in ecclesiae magisterio reponatur (*D.D.T.* 1, 8). Circa vero divinum revelationis fontem, constat sensum alicuius veri ab eius mensurari intelligentia ex quo verum illud procedat. Quare, cum verum revelatum ex ipsa divina intelligentia procedat, a sola divina intelligentia mensuratur. Praeterea, cum his in terris nulli alteri nisi ecclesiæ tradiderit Deus suam revelationem fideliter custodiendam et infallibiliter declarandam, manifestum est theologum non suae sapientiae confidere posse sed semper agnoscere debere ex solo ecclesiae magisterio determinari sensum tum ipsius veri revelati tum sacrorum dogmatum (DB 1788, 1800, 1818). Quod si theologus, uti ipsa rei natura postulat, prompte et libenter sapientiam suam ecclesiae magisterio postponit, remedium simul invenit contra illum morbum, illud peccati vulnus, quod nuperrime indicavimus (*D.D.T.* 11, 32). Denique tandem, cum rerum divinarum sapientia Deo propria sit, ne sapientissimi quidem theologi est de divinis iudicare absolute, sed suum iudicium submittat necesse est ad eum cui Deus his in terris infallibilitatem promisit (*D.D.T.* 11, 53).

The argument is clear enough. It is put with vigorous brevity in the short popular article on the Assumption:

Catholics believe in divine revelation. They believe not merely with their ears, but also with their minds. But they reject to-day, as they rejected in the sixteenth century, the strange notion that a public revelation is to be interpreted by private judgement.[3]

And the principle stated as a general principle in *De Deo Trino* is applied to the Assumption in his more technical article on that dogma:

... ultimately, certitude rests not upon judgement proceeding from merely human understanding but upon the judgement of the church to whom God has promised infallibility in matters of faith and morals.[4]

Now, this view of the relation of divine revelation to the

magisterium assumes a great deal. It identifies a public judgement about revealed doctrine with a judgement exercised by divinely authorised officials, set apart from the ordinary faithful in a hierarchically constituted Church. But public judgements are not limited to hierarchically constituted societies. One can argue that the distinction between the *ecclesia docens* and the *ecclesia discens*, understood as a distinction of permanent hierarchical powers, belonged to a cultural context where the order of society was aristocratic and paternalistic. Nowadays public judgements are—at least ideally—made in a democratic fashion with authority coming from below. The very concept of a magisterium in the hierarchical sense would seem to be an anachronism coming from a past when the ordinary members of a society were considered in principle to be uneducated. The ideal now should be that all become both the *ecclesia docens*—by their participation in the transmission of revelation—and also the *ecclesia discens*—by their attentive submission to that revealed tradition. The procedures for ascertaining and expressing the *consensus* in the Church would vary. I see no inherent reason why God should impart the wisdom needed in judging of revealed truths only through a hierarchically constituted Church.

I am not attempting here to establish the alternative view I have just outlined. That would require an examination of the data of Scripture and tradition, not just the putting forward of a hypothesis. I am merely indicating how much Lonergan assumes. He takes the Roman Catholic view of the magisterium for granted as dealt with elsewhere. Thus in *De Deo Trino* a footnote reads: 'Ex aliis et praeviis tractatibus lectorem iam cognoscere supponimus quotquot specialissimam Dei profidentiam, divinam revelationem, sacrae scripturae inspirationem, ecclesiae magisterium respiciant'.[5] This is reasonable enough in the immediate context; an author cannot deal with everything at once. But the assumption is made generally in Lonergan's writings. True, he argues in *Insight*: 'But the one human means of keeping a collaboration true to its purpose and united in its efforts is to set up an organisation that possesses institutions capable of making necessary judgements and decisions that are binding on all. Accordingly, it follows that God will secure the preservation of faith against heresy through some appropriate institutional organisation of the new and higher collaboration.'[6]

But however one estimates that argument itself, its conclusion falls far short of the Roman Catholic magisterium. I have not found any justification elsewhere of Lonergan's assumption concerning the magisterium of the Church.

If in our minds we bring together the present state of the theology of the Church and Lonergan's unqualified insistence upon the need of the theologian to submit to the magisterium of the Church, we shall see, I think, that his assumption is a very large one for a writer on theological method to make. But this weakness—if I may call it so—provides a hint worth pursuing. According to Lonergan, speculative or systematic theology depends in an essential way upon the magisterium of the Church.

First, whenever this is possible, speculative theology will begin from ecclesiastical definitions and declarations rather than the Bible: 'Attamen, stante dicta identitate veri et sensus, longe propius ad munus officiumque theologiae systematicae accedit declaratio ecclesiastica quam biblica.'[7] The reason for this is that the categories used in ecclesiastical declarations are universal whereas those of the Bible belong to a particular time and place. The Church uses categories expressing the objectively prior (*priora quoad se*), the biblical categories express what was experientially prior (*priora quoad nos*) in a particular historical situation.

Second, the soundness of structure of speculative theology depends upon an accurate and complete formulation of the theoretical elements from which it forms its principles and draws its conclusions. If its selection of these elements from the sources of revelation is defective, then its systematic structure is radically vitiated. A valid selection is the work of wisdom. While the theologian has some wisdom, he looks to the magisterium of the Church as alone possessing an adequate endowment of wisdom in regard to revealed truth. To quote directly from the passage I have been summarising:

In this intermediate position between wisdom and folly, he [the theologian] must take every precaution to arrive at the basic theoretical elements and all of them in as accurate a formulation as he can attain. But the greater his mastery of his subject, the keener will be his realisation of the difficulty of this task and the profounder will be his gratitude that God has vouchsafed us not only a revelation of supernatural truth but also a divinely assisted teaching authority that is not chary in its use of the evangelical *Est, Est* and *Non, Non*.[8]

In brief, speculative theology is subordinated to the magisterium as both understanding and science are subordinated to wisdom.

Third, the speculative theologian depends upon the magisterium for any certitude accruing to the results of his own labours: 'Because the theologian is aware of his inescapable limitations, he propounds even his clearest theorems as merely probable. Because his clearest theorems are only probable, he is ever ready to leave an ultimate judgement upon them to the further exercise of faith that discerns in the church's dogmatic decisions the assistance of divine wisdom.'[9] Such, then, is the close relationship between speculative theology and the teaching authority of the Church.

In so far as Lonergan's account includes the more general thesis of the dependence of theology upon the mediation of revelation through the Christian community I have no quarrel with it. But it includes much more than that, and its specific thesis of a dependence upon a magisterium exercised by authoritatively imposed dogmatic decisions has, I think, important repercussions upon Lonergan's thought.[10] The mentality that comes to expression in Lonergan's thesis is best conveyed by two further points which he adds to it.

First, he has several times made the point that the magisterium in its teaching draws upon the systematic formulations of theologians and, in doing so, confirms, teaches and perhaps defines them. It is in this way that the theological movement from the biblical and patristic understanding and expression to the systematic enters into the dogmatic movement of doctrinal development. Systematic categories are universal and express what is objectively prior. They have a synthetic power and bring many elements under a single view. Their use by the magisterium and their consequent wider use within the Church are the reason for the combination of sureness of doctrine with versatility of expression as found within the Roman Catholic Church. 'So we find', writes Lonergan, 'that non-Catholic clergymen, often more learned in scripture and the fathers, preach from their pulpits the ideas put forward in the latest stimulating book or article, while the Catholic priest, often burdened with sacerdotal duties and administrative tasks, spontaneously expounds the epistle or gospel of the Sunday in the light of an understanding that is common to the ages.'[11]

Second, every new dogmatic decree makes possible a new advance in speculative theology: . . . 'with each new dogmatic pronouncement that basis of the *via inventionis* receives an increment in clarity and precision that is passed on to its conclusions to result in a corresponding increment in the exactitude of the *ordo doctrinae* and in the understanding of revelation.'[12]

There is, I think, no doubt that the theological approach I have just outlined is indissolubly tied to belief in the infallibility of an authoritative magisterium. In other words, it presupposes that the indefectibility of the Christian faith means the infallibility of a teaching authority in issuing dogmatic definitions. Thus, in an approach without such an infallible authority the theologian would have no secure basis for his systematic work. He could not be sure that his basic theoretical elements were accurate and complete. His systematic structure would be open to radical vitiation. Again, the shift to the systematic and the objectively prior would be clouded with uncertainty. There would be no authority to judge the results with complete certitude and thereby give a permanent place in a dogmatic tradition to the systematic formulations of theologians. Further, the lack of certitude would prevent systematic categories from exercising their role in bestowing 'the enviable combination of sureness of doctrine with versatility of expression'[13] upon the work of teaching the faith. At the same time, systematic theologians themselves, unable to rely upon ecclesiastical declarations as providing a ready starting-point and a continual increment of clarity and precision, would be thrown back upon the less manageable biblical and patristic data and the uncertain achievement of their predecessors. In brief, the doctrinal and systematic traditions would be as fluid and confused as among Anglicans and Protestants.

Although the magisterium is not always exercised infallibly, I think it right to say that Lonergan's theological approach as outlined presupposes infallibility, not just authority—first, because Lonergan himself freely refers to the magisterium as infallible; second, because the role assigned to the magisterium would be impossible if the final word of the magisterium were uncertain; third, the whole approach, I suggest, reflects the dogmatic mentality of the Roman Catholic Church, which needs and finds expression in the doctrine of infallibility.

Once again it is not to my purpose here directly to discuss the pros and cons of the doctrine of an infallible magisterium. I do not deny that a case can be made out for it. But Lonergan himself presupposes rather than argues for the doctrine. Because, as I shall shortly suggest, the presupposition underlies much of his philosophical as well as theological thought, his whole impressive system might be taken as an apologetic of the doctrine. However, it remains a presupposition in so far as Lonergan does not himself come to grips with the problem of maintaining the doctrine in the face of the serious arguments that can be brought against it. And it is a large presupposition for him to make, because it does determine the place and importance given to doctrinal certitude in religious faith.

It is by no means obvious that God's purpose in making a revelation would be frustrated without an infallible magisterium. Nothing in the concept of divine revelation necessitates absolute accuracy in its reception and transmission. Some Christian theologians are convinced that the purpose of divine revelation requires no more in regard to errors of reception and transmission than the counteracting and eventual overcoming of them through a variety of means in God's providential ordering of history. There is no sufficient reason for supposing that God prevents the very occurrence of error in some inerrant record of revelation and in the legally authenticated interpretations of an infallible magisterium. Lonergan's own later articles would lead one to regard the expectation of an inerrant record and infallibly defined dogmas as a vestige remaining from classical culture.

To take but a single point from the historical problem. A Catholic historian, Francis Oakley, has recently traced the history and present implications of the conciliar movement which brought the Great Schism of the West to an end at the Council of Constance by declaring the supremacy of an ecumenical council over the Pope. He contends that the various attempts to weaken or destroy the dogmatic validity of *Haec sancta*, the decree of 1415 defining conciliar supremacy, are ungrounded. He also argues that *Haec sancta* and the decrees of the First Vatican Council contradict each other. Hence we have two conciliar pronouncements, both of full dogmatic authority, in direct conflict. This undermines any ecclesiastical claim to infallibility.

While Oakley presents the rehabilitation of Constance and the conciliar movement as offering liberals a chance to seize the initiative again in the Church by calling vigorously for a new ecumenical council even if the Pope does not welcome or encourage this, he sees beyond the liberal interpretation to the radical implications of his findings. He writes:

. . . it is absolutely vital that the coming Vatican III should itself be willing to meet that demand, to renounce, that is—publicly, unambiguously, and in the most solemn terms—the absolutist claims traditionally and currently made on behalf of the Church's teaching authority. So great a renunciation, so abject an admission of fallibility, so radical a commitment to honesty would have an electrifying effect on the whole Christian world.[14]

I have not quoted that passage because I see Oakley's call for a dramatic renunciation as other than quixotic, but because it vividly conveys that the collapse of the doctrine of infallibility means the end of claims to absolute truth. I want to suggest as a hypothesis for the interpretation of Lonergan that his presupposition of an infallible magisterium and of the dogmatic certitude mediated by such a magisterium has led him both to overstress the absolute character of truth and to reach his philosophical conclusions too rapidly.

Lonergan has sufficiently indicated, I think, that behind his whole philosophico-theological enterprise lies a concern to bring one and the same Catholic faith and one and the same Catholic religion into the new context of the modern world. This is made clear in the Epilogue to *Insight*, particularly in regard to the relation of the Catholic faith to modern knowledge. It becomes even clearer in his more recent papers, which express the crisis in terms of the collapse of classical culture and its replacement by modernity. Now, because Lonergan interprets the Christian faith in the dogmatic fashion of the Catholic tradition, his concern takes the form of a search for a secure basis or foundation making possible the affirmation of absolute, unchanging truths in the midst of the historicity and relativity pervading modern culture. However immense the transition bringing the faith from a classical to a modern cultural context, the doctrines must remain the same. The new approach must not be made into 'a device for reducing doctrines to probable opinions'.[15] Although the old foundations will no longer do, this does not 'mean that they are no longer true, for they are as true now as they ever were'.[16]

Catholic dogmas will remain intact; they cannot be relativised or made uncertain. That is taken for granted. It is the belief that governs the whole enterprise. As he puts it in *De Deo Trino* when he rejects *futurismus*, defined as 'tam antiquiori quam recentiori synthesi spreta, novus quidam atque inauditus omnium conspectus':

. . . quia ecclesiae declarationes et definitiones per Spiritus sancti assistentiam infallibiles sunt, intelligentia theologica, inquantum in has declarationes et definitiones intrat, mutationem non admittit. Quare inventiones quas futuristicas nominavimus excluduntur.[17]

Since Catholic dogmas and the systematic theology upon which they draw imply a metaphysics, Lonergan had to find a secure foundation for metaphysics, indeed for traditional metaphysics, in an unmetaphysical age. He claims to have found it in the invariant structures of cognitional activities, structures he thematises in a cognitional theory. These same invariant structures in an isomorphism between the structure of the known and the structure of knowing are then considered as grounding a substantially unrevisable metaphysics, understood as the integral heuristic structure of proportionate being. What we have at the end is the traditional metaphysics, slightly modified but newly grounded.

I think it is fair to wonder at the ease with which Lonergan rejoins the traditional metaphysics. After all, he himself has taught us to consider the mental context or horizon in which a thinker does his thinking. Fr MacKinnon in *Continuum* has this to say about all the transcendental Thomists:

. . . these philosophers have no great difficulty in establishing a metaphysics—and, in fact, re-establishing essentially the same Thomistic metaphysics they held before they took the linguistic turn. Others who have taken a similar turn, e.g., Heidegger and the linguistic Kantians in the analytic tradition do not seem to have this facility at all. The Thomists can assign reasons why they succeed so easily while others fail in spite of a life-time of effort, e.g., because only they really grasp and properly evaluate the distinctive role of judgement in knowledge. A less disposed critic might suggest a different reason. The non-Thomists are sincerely questioning the possibility of a metaphysics while the Thomists are merely using an analysis of questioning as a methodological device for justifying a metaphysics whose validity has not really been questioned. Such questioning is rather readily satisfied by answers that lead from the chosen starting point to the pre-determined conclusion.[18]

The suspicion that Lonergan set out with a firm expectation of rejoining the traditional metaphysics receives some confirmation from his reply to Michael Novak, whose interpretation attempted to push his thought too far in the direction of ethical relativism:

> Now I am completely at one with Professor Novak in his concern for personal ethical decision about the concrete good. But I wish to forestall any misapprehension about my position. Though I did not in *Insight* feel called upon to work out a code of ethics, neither did I exclude such a code. On the contrary I drew a parallel between ethics and metaphysics. In metaphysics I not only assigned a basis in invariant structures but also derived from that basis a metaphysics with a marked family resemblance to traditional views. A similar family resemblance, I believe, would be found to exist between traditional ethics and an ethics that, like the metaphysics, was explicitly aware of itself as a system on the move.[19]

A prior confidence in the vindication of traditional ethics would seem to indicate—some would say *a fortiori*—a prior confidence in traditional metaphysics.

I do not wish to give the impression of going to the other extreme and excluding the traditional metaphysics *a priori*. I am too much of a traditional metaphysician myself to want to do that. But I do suggest that Lonergan's presuppositions and the context of his work justify considerable caution in assessing his vindication of Thomistic metaphysics. The background of the enterprise is dogmatic faith.

While my own thinking is too transitional at present to enter directly into the metaphysical disputes, I must record my conviction that Lonergan's claims for the stability or immunity from revision of his cognitional theory and metaphysics are excessive.

Between the invariant structures of human consciousness and his cognitional theory come the discovery, distinguishing and formulation of those structures. Since these activities may have been carried out with varying success, his cognitional theory is open to debate and revision. The argument by which he endeavours to exclude any but incidental revision is neat, but I think fallacious. He argues that anyone who tries to revise the structure of experience, understanding and judgement refutes his own attempt by invoking experience, understanding and judgement. The fallacy is to suppose that to discover a basic abstract scheme into which all cognitional activities will fit is to have discovered and formulated all the elements of determining importance in human knowledge in the concrete. A revision may be 'incidental' in relation to the basic abstract scheme, but of the weightiest consequence in relation to actual human knowing. There is no need to fall into the trap of denying that cognitional activities can be fitted into his basic scheme, in order to question whether his cognitional theory is sound, adequate and balanced as a thematisation of human knowing in all its concrete richness and complexity. Serious questions have been and will no doubt continue to be raised about it.

It is worth noting that in seeking a new foundation for theology in the objectification of conversion, Lonergan admits various possible objectifications—'though we may not hope', he writes, 'for a single and uniform account of authentic conversion.'[20] The reference is probably too brief for comment, but I am tempted to add that it was too much to hope for a single and uniform account of human knowing.

Lonergan's explicit metaphysics rests upon his cognitional theory. The move from cognitional theory to metaphysics implies a further thematisation, the isomorphism of the known and knowing and indeed a particular conception of what metaphysics is. Together with the cognitional theory itself, all these matters are open to question and debate.

In brief, whatever may be the assessment of Lonergan's particular insights and theories as a contribution to the ongoing philosophical debate, he has not, I think, provided a stable and in principle unrevisable basis in cognitional theory and metaphysics for the affirmation of unchanging truths in the midst of the historicity and relativity of modern culture. Nor has he provided the philosophical support he intended for a dogmatic faith.

Lonergan's more recent work is concerned with a new type of foundation for theology. Theological renewal demands so great a transformation to effect the transition from classical to modern culture that a new foundation is required. In Lonergan's own words, this foundation

. . . is to consist not in objective statement, but in subjective reality. The objective statements of a *de vera religione, de Christo legato, de ecclesia, de inspiratione scripturae, de locis theologicis*, are as much in need of a foundation as are those of other tracts. But behind all statements is the stating subject. What is normative and foundational for subjects stating theology is to be found, I have suggested, in reflection on conversion, where conversion is taken as an ongoing process, concrete and dynamic, personal, communal, and historical.[21]

This is most promising. Unfortunately, until the publication of *Method in Theology*, people like myself are insufficiently informed as yet concerning these latest developments in Lonergan's thought. Certainly, in the recent articles and papers, there are some indications of a wider and much more flexible approach.

However, despite the seeming openness of method, the evidence I have continues to confirm the point I am making. The results are still predetermined. It is still assumed that the method will lead to the same dogmas as before, the same Catholic religion, the same Catholic Church, even indeed substantially the same theology. To such an extent is this taken for granted that Lonergan can even say that the present crisis 'is a crisis not of faith but of culture'[22]—a quote that a devotee of Lonergan would not believe when I referred to it. Here is a longer quotation from that same passage, together with some other quotations:

The crisis, then, that I have been attempting to depict is a crisis not of faith but of culture. There has been no new revelation from on high to replace the revelation given through Christ Jesus. There has been written no new Bible and there has been founded no new church to link us with him. But Catholic philosophy and Catholic theology are matters, not merely of revelation and faith, but also of culture. Both have been fully and deeply involved in classical culture.[23]

In interpreting the last point in the passage, remember that according to Lonergan, in so far as past theological understanding enters into defined dogmas it is not open to change.[24] I have already referred to the passages in 'Theology in Its New Context' where Lonergan states that the new approach must not destroy the certainty of doctrines and that the old foundations remain permanently true. Finally, his attitude comes across most clearly in his paper, *Belief: Today's Issue*, where it is summed up thus: 'In brief, the contemporary issue is, not a new religion, not a new faith, not a substantially new theology, but a belated social and cultural transition.'[25]

In that paper, Lonergan's analysis of the present crisis is most illuminating on his general presuppositions. He distinguishes between the social and the cultural and then between the cultural substance and the cultural superstructure. Although he admits that both social and cultural changes are taking place in general in the modern world, the present situation does not mean for Catholics any doubts about their faith and their religion as their cultural substance, but simply difficulties in theology as their cultural superstructure. Further, though the situation calls for adjustment and adaptation in theology and religion, 'such adjustment and adaptation are in forms and structures much more than in content' (p. 11).

Now, the objection is not merely that the faith remaining one and the same is for Lonergan the Roman Catholic faith with all its dogmas, the religion one and the same Roman Catholic Church and the theology a theology under the guidance of the Roman Catholic magisterium, but also that the very understanding of the present situation presupposes a conception of the Christian faith in which unchanging dogmas are defined by an infallible authority, and a single organised community is the one true Church of Christ. Lonergan's excellent analysis of the transition from classical to modern culture, when read without his presuppositions, urges, I suggest, the opposite conclusion to his own: namely, that the Roman Catholic insistence upon unchanging dogmas, an infallible magisterium and a hierarchically constituted Church belongs to the classical culture and will have to be given up. A different manner of mediating the Christian faith and religion is required.

Schubert Ogden in writing of transcendental Thomism used the phrase, 'adjectivally transcendental and substantively Thomism'.[26] Adapting the phrase, I should say that Lonergan has attempted a theology that is 'adjectivally modern and substantively Roman Catholic'. I do not want a theology that is substantially modern and not substantively Christian. But I think that Lonergan by identifying Christian with Roman Catholic has jeopardised his whole enterprise by an incoherent formulation of the desired goal of a renewed Christian theology. In any event, the assumption of the Roman Catholic faith, which I have argued underlies and pervades his whole work, is for me, even as a believing Christian, too large an assumption to make.

# Empirical Science and Theological Knowing

## LANGDON GILKEY

LET it first be said how great a pleasure it is to participate in this *Fest* for Fr Lonergan. To me he is, of all contemporary thinkers in the realm of theology, the most worthy of such acclaim. His analysis of cognition, it seems to me, is unsurpassed in our epoch. If those of us who came here to honour him are critical of aspects of his thought, it is not without recognition of the transcendent significance of his work as a whole—as it is also a recognition that reiterated praise, even of exciting thought, tends to be unexciting. In the case of this paper, criticism of Lonergan's thought appears only in those areas where apparently his theological assumptions have not quite caught up with the perils and the possibilities of his interpretation of modern science.

George Santayana said in introducing his own way of looking at things, 'Transcendental criticism was a sceptical instrument used by persons who were not sceptics,'[1] a remark that expresses with gentle irony the major theme of our criticism. Fr Lonergan has experienced deeply the empirical and relative character of modernity, and in fact has interpreted its characteristic modes of cognition more perceptively than have any of modernity's more 'stock' representatives.[2] But these experiences have left untouched his classical Catholic sense of the given, substantial, and unproblematic status of the referents of doctrinal language—almost as if his religious existence still reflected the Greek world his cognitive theory had overturned! Thus there arises, as we shall seek to show, a tension, if not a contradiction, between his epistemological and his theological thought. He offers a theological method based on his epistemology which can only subvert rather than establish what he clearly expects theology to talk intelligently about.

Allied with this problem is another, it seems to me. His

analysis of how we know in common sense and in science is well-nigh faultless. Modestly aware of this fact, he mistakenly assumed that veridical theological method, dealing with the *foundations* or *horizons* of our experiencing, knowing and doing, must follow the same pattern as does the cognition of events under or within that horizon. Hence arises another tension between the requirements or obligations of objective scientific knowing, and the requirements implicit in knowing what transcends and so establishes the possibility of such knowing, where a *different* understanding of method may be more helpful. These flaws, let us note, do not concern the analysis of cognition; they relate only to the way in which that analysis is applied to the problems of theological method. After making our case about these problems or flaws, we shall try to suggest another way that this brilliant understanding of the process of knowing can be used constructively in theology.

Our thesis that Fr Lonergan is—like most of us—less sceptical in theology than his understanding of scientific method prescribes that he be if theology is to be understood on the analogy of scientific knowing, and therefore that the analogy itself is a mistake, is borne out, we shall argue, by the fact that at three crucial points in his system he ends up, to our surprise as much as to his, in the counterpositions which he has himself overthrown. Since in theology he does not really accept the relativistic implications of his empiricism (though he does in cognitive theory), he must interject alien and unexplained elements to counteract these relativising tendencies, and those elements in turn throw his method off balance and force that method to represent counterpositions. Let us enunciate these and then get down to our analysis.

1. Lonergan understands well the empirical bent of modern inquiry, and consequently the hypothetical, tentative character of the principles of understanding derived. We know only by means of experience, he insists, and what we know are not objects or laws 'already out there real' to be 'looked at' by the mind through the data, but rather hypotheses created to organise the data—the immanent principles of relations among the data—and judged to be valid only so far as the conditions established by the data themselves are fulfilled. Two fundamental principles or canons of modern science express, Lonergan asserts,

this empirical, hypothetical search for the immanent relations among the data, the canon of relevance and the canon of parsimony. The first maintains that the kind of intelligibility arrived at by modern science is one immanent in the immediate data of sense, and so immanent in the relations between things (not to us but to one another);[3] and the second insists that the empirical scientist cannot affirm anything that, *as empirical scientist*, he does not know, i.e., verification is intrinsic to the intelligibility that is here sought, a verification related again to the data and so an empirical verification.[4] In modern cognition an explanation is not *intelligible*, so Lonergan is here saying, unless it springs from the data, concerns the immanent relations among the data, and is in turn verified in relation to the data.

When, moreover, Lonergan comes to justify philosophical inquiry—as opposed merely to being content with our ordinary language and its usages—his argument reflects the same motif: philosophy, he says, is important because it can help us to dispense with 'idle talk', and eradicate all futile, irrelevant and unrelated 'myth and magic'.[5] Again in expanding the pattern of ordinary and scientific cognition into the arena of philosophy, Lonergan seems to assert this fundamental principle of modernity, defining intelligibility, not as that which answers with apparent rationality or relevance any or all questions, but that alone which arises from experiencing, confines itself to the relations among the data, and verifies itself within them. As the history of thought has been well illustrated, it has been precisely by so confining acceptable explanation to verifiable theories about the data that 'myth and magic' have in fact been eradicated. Finally, he well knows that when other thinkers, equally sympathetic to the aims and methods of modern science, have sought to expand that method into the arena of philosophical inquiry, they have done so precisely by applying the canons of relevance and of parsimony to philosophy itself. Hence have arisen those 'empirical' or 'naturalistic' philosophies which confine relevant and valid philosophical thought to the interrelations among the empirical data, or in ontological terms, to questions concerning the immanent interrelations obtaining between the finite entities that make up the system of our experienced world, or, in Lonergan's language, the realm of proportionate being.[6]

One may conclude from all this that for the modern mind—

as opposed to the Greek—intelligible knowing is defined precisely by its *empirical* character, that is, by its confinement of intelligible questions and explanatory answers to the given system of finite things. Instead of leading beyond that system to require an explanation of it in terms of something beyond it, the modern understanding of the law of sufficient reason seems to require thought to remain within that system and be confined to empirical propositions about the contingent world around us. Thus the modern eros to know, on which Lonergan is intent to build his case, is, to be sure, '*unrestricted*' *in one sense*: namely that at no point in the search for immanent explanations is questioning more than provisionally closed. On the other hand, as the canons Lonergan asserts maintain, the modern eros to know is in another sense very definitely *restricted* to empirical inquiry into the immanent relations between factors within the data. In sum, modern intelligibility affirms rather than denies that matters of fact must remain in this sense 'mere matters of fact' if our talk is to be intelligible and not idle.

Now, if in fact this is the characteristic of modern inquiry,[7] then it follows that the expansion of that understanding of our knowing into the realms of philosophical theology and of theology proper should take account of this restrictive character. If theology is to be understood on the model of modern scientific cognition—and this is Lonergan's proposal—should not its modes of explanation be based on *experiencing* the data, and be confined to what can be so experienced, and so be validated by experiment within the data, if it is to be intelligible? Should not in that case philosophical theological assertions have as their referents, as have scientific ones, the *immanent* relations among the data, and not some principle quite beyond immanence—albeit implied by it? If not, have we not dispensed with the analogy, and surely the authority, of modern scientific cognition?

If in fact the essential structure of modern inquiry is as we have described it (and as Lonergan argues), then two results follow: (i) We cannot claim the authority of cognition as now understood in proceeding in our natural theology *beyond* the empirical, immanent realm—in positing as a demand of sufficient reason, of intelligible explanation and so of knowing itself, that our thought move beyond contingency and immanence in order to explain them.

(ii) Surely in making this move beyond the data and beyond their immanent relations, we are ourselves illustrating another and older understanding of intelligibility and of knowing, namely one which understood cognition as a search for absolute, eternal answers and so objects, and which felt it could find them by 'looking through' the data to another level of being than the one illustrated in the data themselves. Lonergan clearly repudiates *this* view of knowing and of intelligibility in his analysis, and he ostensibly or consciously repudiates it in theology. Theology, he says, is not, as was once assumed, knowing eternal truths or objects, nor is it a deduction of absolutely certain 'doctrines' from these; it is not a *looking at* substantial, changeless structures or objects through the data. It is now 'empirical', and so its results are tentative, hypothetical and probable; its authorities have become merely 'data' and its method is confined to intelligible inferences from these data.[8] Presumably, if theology is now an empirical science, as so defined, and is to be so understood, theological assertions must also be verified in experience, and confined to the immanent interrelations among the data.

These two are, however, precisely the pair of inferences that Lonergan refuses to draw when he seeks to translate theology into these new empirical terms. When he seeks to prove God on the basis and authority of reason as understood in modern terms —as the *unrestricted* desire to know[9]—he reverses this whole modern understanding of intelligibility, and insists (*a*) that mere contingency is unintelligible and so unreal, a 'nothing';[10] and thus (*b*) that the only 'rational' explanation of the contingent is an explanation that in all its aspects quite transcends the immanent relations between contingent things. On the canons of modern intelligibility, the canons of relevance and of parsimony, both (*a*) and (*b*) are totally unintelligible utterances. As expanded into *philosophical* discourse, we may, to be sure, somewhat petulantly call these canons 'restricted philosophy';[11] nevertheless they represent the direct implications of the scientific method Lonergan wishes to use as his theological model. Ironically enough, any Greek would have understood perfectly, and agreed with, this call for a transcendent explanation, and would have regarded as supremely 'rational' this movement, via the law of sufficient reason alone, beyond the contingent to the eternal. Most modern thinkers, however, based on the canons Lonergan has explicated so forcefully, would regard this same movement as an example of the unfortunate perpetuation of the mythical consciousness that Lonergan feels he also dislikes—for such a consciousness habitually used understanding and judgement (explanation) beyond the range of empirical verification and of immanent relations.

Probably most observers would make the shrewd judgement that in applying the law of sufficient reason beyond the system of the data rather than within it, Lonergan was not, as he sought to do, establishing these inferences according to the canons of modern reason—which would precisely deny their possibility. On the contrary, what in fact he was doing—unless a Greek 'wild oat' was here evident—was unpacking the implications of his own *Christian* horizon, according to which horizon the ultimate roots of things, and so their intelligibility, transcend the levels of empirical cognition. But if that be so, then 'natural theology' has at midnight been turned into mere theology—for as he has himself argued, 'horizons' arise from conversion, and as horizons they can be neither established nor disproved by objective reason.[12] In sum, the natural theology presented by Fr Lonergan, in transcending experience on the Pegasus' wings of understanding and judgement alone; in requiring unrestricted explanations which are neither referent to the immanent relations of the data nor referable in any way to concrete experience; and above all, in seeking in the name of 'rationality' to go beyond contingency to explain it in non-contingent terms, reflects a *Greek* understanding of what is rational, in effect a Greek view of cognitive process as beginning with experience but rising far beyond it, and not the modern one with which his analysis began. Thus this natural theology represents one of the 'counter-positions' against which his own thought inveighs, rather than a translation of classical philosophical theology into modern empirical terms.

2. The same implication of the empirical cognitive process that Lonergan so well explicates causes similar difficulties with regard to his 'new' understanding of theology in empirical terms. With regard to questions, not now of ontology but of history, its events, its ideas, its documents, etc., the canons of relevance and of parsimony have had a corresponding effect. Explanations of data are to be confined to the immanent relations among the

data on the one hand, and to those causes or factors verifiably present in our ordinary experience on the other. Thus empirical and so modern explanations of historical events are intrinsically 'naturalistic' and 'humanistic' in their forms, and a scientific understanding of a text concerns only the historical, cultural, psychological and at best religious factors at work in its production by men in a given historical context. If, then, it is the case, as Lonergan maintains, that the former 'authorities' for theology have now become 'data' to be interpreted and understood in the terms of modern science, it is as hard to see how *theological* conclusions can be derived from these data—without the introduction of some new, non-empirical and so 'theological' hermeneutical principle—as it was in the first case. Such a principle, in the introductory stages of his method, Lonergan never explicates, and, in fact, the need for such a principle never seems to have occurred to him.

Correspondingly, Lonergan, in basing the inward or transcendental element in theological inquiry on 'authentic conversion', seems to assume a given, substantial and unchangeable structure to conversion that (*a*) points rational inquiry to a transcendent source, and (*b*) can provide the basis for stable doctrines and stable community, for Catholic language about God, Christ and the Church. To a *merely* empirical or scientific inquiry into religious conversions no such stable, normative or transcendent structure appears or could appear, and for the same reasons. In Lonergan's thought about theology, therefore, as opposed to his thought about science, an alien, classical element seems again to be presupposed. Lonergan seems to assume that in *these* data certain basic principles or realities are 'there' to be seen by objective inquiry, and that in conversion there are certain stable and normative heuristic principles. Such principles, latent in all authentic conversions, are 'there' to be observed and abstracted by transcendental inquiry. But if this is what he means, then he is here enunciating a view of knowing which he has called 'looking at what is already out there real', and which he regards as totally antithetical to the modern mentality. For that mentality generates explanations *out of the data*, interpretations that are merely probable and tentative, and judged to be true only in relation to the data. And such surely are the theological 'doctrines'

Lonergan counts on to be derived by theological inquiry from those data.

If in turn Lonergan is saying that these fundamental doctrines (God, revelation, Christ, the Church as the Mystical Body, and so on) are *not* to be derived from the data, then they must be the premises of the inquiry and not its result, for he gives no *other* mode of their appearance. But if fundamental doctrines are here given as authoritative premises, then Lonergan is advocating *sub rosa* another 'counterposition', namely the very understanding of theology he says has fled with modernity and is impossible for our age.[13] Again he appears to be classical in his view of religion and of doctrine while he seeks to be empirical in his view of thought. And hence the classical keeps thoughtlessly poking its unwanted head around all the corners of this edifice, and grinning slyly at us every time we seek to renovate that edifice into modern form. We shall return to a more detailed analysis of this point later.

3. Logically basic to this whole understanding of theology as patterned after the model of scientific inquiry, is the 'natural' knowledge of God implied by, or extrapolated from, the structures of that inquiry, as we noted in point 1. Thus the knowledge of God here is not directly 'experienced' but extrapolated; and, further, it is conceived on the model of an *object* of cognition, something we know to be there by the process of rational implication, that is of understanding and reflection (as we noted, in this case 'experiencing' is strangely dropped out). We suggest that this model: 'As the object is to cognitive inquiry, so God is to natural and revealed theology,' is a false model. It leads to two unfortunate results:

(i) to the *problematic* character of God's reality as a transcendent and so non-experienced Being, a problem raised in point 1 above;
(ii) it is unable to make intelligible the crucial movement of Lonergan's argument from Being as the *intelligible object* of all true judgements to Being as a transcendent *subject* or *intelligence*.[14] This move from the concept of an intelligible object to that of an intelligent subject has no grounds in the analysis with which it began, which could only point to an unrestricted desire to know on our part, and our penchant as humans to assume that only the rationally established 'is'. Our cognitive practices thus imply (or indicate that in fact we assume) that the real which we seek to

know, and frequently feel we do know, is intelligible. The most that could be postulated (the difficulty of its *proof* has been discussed in point 1 above) from this penchant of ours is that the content of what we do in fact know is intelligible; no ground is given in the argument either for the move to the transcendent, or (which is the point here) for any shift from the object to the subject of understanding and judgement. As a further factor, Lonergan has himself made a very clear distinction between our modes of knowing an object and our mode of being aware of ourselves as subjects; and in emphasising this brilliantly, he quite persuades us of the reality of this distinction.[15] Thus again, he seems to break his own rules in seeking to convert an extrapolated object of implication into a subject of knowing, and to make this conversion without the mediation of any awareness of God congruent with our awareness of ourselves as subjects. That there is some relation of our cognitive processes to the reality of God, Lonergan has proved irrefutably to me. But in proposing to us that this relation is analogous to our knowledge of an object of inquiry, he weakens the intelligibility of his own conclusion, namely that the ultimate there known is both real and an intentional subject.

This is, then, our threefold thesis: the effort to convert theology into an analogue of empirical science is to misconstrue the relation between theology and scientific knowing, and it results in an implicit affirmation of three major counter-theses to Lonergan's own analysis of science: (1) a defiance of the fundamental empirical canons of relevance and parsimony; (2) an affirmation of the 'looking and seeing' version of knowing; and (3) against his own insight, the confusion of the knowledge of an object of inquiry with our awareness of the subject of inquiry, which in turn renders the reality and the subject character of God problematic and unintelligible.

In the above our central critical theses have been stated rather than established by detailed analysis. Since the establishment of all three would more than consume the rest of the paper, and leave no room for our own constructive use of Lonergan's thought, we shall concentrate our analysis on only one, the second. The first, having to do with the conflict between the empirical principle of explanation and the needs of classical natural theology, has been an object of critical discussion for a long time and therefore thoroughly debated in many contexts. The third, having to do with the understanding of God as subject rather than object, will be again broached in our concluding section. Let us turn, therefore, to Lonergan's proposal for a 'scientific' theological methodology and see where its peculiar difficulties lie.

As Lonergan persuasively argues, theology must now understand itself in new terms because of the sudden relativising of its traditional authorities and structures. This process of relativisation has occurred at three crucial points:[16] (1) the traditional *authorities* of theological science, from which as certainties it formerly deduced its conclusions, namely Scripture and tradition, are now *data* and not absolute *authorities*, data to be sifted, judged, re-arranged and finally interpreted by the inquiring mind. Theology is thus fundamentally empirical in its method, drawing probable and tentative inferences from the data as do other sciences, rather than absolutely certain deductions from given premises as does, say, mathematics. (2) The interpretations (or doctrines) of theology from the data are in turn themselves relative, at least in so far as they must be recognised as historical in character, relative to their culture, and changing in their form. Further, any given doctrine is partial in that it develops dialectically over against counter-theses, and can be understood only in that polar, and so relative, role. (3) The inward principle or 'foundation' of theological inquiry is no longer direct divine inspiration or revelation (the direct work of the holy Spirit), as once it was. On the contrary, it is now to be conceived as the human experience of 'conversion', which when passed on to others and stretched out over time, becomes what we mean by 'religion' as a human phenomenon. The historical relativity of conversion vis-à-vis any given doctrinal conclusions that might arise from it lies, for Lonergan, in the following facts: (*a*) that conversion provides only a 'horizon' for theological statements (presumably the sense of ultimacy or transcendence, and possibly the sense of certainty, assurance or belief, though this latter is not clearly stated) and not any given doctrines themselves; and (*b*) that the forms of conversion change from age to age and from culture to culture. Thus everywhere modern theology turns, it seems to encounter only 'data', and so the relative, the changing, even the transient—nothing absolute enough to ground theological certainty, nor concrete enough to provide secure propositions, seems to appear. If, therefore, in our age theology is to be a science, it must be an empirical science, and its certainty and validity must be given to it on the same (or closely analogous) terms as are apparent in empirical science. The question then arises, is *all* in theology thereby inescapably relative and uncertain; is modern *theology* impossible?

Lonergan's answer is no. In empirical science not all is relative, for in empirical knowing we do experience *knowing*, and this is enough. And the reason is that in empirical science we find data dealt with by a mind which reveals to itself an unalterable and undeniable heuristic structure of knowing. And because of the use of this heuristic structure on the data, genuine knowing arises—and none of us can doubt this since we all find ourselves on its basis making claims to know. Although, therefore, the data of science are relative and changing, and its conclusions consequently remain intrinsically probable, tentative, hypothetical and admittedly in flux, we know we know in these terms, and thus we have a virtual certainty that what we there know is true. This is to say, in making positive judgements about even a tentative hypothesis, (*a*) we assert that 'it is so'; (*b*) we do this because it satisfies our rational consciousness (it is virtually unconditioned); and so (*c*) in such assertions we do affirm that we are related to being—to what, in fact, is. If, then, empirical data, plus the operative heuristic structure of the knowing mind, can produce such forms of objective albeit probable truths, why cannot we understand theology on similar lines, namely both as objectively assertive of what is and yet as changing? Why should we as moderns not be satisfied with these results—that is, with empirical 'doctrines' derived scientifically by a converted intelligence from the given data?

Thus Lonergan presents us with a method of theological inquiry divided into 'functional specialisations' patterned roughly on a scientific model. These specialisations within theology represent special activities or enterprises distinguished from one another by being the successive stages in which theological inquiry unfolds and conclusions are reached;[17] and each one is in turn characterised by the fundamental cognitive structure of experiencing, understanding, reflection or judgement, and decision. These stages are: (1) Research into the data; (2) Interpretation of the data: hermeneutics; (3) Historical study of these interpretations (or 'doctrines'); (4) Dialectical interpretation of the conflicts and developments of these interpretations, and therefore how they supplement, reinforce and criticise one another; (5) Conversion, from the objectification of transcendental analysis of which the 'foundations' of theological inquiry, its dynamic, heuristic elements productive of the 'horizon within which the meaning of doctrines can be apprehended'[18] can be derived. The forms of conversion change as culture changes, but apparently the *essential* structure of an 'authentic' conversion does not; (6) 'Doctrines' expressing 'judgements of fact and of value' based on the data as dealt with in (1) to (4), and heuristically apprehended by conversion. Here is found, apparently, the locus of creative theological work where presumably 'insight' or 'understanding' takes place into fundamental theological questions (who God is, what he has done, who Christ is, what the Church is, and so on). Then follow (7) Systematics, the cohering and the testing of these doctrines: that is, a further elaboration of understanding and the application of reflective judgement; and (8) Communications, the problem of translating scientific theology into ethics, sermons, and so on.

Two things, in our view, are awry in this view of theological method:

(1) First of all, the effort to understand theology in such a series of successive stages does not work, and without the category of succession and so of cumulative knowledge, the analogy with science dissipates and this proposal loses its own central structural principle. As we have remarked, and as Lonergan insisted in his canons of relevance and parsimony, on *empirical* principles, that is according to the methods of scientific and historical inquiry as modernly practised, only finite or secondary causes can be used as valid explanations or interpretations. The rational or empirical hermeneutical principles of history and of documentary study (levels one and two) precisely prevent any *theological* interpretation of the data. If we are to find *God*, who transcends the immanent relations of things one to another, in the data concerning historical events, and so to interpret those events *theologically*, some prior religious or theological ingredient must be added—as Troeltsch and a host of others have rightly indicated.

What is needed is precisely the 'theological horizon' in which the meaning, and possibility, of theological doctrines is apprehended, since it adds the dimension of ultimacy and transcendence to the data and thus gives some intelligible basis for a reappraisal of the naturalistic canons of parsimony and of relevance. Without the introduction of the theological horizon, given by conversion,[19] these canons of parsimony and of relevance prevent language about the transcendent, either in natural or in revealed theology. One of the heuristic results of conversion is to rearrange these canons in the light of this new theological horizon. But by the same token, neither natural theology nor a theological study of the data is possible without the presupposition of conversion, for without that presupposition rationality, to be 'modern', must be defined in these empirical terms. Thus conversion is presupposed, both in the natural theological effort to know God through rational implication, and in the theological effort to see his work in the data of special historical events.

Correspondingly, if the study of the Scriptures is to have theological results, if it is in fact to be a listening for God's Word there and so *theologically* relevant, the reality of revelation, and so of a revealer, and the locus of revelation in these events and so in this document, must also be presupposed. Such specifically religious or theological presuppositions are hardly included in the presuppositions of most merely empirical studies of past documents, nor are they at all relevant to a search for the immanent relations among the data presented in these documents. In fact, if the presuppositions of God, of his revelation, of Christ, of Scripture and of Church are essential for a *theological* hermeneutic of the data, they include—if they do not exhaust—most of the basic content of theology, and little is left over to be worked out by the empirical study of the data here described!

The same is true of the historical and the dialectical studies of Church history. Naturalistically interpreted—as, say, a specialised study in the history of ideas—such studies lead not to any positive theological conclusions, but only to historical statements about practices, beliefs and philosophical ideas of people in the past. Only if conversion is already assumed, and with it not only the theological horizon of ultimacy but also a host of concrete theological symbols, can the history of the Church and of its theologies speak to us *theologically*.

Lonergan seems to admit this when he says that research, interpretation, history and dialectics 'mediate an encounter with persons witnessing to Christ'.[20] Clearly, therefore, to him these four first stages of theological method tell us only of *people*, and so do not tell us of the Christ to whom these people saw themselves as bearing witness. And yet, although he thus seems to assume that an empirical and so scientific study of history and its documents, however piously conducted, does not take us beyond the human level and so cannot itself generate the fundamental theological categories of God, revelation, Christ and the Church, Lonergan nevertheless can inexplicably say a moment later: 'It is research, interpretation, history, dialectics that introduce us to knowledge of the Body of Christ [*sic*]. But the second phase is mediated theology. It is knowledge of God and of all things as ordered to God . . . as He is known mediately through the whole Christ, Head and members.'[21]

Clearly Lonergan in this passage is enunciating theological categories that are not derivable empirically from the data themselves, but only appear at best when the data are interpreted in the light of some attachment to these very theological symbols of God, revelation and sacred community. If this be so, Lonergan must either give up his analogy of a *cumulative* process of objective inquiry, or else hold, as he seems to, that these theological doctrines can be 'seen' in the data when the latter are properly studied. In so far, then, as he implies here that such inquiry 'introduces' us to, or mediates to us, knowledge of God, Christ, and the Mystical Body, he seems to hold that these doctrines are inherent in the data as their objective principles, to be discovered in these data by careful 'looking'—a form of inquiry he abhors.

Theological judgements are, to be sure, in strange ways related to and dependent on objective scientific research. Still these theological judgements cannot be simply understood as the cumulative results of that research as are the conclusions of science. For religious attitudes and commitments, expressed or thematised in theological symbols or doctrines, determine (as do all foundational principles) the criteria, the data, and the hermeneutical principles of our research. Thus are theological symbols, and especially the presence of a theological horizon as our fundamental hermeneutical principle, similar in form to the heuristic principles of cognition itself; neither one is the *conclusion* of inquiry but rather each is expressive of its *prior structures*. For this reason the notion of cumulative stages is here radically subverted; for now we need to move conversion and its horizon (or some surrogate thereof) forward as the presupposition for any type of theological inquiry at all.[22]

(2) Lonergan seems to realise this subversion of his proposed 'stages' in his emphasis on conversion as the foundation of heuristic principle of theology, which it surely is. Our next question is, therefore, is it possible to derive fundamental theological principles from *this* element in the method, and so maintain the analogy: as heuristic principles are uncovered by transcendental analysis, so fundamental theological principles (essential doctrines) are derivable from a similar analysis of the experience of conversion? Surely this was roughly Schleiermacher's method; is Lonergan proposing a modern version of this sort of phenomenological analysis of normative Christian experience leading to doctrinal statement?

Lonergan, it seems to me, is more elusive, undecided and double-minded on this issue than on any other, and thus no one answer is clear. On the one hand he recognises that conversion as an object of inquiry, if not as an ontic fact, is a *human* phenomenon and therefore historical and cultural in its forms, changing as the age in which it appears changes.[23] Also, as a human phenomenon, it seems to offer to our inquiry no clear *doctrinal* content when studied either empirically in others or transcendentally in ourselves. An empirical study of conversion in others, even among Christians, will reveal only the varieties of the human responses to grace, and tell us little more than the vastness of the possibilities of religious life and of intellectual formulation resident even in a similar 'dispensation'. A transcendental study of conversion in ourselves, and in others like us—though on what principle can it be so confined?—could at best reveal only the essential structures (for us) of the religious life, of our *human response*: a sense of dependence, a sense of sin and judgement, a sense of acceptance, of healing and of hope. Schleiermacher began here, on the basic assumption that religious feeling (*Gefühl*) was an avenue to what really is, could describe the 'whence' of these feelings in doctrinal statements reflective of those feelings. In the first place, I wonder if Fr Lonergan has even remotely in mind as *radical* a theology as Schleiermacher's? But even more to his discomfort, a twentieth-century man (to my mind) would be lucky even to approach Schleiermacher's 'orthodoxy' on the basis of phenomenological analysis of our religious experience: (a) numinous experiences are less frequent, certain and evident now; (b) experience has been so relativised since then that any 'normal' or 'standard' model is hard to find; and (c) above all, no experience, however 'illuminating' or 'revealing', is able to be taken by us, *per se* and on its own terms alone, as irrefutably indicative of what is real, of its own transcendent causes. Experience has for us been too subjectivised to lead, without other factors, to ontological conclusions; it remains for us more an *anthropological* than an *ontological* or *theological* category. For all these reasons, once he admits the 'human' and so variable character of conversion as it has happened historically, it is difficult to see how Lonergan expects to generate fundamental *theological* doctrines out of its analysis.

Finally, as Lonergan reiterates, conversion gives us the horizon in which doctrines can be apprehended, not the doctrines themselves. Apparently, therefore, Lonergan, uneasily suspects that an analysis of conversion, even Christian conversion, will not produce doctrines about God, but merely insight into (a) the religious dimension of human experience, and (b) the varieties of the human reaction to this dimension. As an empirical analysis of the historical and literary data of religion by no means necessarily grounds a *theological* interpretation of these data, so a thematisation of changing patterns of conversion, even by one who believes religion to be no illusion, cannot yield any theological assertions about God and his means of salvation. In both cases—i.e., in the case of scientific study of the data and that of a transcendental analysis of conversion—it seems true that for Lonergan fundamental doctrines are not only already presupposed but, even more, derived elsewhere. Thus we have argued that this picture of an 'empirical' method with a heuristic foundation does not in itself at all disclose the *real* sources for him of a valid theology.

Lonergan, however, has other things to say about conversion that mitigate, and in fact subvert, this empirical view of its role in theology. First of all, he speaks of 'authentic and inauthentic conversions', and so of authentic and inauthentic horizons arising out of conversion. The criteria by which he thinks conversion and its theological horizons are to be assessed for their authenticity are presumably derivative from *theological* doctrines of some sort;

certainly it is hard to see what other considerations, besides possibly ethical ones, Lonergan here has in mind. But where such theological criteria might arise is left quite unanswered. They cannot arise from any given experience of conversion itself, for they are in each case to be the judges of the authenticity of that experience. Formerly, of course, such criteria of the authenticity of conversion were derived from the Bible and from creeds; could he think they arise there? Clearly, however, such derivation presupposes precisely the 'deductive theology' from given absolute authorities that Lonergan has rejected from the outset.

Allied to this conception of an 'authentic' conversion is Lonergan's belief that there apparently is a structure of authentic conversion that remains relatively stable as it passes from person to person and even as it moves through the changing forms of historical epochs and of cultures. For, says Lonergan, out of conversion arises the community (a strangely Baptist notion) and out of the unbroken sequence of such structurally similar converts arises the Body of Christ. In both instances, when he speaks of authentic conversion and of a historically stable continuum of conversions, Lonergan clearly assumes a given and stable structure of conversion, authentically Christian and presumably Catholic in form, which gives stability to the varied life of man's religion, which in turn provides grounding for the continuity of the Church, and a universal and Christian foundation to theological inquiry. In other words, a given, stable, *a priori* structure that roughly corresponds to the heuristic structure of cognition evident in all our knowing, each one *quod semper et ubique est.* But while such a universal heuristic structure is derivable by transcendental analysis of our natural cognitive powers, such a 'theological' structure of authentic conversion can be neither empirically nor transcendentally derived. For this structure is available neither to inquiry into the *historical* data nor to a transcendental analysis of any given type of *human* religious experience. And even if it were, it would only tell us of the human response to grace, not of its divine 'whence'.

Again, a basic theological presupposition, in this case a doctrine concerning the continuity of the work of the holy Spirit in the varied life of Christian faith, is presupposed in the method and not produced by it. This presupposition, arising from 'nowhere', functions to give theological credibility, and certainly Catholic orthodoxy, to this empirical method. But if the categories of God, Christ, Church and now holy Spirit are the *presuppositions* and not the *results* of a proposed theological method, what is there left for such a method to reflect upon, and what of significance remains for theology to establish and to define? Have we not in fact returned to a *deductive* theology, whose fundamental premises are deduced from a given tradition and its doctrines, and then elaborated and assessed in terms of the varying, unstable data of empirical analysis and a study of religious experience?

In sum, the fundamental theological principles of Lonergan's theology are 'sneaked in', imported clandestinely, and not produced by his method, and so the radically empirical method he proposes seems to bear little relation to the actual theological structure he envisions to be true and in fact uses. I have suggested, therefore, that (1) the radical and explosive relativist implications of his empiricism have not penetrated to the heart of his own theological consciousness, so that 'doctrines' and 'authentic conversion' seem to him possible resultants from an empirical theology; and (2) that in fact his theology represents, therefore, a view of doctrines as latent or resident in the data, there to be 'seen' when objective research, motivated by pious concern for religious truths, has conducted its inquiries—a view of knowing he has repudiated as a vast misunderstanding of what empiricism in science really means. One thing seems established, namely that a direct and isomorphic analogue between (a) scientific cognition as Lonergan spells it out, and (b) theology as he wishes to conduct it, is more misleading than illuminative of what a Christian theology can really be about. The question is, is there another use of his cognitive theory that may be more helpful in understanding theology and its methods?

Our purpose in this last section is to suggest how this brilliant analysis of cognition can be more creatively used in theology. Our argument with Lonergan is firstly that he has failed to sense the really radical implications of his empirical understanding of science, implications which entail that theological doctrines could not be interpreted as the results of an objective scientific enterprise; and secondly that this criticism applies to his view both of our natural knowledge of God and of our knowledge of God through revelation. How else, then, can we interpret fundamental theological concepts or doctrines and yet remain within the orbit of Lonergan's analysis of cognition? Our suggestion is that we interpret his view of knowing more in an Augustinian than in a Thomistic fashion—though between Professors Gilson and Mascall on the one hand and Fathers Rahner and Lonergan on the other, the layman in these matters tends to wonder what it was on the issue of knowing that Thomas really meant to say! In any case, if Fr Rahner is right about a pre-thematic apprehension of Absolute Esse in Thomas, then the interpretation which follows can be said to be Thomistic as well as Augustinian—but then it looks as if Lonergan had better check over once again his own understanding of Thomism!

Lonergan has established beyond question, so it seems to me, that the process of human knowing manifests at three basic points a relatedness of the knowing mind to a dimension of ultimacy or of unconditionedness. And he makes clear that an apprehension, however unthematised and 'unlooked at' it may be, of this dimension of the unconditioned is absolutely requisite as a part of the dynamic process of knowing if we are to understand that process correctly. Because man is thus related to the unconditioned, and aware that he is so related, man is enabled to know; a relation to ultimacy is one of the transcendental conditions for the possibility of empirical knowledge. *What* modern empirical man knows is tentative, hypothetical and probable—the object of his inquiry is not itself absolute; here possibly Augustine was wrong and modernity right (and here Lonergan, strangely, is in his own thought incurably Greek!). But *that* modern man knows the tentative and hypothetical truths that he does know is itself dependent on a relation to ultimacy, not as an object to be looked at but as a qualification of our knowing capacity, as an awareness that makes it possible that we know at all; or, to use Augustine's language, we know because of the presence of a Divine Light that illumines our minds so that they can know.[24]

At three places, according to Lonergan's analysis,[25] this dimension of ultimacy appears:

(1.) In the unrestricted desire to know, the unremitting eros to understand, the ultimate concern with the truth, as Tillich would have put it, that is foundational for science as an enterprise. Without this ultimate passion for knowing and this ultimate confidence that such knowing is possible, either on the individual or communal level, inquiry would not be possible, for then other interests would dominate, exactitude would vanish, and perseverance flag; and, above all, the confidence in the work of others necessary for the cumulative community of science would have no basis in the commitments that the members of the community of inquiry share.[26]

(2.) As Lonergan has brilliantly demonstrated, no judgement is possible without a 'grasp of the virtually unconditioned character of our prospective judgements'.[27] When we see that the conditions relevant to a judgement are fulfilled, not that they are necessarily so fulfilled but are in fact so, then with this apprehension of the *unconditioned* in relation to our proposition, we judge our hypothetical proposition 'to be so'—and that judgement, that apprehension of a virtual or 'conditional' certainty, is basic to any meaning which the processes of verification or falsification may be given. If no such apprehension were characteristic of our knowing process, if we never achieved in this limited and contingent sense an apprehension of the unconditioned, we would never either *know* or *know that we know*. To know that something is so, that a proposition is verified as probable or falsified as improbable—not that it is necessarily so but only in fact so—is to know that the conditions for the making of the judgement are in fact fulfilled; it is to know that this judgement is not in fact subverted by an endless sea of further internal relations, of further conditions that qualify and may finally subvert the judgement. To know is to apprehend this stopping of the flow of relativity, this fulfilment of the requisite conditions: it is to apprehend the virtually unconditioned character of this judgement. The possibility of that stopping of endlessly qualifying conditions, of saying, 'Here the conditions *are* fulfilled and so here I *know* that it is so,' is this apprehension that now this judgement is in fact, and so virtually, *un*conditioned —that is, that no further conditions are outstanding. Without this quality of the unconditioned, no certain knowledge about the finite and so the internally related would be possible. Thus an apprehension of the dimension of ultimacy—in a virtual or conditioned form appropriate to a contingent creature—is basic to the possibility of finite truth and so to scientific inquiry.

(3.) In grasping by the rational consciousness the virtually unconditioned character of our proximate judgements, we know, says Lonergan, that we know, and this apprehension is utterly certain, totally indubitable, and thus in its own way absolute.[28] We cannot question or doubt this, for such doubt itself depends on what is doubted, namely the self-knowledge or self-awareness that I understand my doubt and affirm it. Thus a doubting self is a self that is self-aware that it understands and knows the truth of its own doubt.

In this self-awareness of the self as here a knower lies the ground of all certainty and so of all knowing. Our ability to know that the conditions are fulfilled and so to make rational (conscious and not compulsive) judgements is dependent on the certain grasp of our rational consciousness that here we are knowers, that here we do know, have had insight and have seen the conditions as fulfilled. This fundamental self-awareness and its resultant sense of certainty are themselves unconditioned; they are the grounds of all other certainties, and are themselves indubitable. For on this bedrock of self-awareness that here I do know, and experience myself as such, all verification and falsification of our hypotheses about objects, and so all cumulative scientific knowledge, phenomenologically rest. The greatest certainty *for Lonergan*, and that which grounds all other knowledge, comes to us by the mode of our self-awareness of ourselves as subjects rather than through the mode of 'knowledge' of objects outside and beyond us.

Thus at three points there is a prehension of the unconditioned grounds of our knowing: as the quality of our own commitment to the value of, and confidence in the reality of, the rationality of being and so its knowability; as the quality of our proximate judgements when we apprehend them as virtually unconditioned; and as the quality of our self-awareness in making such judgements, an awareness that here we do in fact know. This dimension of ultimacy as an element of the cognitive process is not a result of knowing but a condition of knowing. Nor is it known as are the objects of our inquiries, but rather is it apprehended in our modes of self-awareness. It seems an aspect of the self, present clearly to it as the self is to itself. On the other hand, in its phenomenological shape and quality—and in its function (as Augustine said) of drawing us to itself, of judging our minds, and of making our own judgements possible—the 'referent' or 'whence' of this prehension seems to transcend the mind, giving to it the possibility of the empirical, finite, tentative truths the mind does know. This element, we suggest, is the central way our cognitive powers are related to the Divine; though, as far as I know, Lonergan—having pointed all this out to everyone else—fails to draw this conclusion! But, as Augustine insisted, in our knowing, as in our being, valuing, hoping and loving, we relate essentially to the God who made and so transcends us, and that relation makes possible all we are and do. Our nature is to be so related, and a dim awareness of this dependence penetrates all our capacities, in this case our unrestricted eros to know, our awareness of the virtually unconditioned character of a given judgement, and our totally non-tentative apprehension that here in this case we do know.

This is not natural theology, for only the *horizon* of ultimacy and unconditionedness vis-à-vis truth appears here; 'God' has not yet appeared. But the presence of this horizon not only illustrates the religious character of man; it also provides part of the essential grounding to our religious and theological discourse. Further, if in fact this is a pre-thematic apprehension of 'God' as providing the condition for our knowing, it is to be understood not on the analogy of the uncovering of an *object* of our inquiry, but on the analogy of our awareness of *ourselves* as knowers. As unthematic, it provides no doctrines about God. It is an apprehension of the dimension of ultimacy in which we naturally live, the basis in the cognitive aspect of our ordinary or 'secular' experience for the horizon of ultimacy that makes possible the reception of revelation on conversion—and so the theological interpretation of its data. And thus we are led to the second 'reconstruction'.

As we saw, neither the empirical and interpretative study of the data of theology outlined in the first section of Lonergan's method, nor a transcendental analysis of the inward principle of conversion dominant in the second section, could establish the possibility of *theology*, namely reflective Christian discourse about *God* and his works among men. A method of this sort could, to be sure, tell us much about the social, historical and psychological varieties of human religions; but such conclusions about man and his gods, history and its events, documents and their images, movements and their ideological conflicts, do not, even together, make up *theology*, which intends reflectively to speak in a

Christian way about *God*, Christ, the Mystical Body and all things in relation to them—as Lonergan makes very clear when he says what theology is about.[29] The problem, we suggested, was the analogy with scientific inquiry. As Lonergan has clearly shown us, science is intent on discovering the immanent relations of things to one another manifested in the data, and it is a process directed and carried on by an invariant heuristic structure characteristic of man. Thus scientific inquiry in the natural and human 'sciences' *can* reach its goal in terms of a rational interpretation of the given data, and it can in turn be understood as a process through a transcendental analysis of how we thus know.

Theology, however, is not in this sense like science: a *rational* inquiry into *given* data seeking thereby to uncover the *immanent* principles of the data; nor are all the essential foundations of theology to be found by any sort of *transcendental* analysis. First of all, it is not like a science because it concerns the foundations of all inquiry, the shape of the ultimate horizon men live and think in, and thus its rationality takes a different form from that of science. As an inquiry into what founds inquiry, theology's principles cannot be the results of inquiry, nor its structure appear as one among many examples of inquiry. Lonergan sees this when he says that 'horizons' cannot be established by proof, nor cognitive structures discovered by an inquiry into objects. Theology's principles, further, are to be uncovered neither by objective inquiry nor by transcendental analysis because theological reflection concerns much more than the immanent structures within the data, and much more than the immanent capacities of the rational consciousness. Rather theology, by its nature as reflection on our foundational *religious* symbols with regard to their meaning and validity for us, essentially concerns the impingement of *transcendence* (or 'God') on our existence— and hence neither an empirical inquiry into the 'facts' around us nor an analysis of our own 'immanent' powers of cognition will in and of themselves manifest the object of theology, which is the sacred or the divine. On both counts, then, the analogy is misleading.

Conversion, however, is the place to begin, as Lonergan suggests.[30] But, for theological inquiry, conversion is the prius for the whole process, not its mid-point result. Thus its inception is to be understood, not as a result of inquiry into data, but in another mode entirely. Its *possibility* as a meaningful human experience arises, we have suggested, because of the universal and omnipresent impingement of transcendence or of ultimacy in all facets and on all levels of our human existence, one of which was the cognitive facet. But for many reasons, this impingement and the awareness that accompanies it, are not 'conversion', nor taken alone could they (because, among other things, of their vagueness, variety and non-specificity) result in *theology*, positive affirmative statements about the sacred or the divine.

Positive affirmations about this ultimacy and its character, reflection upon which is theology, arise out of special historical constellations giving rise to special experiences, although they arise universally. Each such experience is always specific, resulting in a *particular* view of our world, of ourselves, and of the ultimate that lies behind them. Each arises in a particular community and through a particular set of symbolic forms which mediate this apprehension of ultimacy. And each potent 'hierophony', because creative of a stance vis-à-vis ourselves, others, and the world, founds not only a religious community but also an entire cultural form. The symbols, both substantial and verbal, of the community in whose ethos we spiritually exist—be it the Christian or the Jewish communities, or the liberal political or the scientific communities—mediate ultimacy to us. In this process of mediation they shape our consciousness, the horizon in which we live, and they provide for our community and so for us, the ultimate norms that mould our behavioural life and the apprehensions that ground our confidence and hopes. Through these symbols we are given, in so far as this is possible to men, ultimate clarification and healing. Thus are our ultimate religious symbols meaningful and valid for us; and thus are we inescapably involved in them. All of this together, we suggest, makes up what Lonergan really means by 'conversion', and, as he notes, on a communal and more permanent basis this complex is what he means by 'religion'. Conversion 'happens' *in community* and *through symbols*. Our sense of the reality and relevance of what is there mediated to us, and so our apprehension of the meaning and the validity of these communal symbols, comes to each of us in a grasp of our existential consciousness when 'in conversion' we experience the reality with which we must ultimately deal, clarification, healing, transformation, and hope.

It is here, we also suggest, that the analogy of science with theology becomes most clear. For the scientific community is, as a community, committed to certain fundamental symbols concerning human existence and human truth, and to certain standards and canons resulting from these symbols; also as a community it is grounded in repeated and transmissible experiences of clarification and renewal, experiences passed on in the community from master to student as the ultimate telos of education because the ultimate spiritual basis of this community in history. Here again, as the *cultural* basis of inquiry itself, *symbolic forms* appear, *community*, *tradition* and *commitment*, all of them the 'secular' counterparts of the religious conversion of which Lonergan writes.

The fundamental symbols of a religious community, like the basic symbols that direct scientific inquiry, are not known and believed through objective rational inquiry, but through existential conversion—for in each community they guide and direct inquiry rather than appear as its results. Thus, returning to the sphere of religion *per se*, these symbols and the community that bears them do not arise out of conversion but mediate it to men (Lonergan, as we noted, has a strangely 'spiritualist' view of theological symbols as well as a far too 'Baptist' view of the Church).[31] For any theological reflection, therefore, the fundamental symbols on which reflection concentrates are already given in the community as mediating ultimacy and healing to us. Through them, and through the community that bears them, ultimacy has been apprehended and so is named, clarification and healing have been and are experienced, and hopes are born and nourished. Hence the essential structure of theological symbolism: God, Christ, Spirit and Church, arises *neither* from conversion *nor* from the data; rather that symbolism appears as the prius of understanding the data theologically—which is really, I think what Lonergan wished to say.[32] Language about God is, to be sure, a union of data with converted intelligence, but it is a union that takes place in a given historical community and in relation to a given set of communal and traditional symbols. Its central task is therefore not merely inquiry into the data, but reflection on the meaning and the validity for us and for our time of these communal and traditional symbols.

On these terms the other unexplicated and so unintelligible

elements of Lonergan's view become clearer. The fact of the change and development of religious experience and of theology in cultural process is obvious to any modern. Conversion as a human experience and phenomenon can, however, have a hint of stability amidst change and of authenticity amidst its omnipresent waywardness, both of which Lonergan specifies as its 'essential' character, only if we see religious apprehension as a union of historical community, traditional symbols, and personal existence. Theology is reflection for its time on the meaning and validity for us of these symbols communicative of ultimacy, healing and hope. It seeks to express through a union of traditional symbols and present experience the contemporary ethos of its community with regard to ultimate issues. As Lonergan notes, the roots of objectivity and knowledge in science are threefold: experience, insight and judgement. So here, as well, the essential structures of conversion and religion, varied as they are historically and phenomenologically, are threefold. Together these three elements provide the aspects of stability and authenticity Lonergan is looking for: community, symbols and personal existence, which together mediate to us the ultimacy of which theology reflectively speaks and on which man in all the facets of his living and knowing depends. Theology can only be understood as cognitive talk about the transcendent if this mediation of ultimacy (conversion) is understood as coming to us through certain central symbols and through a given historical community. In sum, theology presupposes as its basis a threefold structure which is more 'Trinitarian' than it is 'heuristic' in its origin and in its form.

# The Reception of Church Councils

## A. GRILLMEIER

IN recent times the concept of 'reception' as applied to Church synods or councils has taken on a new significance, especially in ecumenical dialogue.[1] Historically as well as systematically we can ask what the double concept 'council-reception' could mean for the unity of Christians. In this context there is an interesting parallel in the history of law. The phenomenon of reception has played an important role in the development of law and for a long time there has been a discussion among scholars about its interpretation. Indeed, this word has tended to become almost a technical term in the history of law, where it is used without further qualification.[2] The history of the councils, however, and in fact the entire Christian tradition have relied upon the same idea as a concrete expression of a reality of Church life and community consciousness.

For that very reason it can become a topic in ecumenical discussion. Reception should be a way to unity. Here recourse to the history of law can be quite helpful.[3] Both lawyers and theologians discover that the reception processes, which they have to interpret, either involve a juridical and theological aspect of their own or are, in any case, of great cultural importance.[4] Therefore it would be useful for theologians to question lawyers about their experience in the study of reception, since they already have a hermeneutic and a method for the interpretation of the processes they observe, whereas the theologians are only now beginning to tackle the theme of reception in all its implications.

Because reflection about *method* is a theme of Fr Lonergan's life work, it is proper that this ecumenically important problem be unfolded, as it were, before his eyes in order to bring his experience with the methodological question to bear in this area of study.

The first part of this paper will deal with the methodological experience of the legal historians in their own field. The intention here is only this: to focus the attention of theologians on the fact that there are important methodological experiences made by non-theologians which might cast light on the topic. We cannot here develop in detail the direct application of this method to the problem of reception in conciliar history, but I have considered the problem in an article written for *Theologie und Philosophie*, XLV (1970). The second part of this paper will attempt to show the significance of reception for present and future theology.

## I. THE METHODOLOGICAL EXPERIENCE OF HISTORIANS OF LAW IN THE INTERPRETATION OF LAW RECEPTION

*What is Reception in the Field of Juridical History?*

Undoubtedly this question is quite remote from Fr Lonergan's area of research. Nevertheless his interest extends, precisely because of the methodology involved, to all important manifestations of intellectual culture. Therefore juridical history, even European juridical history, should also be subjected to scrutiny. Our particular object of inquiry, then, is the reception of Roman law in Germany and in certain other parts of Europe. The medieval idealisation of ancient Rome, which inspired the Christian emperors of the Holy Roman Empire, prepared the way for the process of reception. According to common theory the German emperors were, by the *translatio imperii*,[5] the successors of their Roman counterparts, including the Christian Byzantine Emperor Justinian, whose legislation was of great significance for the history of the councils. This idea of Rome was a bridge between the two dominant cultural spheres of the time, i.e. the German culture on the one hand and the Roman culture, centred around Rome and Constantinople, on the other. The resulting feeling of spiritual kinship bore fruit. From the twelfth to the fourteenth century Bologna sent its students of canon and civil law over the Alps into Germany.[6] Here their legal knowledge found ample opportunity for implementation, since the early medieval German law, developed in and for an agrarian society, could no longer meet the demands of the new economic and social relationships. This period from the twelfth to the fourteenth century was only a prelude, however, to the so-called 'total reception' of Roman law, beginning at the end of the fifteenth century when Germany abandoned her own law system and employed instead the Roman *jus civile* in the common civil courts and in general legislation.[7] Such an exchange of law systems, even though it was not everywhere equally carried through, was a cultural phenomenon which has engaged whole generations of researchers and still occupies their efforts.[8] In the analysis of this process, which has been interpreted and evaluated in various ways, the concept of reception received a sharper definition, as its field of application was marked out.

*When can one speak of reception?*

Generally speaking reception is present when one people takes over from another people cultural elements which it did not previously possess. This provisional definition, however, can easily mislead if not handled carefully. For reception, in the strict sense of the word, can only occur when this is a giving and taking between cultures which are truly different and separate.

One cannot consider receptions the penetration of ancient Roman law into the west provinces of the empire, nor the diffusion of the Islamic law in the wake of the Arabian conquests, nor for that matter the propagation of the Franco-Norman law in England, nor of German law in the colonisation of eastern Europe. Rather, receptions are exemplified in the acceptance of Christianity by the majority of German peoples as well as in the acceptance of Buddhism in the Far East. Reception is thus in particular the acceptance of Roman law in Germany, Scotland or the Netherlands.[9]

If reception is in general a process between group A and group B, it is nevertheless also true that certain further conditions for the relationship of A to B and B to A are called for; namely, both must be antithetically opposed with respect to the cultural object to be exchanged. Or if we consider A and B as two areas of cultural influence, then in the exchange A must give something to the foreign cultural sphere of B, and B must take something foreign from outside its own cultural sphere. Reception is therefore an 'exogenous' process and not an 'endogenous' process, an 'epidemic' and not an 'endemic' phenomenon.[10]

*The question of method in the interpretation of this process*

Let us note carefully the word 'process'. It is not merely the *bonum recipiendum*, materially considered, that is the object of inquiry. When it is a question of the adoption of law statutes, one might be tempted to conceive of the reception process in purely quantitative and mechanical terms, similar to a chemical or mechanical process: nation A takes over from nation B this or that set of legal statutes. It was in this external way that the juridical positivism of the nineteenth century understood the reception of Roman law in the German nations. But we can see immediately what kind of interpretation such a view would yield when applied to the reception of Christian dogma: Church A takes over from Church B this or that council decree or this or that council.

Consequently it is not unimportant for our topic that the recent research on the reception of law deliberately insists on overcoming the positivistic interpretation and evaluation. Besides the object of the *recipere*, the *bonum recipiendum*, the *recipere* itself must also be considered. Only in this way will we understand the reception process and its cultural and historical importance. So modern scholars have envisioned the reception of Roman law not so much in terms of 'the introduction of new individual laws', but rather as 'the seizure of power by the educated lawyer and the juridical application of his methods in the whole of public life' from the end of the fifteenth century on.[11] In other words, the law-transforming activity of an entire social class as well as the material object must be taken into account in order to grasp the reception process in its uniqueness. Reception is the sum of 'countless deeds, events and internal processes; of legal statutes, judgements and juridical education, even of the change in juridical conviction on the part of many millions of people.'[12]

The method is also determined by the above-mentioned facts. Juridical positivism made the interpretation very easy for itself. It compares, as it were, two lawbooks and asserts: this is from there (exactly like the theologian, for example, who places Denzinger next to the Protestant creeds and ascertains: this sentence is also there, this sentence is missing there). It is certainly true that positivism has performed a valuable service. It has reduced the large number of instances which must be interpreted to a simplified *model*. Nation A receives from nation B an object, namely B's self-contained national law system.[13] Even the historians who want to overcome positivism have to make themselves a simplified model; however, it must be a model that guarantees an essential grasp of the entire process. Thus they place beside positivism's model X their own models Y and Z. For example, nation A changes of itself and passes over from an earlier phase into a new phase (model Y). Or, the present nation A (that is, the present political condition of this nation) has only come into existence through the reception process (model Z).[14] Juridical positivism, similar to dogmatic positivism in this respect, stops at model X, without considering the structure of manifold historical, social, intellectual, psychological—and in our case of conciliar reception also theological—group processes. The point is that the formula, 'the reception of Roman law', understood according to model X is too simplistic. And it would be just as superficial to understand conciliar reception as the literal taking over of dogmatic propositions.

Consequently the interpretation of important cultural and theological receptions must rely upon models Y and Z. Attention should be given to the change which the subject of the reception experiences in the process. Hence, one has to choose a model 'that encompasses the social, political, cultural, and religious significance of reception'.[15] In the judgement of recent research the changes which the reception of law called forth in the German realm were so fundamental that political and private disputes were no longer settled through force, emotions, or instinctive patterns of behaviour, but rather 'by a universally valid decision resulting from a logical discussion of the autonomous juridical problematic'.[16] This event created in its turn the essential conditions 'for the advance of the material culture, especially in the art of administration, in the establishment of a well thought out economic structure in society and even in the modern technical control of nature'.[17] So the examination of the data within the framework of models Y and Z borrowed from the social and historical sciences permits the interpretation of the entirety of a juridical system that is integrated into and simultaneously changing the concrete historical society.

The reference made to 'models' becomes important when we consider the treatise *De Methodo* as Fr Lonergan has proposed it.

An analysis of the process of reception with regard to these models should replace the inquiry into causes as conducted by the positivists. We are all aware of the role which the word 'cause' plays for Aristotle and Thomas, and consequently for Fr Lonergan also. The effectiveness of this type of investigation, however, is not always clear. For the assessment of conciliar history and the reception of the councils it would be worth while considering the validity of Franz Wieacker's comments about the method of research in the area of the reception of law.

The replacement of an explanation in terms of effective causes by an explanation through an exact description of the processes which take place has been proved a very effective instrument in every area of historical research. Practically speaking, the cause-effect relation cannot be carried through when one is considering such complicated developments as we have to deal with in reception, where social and ideological pressures are continually entangled in the free actions of individuals. This relation is totally inapplicable on the level of historical processes which come about through the conscious decisions and actions of individual persons. These are actions which are not mechanically or biologically determined, and therefore should not be explained, but rather understood.[18]

A model must naturally be of such a character that it captures the essential elements of the process under consideration. To determine which of the many possible methods available is the one best suited for application the ultimate criterion can only be its usefulness in clarifying the concrete situation to be understood. Once the correct method has been discovered, it is then possible to ascertain variations and thus distinguish genuine and deficient forms of the reception process.

## The reception of law and the reception of the councils

Are the methodological insights which we acquired from an analysis of the reception of law directly applicable in theological and ecclesiological areas? I think we can answer this question with a qualified 'Yes', especially if we bear in mind the canonical and historical function and significance of the councils. The councils were an integral part of Justinian's system of ecclesiastical law, and as such could automatically become an immediate object of investigation in the study of juridical reception, which we have been discussing up to now. The early period of juridical reception in Germany was concerned principally with canon law. Whether a reception of synodal Church law actually took place and what changes it brought about in the recipient remain open questions that can only be answered in a further study treating this matter specifically.

The significance of Church councils is not exhausted in the realm of juridical history. Obviously councils are also significant events in the cultural and intellectual history of Christian nations. If we are dealing with the reception of culturally significant councils, then the same methods as are employed in the evaluation of the reception of law easily lend themselves to the interpretation of this conciliar type of reception. This touches a point which in Fr Lonergan's view is very important. It almost sounds as if it were written for this context, when he remarks in connection with something entirely different (the matter of conversion): '. . . what can become communal, can become historical. It can pass from generation to generation. It can spread from one cultural milieu to another. It can adapt to changing circumstances, confront new situations, survive into a different age, flourish in another period or epoch.'[19] This undoubtedly creates a very difficult question for conciliar reception today. In ecumenical dialogue the issue is still the reception of old synods convened by the separated Churches. Fifteen hundred years, however, now divide us from these synods. The reception of such a synod is today something entirely different from the reception of exactly the same synod 1,500 years ago when the different Churches lived in the same cultural milieu.

In his article 'Dimensions of Meaning' Fr Lonergan says something which I believe to be of importance for our topic.[20] Although he dismisses a purely philosophical understanding of the historical problem, he does nevertheless use philosophical categories in 'Dimensions of Meaning' to differentiate various historical periods. He talks about the difference in cultural levels. On the first level man lives in a world whose substance is meaning. At the second level man accomplishes a mediation of meaning. When the mediation of meaning changes, the culture is altered and a new historical era begins. 'For if social and cultural changes are, at root, changes in the meanings that are grasped and accepted, changes in the control of meaning mark off the great epochs in human history.'[21] Lonergan can therefore speak of a primitive epoch when there was still no reflective mediation of meaning, a classical epoch which was determined by the ideal of Aristotelian science, and finally a new epoch which is determined by new ways of mediation.

When the educated, or the cultured, or the gentlemanly, or the saintly man was standardised by classical culture, then it was recognised that definitions were to be explained but not disputed. Today terms are still defined, but the definitions are not unique: on the contrary, for each term there is a historical sequence of different definitions; there is a learned explanation for each change of definition; [one can illustrate this with ideas which have played an important role in conciliar history, e.g. the concepts of persons and nature] and there is no encouragement for the sanguine view that would exclude further developments in this changing series.

What is true of definitions is also true of doctrines. They exist, but they no longer enjoy the splendid isolation that compels their acceptance. We know their histories, the moment of their births, the course of their development, their interweaving, their moments of high synthesis, their periods of stagnation, decline, dissolution . . . In brief, the classical mediation of meaning has broken down. It is being replaced by a modern mediation of meaning that interprets our dreams and our symbols, that thematises our wan smiles and limp gestures, that analyses our minds and charts our soul, that takes the whole of human history for its kingdom to compare and relate languages and literatures, art forms and religions, family arrangements and customary morals, political, legal, educational, economic systems, sciences, philosophies, theologies, and histories . . . (Now) Catholic philosophy and Catholic theology are matters, not merely of revelation and faith, but also of culture. The breakdown of classical culture and, at last in our day, the manifest comprehensiveness and exclusiveness of modern culture confront Catholic philosophy and Catholic theology with the gravest problems, impose upon them mountainous tasks, invite them to Herculean labors . . .[22]

The legal historians who developed the methods for the interpretation of reception are dealing with an epoch that can still be termed classical. They are dealing with a cultural phenomenon that despite its temporal duration can still be interpreted in categories that remain basically constant. Conciliar reception makes different demands and consequently the method of interpretation must allow the following:

1. In conciliar decisions it is always a question of religious

9

belief. In the Christian tradition the synods are constituents of faith; they are events in the life of the Church and the Churches. However, they are events which cannot be pigeon-holed in the category 'cultural history'. Therefore the first methodological requirement is this: conciliar reception must be considered at the level of Christian understanding of the nature of Church. From this centre of the Church's understanding of herself, it is necessary to develop a model which makes possible the consideration of conciliar reception under a twofold aspect: i.e., as a past fact, to be analysed, and as a future event, to be realised.

In this analysis it should be noted that a change in the Church's understanding of herself implies a change in her understanding of the synods. Further, because the Church always remains bound to human culture, changes in this relation must be carefully evaluated. These are due to fluctuations in the relationship between Church and state as well as to the variations in the relationship between Church and culture.

So it is evident that conciliar reception in its entirety is a more complex entity than juridical reception, which was sufficiently complicated in itself. If research in the area of juridical reception required more than a hundred years to find an adequate method, it is to be expected that the difficulties in the determination and interpretation of conciliar reception will increase.

On the other hand, conciliar reception and research in this field are intimately connected to Church history and the history of dogma; these, however, already have a long tradition. Reflection on the methods employed in these disciplines is of immediate advantage in the study of synods and councils, even though they are only now for the first time being studied systematically from this point of view. The interpretation of post-synodal history is likewise an instance of historical reception. However, when reception is treated thematically in its own right, it makes special demands upon us. The ecumenical situation is an obvious case in point and considerable difficulties do arise.

2. The Churches which speak about the reception of old Church councils are the Churches which are bound together in the World Council of Churches. Catholic theologians are also present as consultors in this organisation. It is clear to everyone there that dialogue in such a gathering is difficult not only because the subject matter lies some 1,500 years in the past, but also

because the participating Churches each have a special relationship to these events. Consider, for example, the Council of Chalcedon. What does it mean to the Orthodox Church, to the various Monophysite Churches still existing today, to the Lutheran and Reformed Churches and finally to modern liberal Protestantism? In view of such a variety of traditions, is it sensible to talk about the reception of one or other synod?

## II. SIGNIFICANCE OF THE QUESTION OF CONCILIAR RECEPTION FOR THE DIRECTION OF THEOLOGY TODAY AND IN THE FUTURE

The study of the reception of the ancient councils may appear to us today as a low priority task. One may even get the impression from Fr Lonergan's 'Dimensions of Meaning' that theology today must devote itself primarily to the task of leading the Christian tradition into the new epoch already upon us by finding an expression for Christianity suitable to the new mentality. It is quite possible that none of us knows how the *kerygma* and Christian theology will adapt themselves in order to appear credible. The peculiar handicap in the fulfilment of this task is the lack of a common philosophy to serve as a basis for theological speculation and reflection.

We should not, however, lose sight of an ecumenical concern that presents itself to us in the subject 'reception of councils'. The Churches joined together in the World Council of Churches are clearly determined to work out patiently the implications of this topic. Catholic theology should not stand in the way of the realisation of this desire. What then does this task demand?

Involved in the discussion are first of all the Churches which cut themselves off from the main Church after the Councils of Ephesus and Chalcedon. The first of these are the Nestorians, who after the year 431 migrated to the East, beyond the Byzantine empire; the second are the Monophysites, who emerged in the years following 451 and who survive today as the Armenian, West Syrian, Coptic and Ethiopian Churches. The various Protestant Churches in the West are also involved in this dialogue, as are Catholic theologians, though in an unofficial capacity. Somewhat unexpectedly a new confrontation with Nestorianism, Monophysitism, and Chalcedonian Orthodoxy in all their forms has arisen. Alexandria, Constantinople, Rome, Wittenberg and

Geneva are again speaking to one another. Some of these
Churches still speak their ancient language, so we have to travel
back 1,500 years to understand clearly what a certain dogmatic
formula means to them. The formula: Christ, one nature, one
person, one hypostasis, stands in sharp contrast to the other
formula: Christ, one person in two natures. Whoever enters this
dialogue with official representatives of these Churches, realises
immediately how slow they have been in developing a reflective,
critical theology. They have neither a historical understanding of
their own tradition, nor a dialectic, which would enable them
to reconcile seemingly contradictory statements. On the other
hand one also meets theologians in these dialogues who have
adopted the hermeneutics of Rudolf Bultmann. For them
Chalcedon is no problem at all; it's not even worth talking about.

In face of all this, the theologian's task is extremely complicated,
but also extremely important. Another reference to the notion
of juridical reception, from which we began, can be of assistance
here. Franz Wieacker emphasises very strongly that to interpret
the process correctly account must also be taken of the theoretical
and practical work of lawyers: reception was not simply a process
of adopting foreign legal statutes, but it took place above all in
the way lawyers went about their work, both theoretically and
in practice. If conciliar reception, on the ecumenical level, is to
take place today and in the future, then it is the theologians who
will have to take the lead. There are examples of this already in
the history of the councils, especially in the period following
Chalcedon. Theology, as a serious scholarly discipline, was really
first developed by the Chalcedonians or the followers of that
council and their successors; it was born out of the dialectic
between the Monophysite and Dyophysite Christological
formulas. The result of this theological discussion was both the
clarifying and the deepening of the more important concepts in
which the Christological dogma was expressed and consequently
a deepening of the way in which dogma itself was understood.
The Monophysites, on the other hand, by excluding themselves
from taking part in this work and arguing purely from tradition,
shut off the possibility of discovering behind the varying, at
times contradictory formulas the common meaning—the
common faith in Christ. This necessary task of reflection has
still to be accomplished today.

This is only one example of the work theologians have before them with regard to the reception of the councils. Similar, perhaps more difficult, tasks of interpretation remain for Trent and for Vatican I, if these Councils are not simply to exist as a stumbling block and a wall of division, but are to become, at least to some extent, the common possession of the Christian Churches.

Fr Lonergan has given us, under the general heading 'History and Dialectic', an excellent description of the role of theologians in this sort of process.[23] Only when the theologians have done their work will it be possible for responsible leadership in the Churches to make decisions, according to their own consciences, on the possibilities of reception, and to recommend their decisions to the faithful. Of course such a step as the reception of the Council of Chalcedon by the Monophysite Churches and a subsequent union with the Greek Orthodox Church, if it were to be accomplished successfully while preserving the good conscience of all the Monophysite faithful, would call for an intensive preparation of the people by their bishops, priests and theologians; pastoral effort here must be itself essentially ecumenical and pastoral in orientation.

The whole subject of reception, as it is presented in the thematic foreground of ecumenical efforts at dialogue, opens up many theological perspectives that cannot be developed here.[24] One thing, at least, will surely be asked from the Catholic theologian in such dialogue: that he only allow himself to participate if he can interpret the process of dogmatic development in the Church with understanding, sympathy and inner assent. He must be able to recognise the tension between meaning and expression, in order to judge similarities and differences in both correctly, and to distinguish what is important from what is only secondary. He must understand the stages of development in the history of Christian faith, and recognise also the demands of the future, so that he can not only find solutions to problems *pro hic et nunc*, but also help prepare the way towards unity for coming generations. Purely factual knowledge of history will be just as useless as a theology which fully overlooks history and tradition in the hopes of being a purely 'political' theology or something else of that sort. Only when the whole Christian tradition—if in a purified form—is brought into the newest developments in Christian language and Christian living, will contemporary theology have fulfilled its task for the future. And this theological and kerygmatic struggle to grasp the truth of faith will itself bring about *a new process of spiritual reception of the ancient councils and their statements, within Catholic theology itself.* All of which is but another indication of the essential historicity of the truth which God has entrusted to us in Christ: a truth which does not float over our heads as some vague sort of absolute, but which lives within us—within us and, indeed, before us, if only because we are never finished with the task of grasping it and 'receiving' it more profoundly than we have done before.

# Protestant Problems with Lonergan on Development of Dogma

## GEORGE A. LINDBECK

THIS paper sets out to be a contribution to the ecumenically-orientated theological discipline which Lonergan has called 'dialectic',[1] and which he proposes as a replacement for the apologetics of the past.

It is limited to one part of a single question: is Lonergan's basic cognitional and metaphysical analysis as this is developed chiefly in the revised edition of *Insight* confessionally (ecumenically) neutral on the question of the development of dogma? Would it be possible for a Protestant to adopt it while still remaining dogmatically a Protestant? More precisely, could he consistently continue to adhere to the *sola scriptura* as this currently still continues to be affirmed by theologians standing in the Reformation tradition? Or would he be induced to adopt that view of theological understanding which, for Lonergan, eliminates the need for the *sola scriptura* and sanctions what the Protestant considers a dangerously extended view of the possibilities of development? Put in still another way, could a Protestant 'Lonerganian' develop a 'Protestant' view of theological method without abandoning the basic position and falling into what Lonergan calls 'counter-positions'?

One's assessment of the possible ecumenical importance of Lonergan's work depends in part on the answer to this question. If his basic position is ecumenically neutral, capable of being used to formulate either Protestant or Roman Catholic views of theological understanding, method and development, then it could perhaps serve as a useful common tool in the ecumenical discussion. This, on the other hand, is not likely to happen if the cognitional and metaphysical analysis inevitably has what the Protestant considers heretical biases, for the Protestant, no less than the Catholic, is disinclined seriously to consider philosophical views which seem to him inimical to the faith.

Only the most schematic treatment is possible in this brief paper. The thesis is that Lonergan's basic position is ecumenically neutral on the specific points of *sola scriptura* and dogmatic development; or, to put it another way, those aspects of his theory of theological understanding and method which are not ecumenically neutral on these points are not entailed by his basic position. Little more can be done here, however, than to identify the main issues involved in an argument for this thesis, rather than actually to argue it *in extenso*.

One other preliminary comment: the points we are considering are not the only ones relevant to the question of ecumenical neutrality. I happen to think that they are the crucial ones. I do not see that Reformation dogmatic commitments on, e.g., the *sola fide*, the role of 'natural theology' or the nature of the Church are in any way imperilled by Lonergan's basic position unless that position favours his specifically Roman Catholic view of dogmatic development. This presupposes a rather 'Catholic' reading of the Reformation, but one which is thoroughly compatible, as historians would almost unanimously agree, with the official Confessional writings[2] of the Lutheran tradition to which I belong.

As is hinted by the last remarks, we are discussing in this paper a kind of Protestantism which is orthodox (or neo-orthodox) in a sense comparable to the way Lonergan is an orthodox Catholic. Protestants of this sort, unreservedly accept modern science and historical work and the need for constant re-interpretation of the revelation 'once for all delivered to the saints', but at the same time they seriously believe that they are in basic agreement with their forefathers in the faith (just as Lonergan does with his). They adhere, as did the Reformers, to the three Catholic Creeds (Apostolic, Nicene and Athanasian). They believe that it is 'objectively' true that Jesus Christ is the God-Man whose life, death and resurrection is the definitive, never-to-be-surpassed revelation of God in the space-time world of human experience and history which we now inhabit. On this central issue they side with Lonergan against modernists and extreme relativists, historicists, liberals, idealists or existentialists and also, if I understand the issue rightly, against a Catholic such as Leslie Dewart.[3]

In short, we are speaking in the company of 'neo-orthodox' writers like Barth or Brunner, or a theologian of hope such as Pannenberg, or, to mention some neo-Germans, men like the authors of the two most recent complete systematic theologies to be written in America, Gordon Kaufman of Harvard and John Macquarrie, formerly of Union.

Now Protestants such as these, even when they are not very explicit about it, still adhere to the substance of the Reformation *sola scriptura* as this was understood by Luther. For him, Scripture is the sole *norma normans non normanta* because it is, to use his phrase, 'the cradle of Christ'.[4] It contains the primary testimony to the definitive revelation, and so, in order to protect the definitiveness of that revelation, the exclusive Lordship of Christ, dogmatic development cannot be allowed 'to go beyond' Scripture.

Of course, all historically responsible contemporary Protestant theologians recognise that dogmas such as the Nicene Creed in one sense do 'go beyond' Scripture. The force of the exclusion of extra-scriptural developments, therefore, is that 'new' dogmas must not only be *compatible* with Scripture (with this Roman Catholics agree), but they must also be *required* by faithfulness to scriptural witness to Christ. Thus dogmatic development is legitimate only (1) when a new question of vital importance to the faithfulness of the Church must be decided one way or another, and (2) when one of the answers concretely available at the time is objectively more in accord with scriptural testimony than are the others.[5]

Neither of these two conditions are necessary for Lonergan nor for Roman Catholics in general. They were, to be sure, fulfilled at Nicea and Chalcedon, but clearly not at the time of the definition of the Assumption. Lonergan, in his essay on the definability of the latter dogma,[6] does not so much as hint that either of these conditions was even minimally present. He does not suggest that decision was necessary in order, for example, to preserve the peace and unity of the Church (ecumenically viewed, indeed, it did the opposite). Even if it had been, this would have justified only a kind of negative judgement similar to that which ended the disputes on *de auxiliis* (DS 1997)—e.g., 'Let no one affirm that belief in the Assumption is inconsistent with Christian faith.' In reference to the second condition, not

even the most fool-hardy, much less Lonergan, have argued
that the Assumption is in *greater* accord than are alternatives with
Scripture when the exegesis is objectively done rather than
mystically or allegorically. Thus this dogma, not to mention
others which Catholics (but not Protestants nor Eastern
Orthodox) accept, is not claimed to be *objectively* contained in
or *required* by our records of the original 'deposit of faith'.

Yet it must, so Catholics agree, somehow be in that deposit.
There has been no publicly binding revelation since, in the
classic phrase, 'the death of the last apostle'. Any other view
imperils the definitiveness of the revelation in Christ. Thus
*de fide* pronouncements which go beyond what is explicitly
required by the early tradition and Scripture must somehow be
implicitly or virtually revealed. The problem, therefore, is to
give a meaningful explanation of how through the growth of
theological understanding the implicitly revealed can become the
object of explicit awareness and belief.

Lonergan's solution is thoroughly original.[7] If I understand
him rightly, the core suggestion is that theological reflection can
be understood as structurally analogous to scientific investigation.
Crudely stated, his argument is that just as the new truths (e.g.,
that light bends or that there must be a previously unknown
element, or planet, or sub-atomic particle) deduced from a
scientific hypothesis can be said to be implicitly contained in the
already known facts which the hypothesis was designed to
explain, so the new conclusions derived from a theological
'theory' can be said, if they prove veridical, to be implicit in the
revealed truths the theory was designed to 'interpret' (i.e., quasi-
deductively unify). Further, just as a scientific hypothesis is
verified by actually observing the unknowns it predicts, so a
theological theory is verified in a structually (though not
materially) similar way when one of its derivates is dogmatically
defined. According to this, a developmentally arrived at dogma
is implicit in the original revelation, but at two steps removed.
First, it is contained in the 'hypothesis' from which it is derived
'synthetically' (or *via doctrinae*). But this hypothesis is not itself
explicitly revealed. It in its turn is implicit in the revealed data
from which it is obtained 'analytically' (or *via inventionis*). This
is known to be so, however, as we have already said, only if the
hypothesis is confirmed by the theological equivalent of a crucial

experiment, namely, a dogmatic definition. Only then can one affirm that this hypothesis, rather than one of the many other logically possible ways of unifying the same original data, is true—i.e., expresses, corresponds to, or reveals the divine reality to which it refers; and therefore also only thus can the new conclusions derived from such a hypothesis be known to be implicitly contained in the truths already known to be revealed. Finally, because new dogmas can serve as additional data for further hypothesis, doctrinal development is in principle not only never-ending (Protestants can agree to this), but also can be irreversibly cumulative (which Protestants deny).[8]

One question which can be raised regarding this view is whether it rightly construes the relation of higher order scientific theories to reality. Fr MacKinnon has argued at length that Lonergan does not sufficiently distinguish laws from theories, and that he therefore wrongly extends to theories that isomorphism with reality which laws possess. Theories, in contrast to laws, should not be said to express the intelligibility immanent in things so much as the intelligibility projected by the ordering mind into the data of experience. The entities to which theories refer are constructs, not objectively real. As MacKinnon puts it in reference to a specific case, 'the physicist uses concepts derived from more familiar realms, concepts whose proper objects are not the objects treated in quantum physics, but which admit of analogous application in theories concerning atomic data.'[9]

If this is a sound objection, then although MacKinnon does not make this further point, it suggests an alternative 'Lonerganian' way of analysing theological understanding which would greatly restrict his highly generous interpretation of what can be implicitly revealed. For example, in the Thomistic Trinitarian hypothesis, the immanent processions of love and will and the the correlated subsistent relations could, on analogy with MacKinnon's interpretation of scientific theories, be understood as 'theoretical entities' which can be helpful in removing the logical or imaginative difficulties created by Trinitarian formulas, but ought not be regarded as, even in some highly analogous way, 'corresponding to' God's inner being. They are *quoad nos*, not *quoad se*, reveal nothing new about God, and so, though based on the data of faith, cannot be viewed as revelations implicit in the original deposit nor as the possible source of dogmatisable consequences.[10]

If this view were adopted, then much of what Lonergan has so far said about theological understanding and method would have to be revised. Speculative theology would no longer be understood as the exploration of the truths of the faith *quoad se*, and so would lose its primacy. It would still retain some usefulness in untangling purely conceptual knots and problems in the understanding of the faith, but this would be seen as a detour to be traversed as quickly as possible in order to get on with the more important aspects of doing theology *quoad nos*. One would not, for example, tarry long on speculations about the immanent Trinity à la St Thomas, but would agree with Karl Rahner, Karl Barth and a strong Eastern tradition that the economic and immanent Trinity are one and same and should normally be treated as such.

Some of Lonergan's most recent writings contain similar emphases.[11] It will be interesting to see whether this leads him to modify what he has earlier said about speculative theology *quoad se*, and perhaps even about doctrinal development, or whether he will find ways of reconciling the old and the new.

Nevertheless, in the absence of fuller explanations, it seems that Lonergan's stress on *quoad se* speculation in theology must be viewed as *ad hoc*, motivated in part no doubt by his admiration for St Thomas, but also perhaps by a search for a solution for the specifically Roman Catholic problem of doctrinal development. A Protestant follower would not need to follow this path. Nor, for that matter, would a Roman Catholic. He could always try to deal with the question of development by other means.

These critical comments apply only to one part of Lonergan's theory of development — viz., to that part which applies to dogmas which are reached 'synthetically' or, as a Protestant would say, are 'extra-scriptural' in the sense of not being 'objectively required' by Scripture in the sense already described. The situation is entirely different when we turn to the Christological and Trinitarian dogmas which Protestants, as well as Eastern Orthodox, have historically accepted and which can be responsibly defended, even if not fully demonstrated, as scripturally required. These are, in Lonergan's terms, the products of 'analysis' rather than synthesis. The difficulties which many Protestants would have at this point with Lonergan's theory of development seem to me not insuperable.

The issue here is whether these dogmas are to be understood as simply the result of 'trans-cultural transposition', of a movement from one relative 'experiential priority' to another, or whether they also involve a movement 'toward the absolute of the objective priority'.[12] If only the former, the most that could be said about the permanence or enduring validity of these dogmas is that they represent *irreversible decisions* of the Church; but if also the latter, one could go on and add that these dogmas, considered as propositions or formulations, are *unrepealable*, i.e., affirmations which in reference to the questions they address, can never be superseded by more adequate affirmations.

Protestants in practice accept the irreversibility of dogmatic decisions. They do not think that the *sola scriptura* implies that perhaps Arianism was, is or will be right after all. They believe that the Church rightly responded to scriptural requirements when it forever excluded that heresy. They can also accept the historical argument (which Lonergan also adopts) that the homoousion was the only conceptual device available at the time for doing this job. It was the only 'formula which would compel all who professed that Christ was truly God to mean what they were saying and to mean it seriously.'[13]

To say all this, however—to grant the irreversible rightness of the Nicene decision—does not logically imply that the Nicene formulation, the homoousion, might not need at some time to be repealed, 'de-developed'[14] and abandoned. This would be necessary if, for example, (1) a scripturally more accurate answer to the point at issue were ever to be developed, (2) no way were seen of reconciling the Nicene formulation with this new and better one, and (3) the tension between the two were dangerous to the Church's life. Under these circumstances, obedience to Scripture and to the Lord to whom it testifies would require repudiation of a dogmatic formulation which one would still recognise as having been right in its day.[15]

Such a Protestant position is perhaps also reconcilable with Roman Catholic orthodoxy. Once a distinction is made between 'irreversibility' of dogmatic decisions and 'unrepealability' of formulations, it is no longer entirely clear whether the 'irreformability' of dogma affirms both these notions, or only the first and weaker one.

Lonergan, however, leaves no room for such doubts. His theory requires one to understand dogmatic propositions such as the homoousion and the 'two natures' as unrepealable. They represent permanently valid and valuable advances in the understanding of revelation which hold good in all times and places, in all cultures and historical periods which are intellectually capable of grasping what they assert.

His argument depends on an interpretation of these doctrines which makes them far more 'formal' and therefore less culturally conditioned than most historians have supposed they were. What is binding in the homoousion is no less and no *more* than the Athanasian formula: 'eadem de Filio quae de Patre dicuntur, excepto Patris nomine'.[16] He agrees with Augustine that *persona* or *substantia* was an undefined heuristic concept' saying no more than that 'as long as the Trinity is acknowledged, there are acknowledged three of something.'[17] In reference to Christology, he asks, in effect: Do you grant that some things should be said of Jesus Christ which can be said truly only of God, and others which can be said only of one who is truly man? If so, you acknowledge the two natures. Do you accept that these two sets of statements refer to *one and the same* Jesus Christ? If so, you acknowledge what is meant by one hypostasis.[18] He concludes that this understanding of the dogmas 'leaves the believer free to conceive the Father and Son and Holy Spirit in scriptural, patristic or modern terms.'[19]

When thus interpreted, I see no dogmatic conflict between the Protestant *sola scriptura* and this aspect of Lonergan's theory of development. This does not imperil the primacy of Scripture because the dogmatic propositions, even though they represent a genuine and unrepealable advance in understanding beyond what was explicitly revealed, nevertheless do this by identifying formal rules of right belief and speech. The 'substance' of orthodoxy is still to be looked for in 'the ordinary language' of prayer, worship and preaching and must be constantly and primarily nourished by other sources, above all Scripture. Dogmas are 'second-level propositions'[20] which guide the use of primary religious language. They should not become the 'content' of piety, serving as a warrant (or imperative) for praying, for example, equally to all three members of the Trinity, rather than to the Father, through the Son, in the power of the holy Spirit.[21] If this is Lonergan's position, then there need be no quarrel with the thesis that these dogmas represent a movement towards 'the absolute of the objective priority'.

Indeed, not only would this view seem to be compatible with classical Protestantism, but it can serve as a major ecumenical contribution. It can enable the Protestant, without sacrificing the *sola scriptura* with its emphasis on the definitiveness of the revelation in Christ, more highly to value the role of dogma, when it is properly used, in serving the unity and continuity of the Church.

# History as the Word of God

## JOHN NAVONE

THE progressive revelation of God has been emphasised in recent theology as well as figuring prominently in the documents of Vatican II. There has also appeared in recent years a profound interest in the notion of development. This latter has ranged from the work connected with the development of dogma to the theological implications of human development. With the anthropomorphic theology there has been a movement away from the static concepts of the scholastic manuals to the suitable categories of existential and personalistic philosophies. From the phenomenon of man we see the phenomena of God. Two points stand out in need of reconciliation or rather integration: human history, with its progress and decline, and God's word which constitutes that history. It is said that God speaks *in* history; however, it is more exact to say that history *is* the speech, the word, of God. Aquinas implied this when he said that all creation is a type of emanation from God. In this respect, God is not so much *in* history; rather, history is sustained and constituted by God. As long as we continue to *describe* God's action in history and *describe* man's response, we have not achieved the aim of theology as science in its efforts at an explanatory answer to the question 'Quid sit?'

This paper treats of history as the vehicle of revelation. If we say that God speaks in history, a basic metaphysics is presupposed. To speak or not to speak is ultimately a question of being.

Metaphysics is neither some vague view of life nor some subtle intuition of Being. It is not a general account of reality, nor a process of linguistic clarification. Metaphysics is a structured anticipation of what is to be known, and the basic component in that structure is human wonder about human experience.[1]

This wonder is expressed in two complementing types of

question: a what-question or a why-question, and in another mode whose satisfaction is expressed in a simple Yes or No.

The structured wonder of man is often unformulated or thematised as it was by Aristotle; nevertheless, it is an invariant structure which grounds metaphysics. This unchanging structure is shared by all mankind, always and everywhere. It is a dynamic structure which pushes for reasons (why?) and for truth (is it so?)

The dynamic structure of human knowing involves many distinct activities of which none by itself may be named human knowing. It is the total combination of experience, understanding and judgement, which assembles itself consciously, intelligently, and rationally.[2] One part summons forth the next until the whole is reached: experience stimulates inquiry, and inquiry (i.e. intelligence bringing itself to act) leads from experience through imagination to insight, and from insight to concepts, which stimulate reflection (the conscious exigence of rationality). Reflection marshals the evidence to judge Yes or No, or else to doubt and so renew inquiry.

Man is a part of history. Because of his structured dynamism of wonder, he inevitably questions his historical experience and is also questioned by it. The objective, dynamic world-order of which he is a part raises questions for his understanding. The human dynamism of inquiry is an integral part of the developing world-order, of the interlocking, created, temporal universe which is history.

How does God 'speak' in history? Although other biblical categories have been subjected to demythologisation, the category of 'word' seems to have been exempted.[3] The 'word of God' in its material aspect is just as anthropomorphic as the 'arm of God' and as open to magical interpretation as the sacraments. There is no need to maintain the mystique of the 'word of God'. Departing from the material aspect for the meaning and truth of this expression, we can understand the prophetic dictum, 'The word of the Lord came to me,' as an interpretation of history in which the proper judgemental element is supplied by prophetic light and the formal element by the ideas conceived in a human way by the prophet or writer.[4]

God uses the things of the universe to convey his mind, as men use the written or spoken word to convey theirs. For Aquinas, the movement of pen or vocal chord is not less subject to man's dominion than the course of events is subject to divine providence. The intelligibility of things derives from what they are, and from the Mind that is using them to express Itself.

Generalising this Thomistic principle, we may say that the totality of history is God's word.[5] Nor is history, the totality of the created, developing, world-order, an inferior means of communication, as if words openly stated the mind of the speaker, whereas one could only infer from events the mind of God. Words are just black marks on white paper or vibrations in the air apart from the intelligence of the speaker or receiver. In themselves they are just data, potentially intelligible, on the immediate level. The totality of history is a divine creation, no more unwieldy an instrument of meaning than the human artifact of language.

Both truth and meaning are, strictly speaking, in the minds of persons and in their minds only.[6] Words in an unknown language, whether written or spoken, have no meaning for us. The lack is not on the page, in the transmitted vibrations, in history, but in ourselves. We are the basic source of meaning for the document, the vibrations, the events, and the greater our understanding of the language and of the subject written or spoken about, the more meaning they will have for us. This does not imply that meaning is subjective; rather, the ink-marks on paper, the vibrations, the events, all are only *signs* of meaning and not the meaning of truth itself.

The marks, vibrations, and events can be signs of meaning, and there can be a correct meaning, which comes only through long efforts at understanding. Over a period of time the document, words, or events, might have meant something different to each successive generation; however, the meaning need not be opposed. The first understanding might have been correct but inadequate; and basically what was developing was not certainty but understanding.

Our understanding of documents, and of the dynamic world-order of the created universe (of God's word, history) can develop. Our growth in understanding can be expressed in several ways. The words and actions of Christ, for example, express his mind and meaning. These may be understood feebly by one generation; however, after several generations of centuries there has been a growth in the understanding of Christ, of his words and actions.

This deeper understanding of his meaning has been reflected in various ways in the structures of the world, and in a series of documents, in the writings of the Fathers and in the affirmations of the councils.

Theory is relevant to our developing understanding of the signs of meaning, whether these signs be the written or spoken words of men or the word of God that is history. It might be objected that theory is not really relevant to human living; that it is better to be in history than to be able to understand it.

Human development, however, demands and involves a theoretic element. This point can be illustrated from the field of theology: Bultmann could not call Jesus God because he lacked the metaphysical basis for it; hence he called him Lord. If we renounce theory, we cannot solve theoretical problems when they arise. Catholic theology reacted against the Protestant Reformation by attaching enormous importance to the external and juridical concepts of the Church itself. Gallicanism, Jansenism, Febronianism, and Josephism served only to strengthen a juridical preoccupation with the nature of the Church. This understandable, though unfortunate, theological preoccupation in ecclesiology began to be challenged and reversed in the nineteenth century by the work of the Tübingen theologian Johann Moehler (1796–1838), which marked the beginning of modern ecclesiology, characterised by the belief that through the operation of the holy Spirit the Church is the continuation of the Incarnation. Moehler is the father of the incarnational theologians (e.g. Passaglia, Schrader, Scheeben, Franzelin, Karl Adam, Congar, de Lubac, de Chardin, and others) who created a new climate of opinion within the Church, fostering natural values, human progress, the duty of the Christian to work for a better world, the natural sub-structure of a world spiritualised by grace.[7] The Incarnation is seen as Christ's invitation to us to make of this world a genuine anticipation of, a beginning of, the world to come. The theoretic contribution of Moehler led to a universal reaffirmation within the Church of the particular value of human activity in the plan of God, and of our cooperation in this plan by engagement in the world. It has modified and deepened the Catholic view of history.

Theory concerning revelation must account for revelation as

objective and historical, on the one hand, and as subjective, on the other.[8]

On the other side, God reveals himself as the ultimate source of revelation in all its phases. His primary revelation for men is the visible world he created and through which he speaks. The totality of history is God's word; the one universe with both its natural and supernatural components, the *magnalia Dei* in history and the operations of men; the entire dynamic world-order from beginning to end with its sacred and secular aspects.

The form, or structure, of universal history has already been given in Christ, its permanent meaning through all material changes. The Father sends the Son, whose Incarnation assumes the material universe (history) into the Trinitarian life. The Father and the Son send the Spirit for the definitive work of sanctification. The three Persons come to inhabit the souls of the just. The events of history, the material element of this phase of revelation, will be completed at the end of time when the number of the just has been completed.

On the subjective side, there is the inner light needed to interpret the objective and historical. This light is necessary because the supernatural component of history is beyond the penetration of native human intelligence and judgement on the subjective side.

In *Offenbarung als Geschichte*, W. Pannenberg affirms that the idea of the supernatural in history should be excluded because everything that happens in history is the expression of the working of the one triune God. He affirms that God's self-revelation through his deeds is open for everyone to see in 'ordinary history'. There is no need of faith or supernatural aid to recognise this. Ultimately, it takes the whole of history to manifest God.

The whole of history cannot adequately manifest God. Only proper knowledge of God can fully meet the question of what God is. Reception in the intellect of an intelligible form proportionate to the object that is understood is necessary for proper knowledge. This knowledge is an act of understanding in virtue of a form proportionate to the object; hence, proper knowledge of God must be in virtue of an infinite form, in virtue of God himself. Such knowledge surpasses the natural proportion of any possible, created, finite substance and so is strictly supernatural.[9]

Whatever knowledge history mediates of God will be analogous. The sacred is always beyond whatever knowledge we have of it. Analogous knowledge provides the intellect with some lesser form that bears some resemblance to the object to be understood and thereby yields some understanding of it. Because history which mediates our knowledge of God, differs from the object to be understood, which is God himself, it must be complemented by the corrections of the *via affirmationis, negationis, et eminentiae* as in natural theology.[10]

All spheres of the profane mediate the sacred; the character of the mediated knowledge is analogous. Knowledge of God, mediated through history, does not and cannot fully satisfy the human intellect. Such knowledge answers some questions and raises others. Because it is analogous knowledge, the more man learns about God through the mediation of history, the clearer it becomes that there is much he does not know.

The meaning of history is measured by the infinite mind of God and unrestricted by human conceptions. Because the meaning of the divine word cannot be exhausted, the meaning in revelation will never be exhausted. God alone knows the meaning of history. Paul spoke a word which is his and God's, however the meaning is limited by the meaning which Paul gave it.[11] History, as the totality of creation with its natural and supernatural components, is the word which God alone speaks in much the same way that men move pen and vocal chords in revealing themselves.

Within the word, history, which God speaks, is man. His spirit is marked by its questioning character and almost constituted by inquiry. His understanding of God will be mediated by the word, by the totality of history, in which his existence is rooted. It will be mediated by the dynamic world-order; consequently, man's performance in questioning history implicitly manifests his dialogue with God, who speaks it. Implicit in every human inquiry is a natural desire to know God by his essence; implicit in every human judgement about contingent things is the formally unconditioned that is God; implicit in every human choice of values is the absolute good that is God.[12] Man is a component of the word and questions it. In the dynamic of the question God speaks in human history, even if implicitly and anonymously.

History, the word which God speaks, triggers the human dynamics of the question. It raises questions and stimulates inquiry. It constitutes man's precarious situation with the possibility of a failure or of fuller development. The word, which God speaks to man and which 'contains' him, offers possibilities of human development in the dynamism constituting human consciousness which may be expressed by the imperatives: be intelligent, be reasonable, be responsible. The imperatives regard every human inquiry, judgement, decision, and choice.[13]

Any failure to be human implies an abdication from history. Man's dynamism for inquiry is a part of history which makes him responsible to history as God's word. As a part of God's historical word, man transcends himself in answering that word through the intelligence of his inquiry, the reasonableness of his judgements, the responsibility of his decisions and choices. The absence of intelligence, of reason, of responsibility in man's inquiry, judgement, decision and choice, distances him from history, from the meaning with which God actually constitutes history as his temporal self-expression.

History *is* ultimately what it means to God; who freely speaks it. In this respect, history *is* what it means and history *means* what it is. Meaning constitutes history. Meaning and existence are convertible. God is uncreated Meaning creating meaning; He is eternal Meaning creating historical meaning. All the spheres of the profane mediate the sacred; all spheres of historical meaning mediate the meaning of the supra-historical from which it derives. Limited meaning bespeaks infinite Meaning; historical meaning bespeaks eternal Meaning. In this way, history is God's limited, temporal self-expression: it is the limited, temporal expression of his meaning. Meaning is God's 'speaking' in history; rather, God 'speaks' history as Eternal Meaning expressing Itself in temporal meaning.

In virtue of his existence, man participates in history; in virtue of his meaning, man expresses God's historical self-revelation. Only the meaningful is desirable (lovable); therefore, only the lovable mediates God's self-revelation. The pure desire to know the meaningful is an intrinsic component of man's make-up, even if it does not consistently and completely dominate his consciousness. It is man's openness to history as fact and decision, for love is the proper emanation of desire. The achievement which is always implied in man's openness to history is a question of the pure, unrestricted desire's full functioning, of its dominating consciousness through precepts, methods, criticism, a formulated view of knowledge and of the reality man's knowledge can attain.

Divine grace brings openness as gift, when man's pure desire to know the meaningful is no longer restricted to the limited and the historical, even though it conditions it and is conditioned by it. Openness as fact (the self as ground of all higher aspiration) and openness as achievement (self-appropriation) which arises from the fact, are an openness to history, to created meaning extending from the beginning to the end of time, the finite expression of uncreated Meaning.

The possibility of openness defined by the pure desire for meaning is intended for openness as gift, which implies the enlargement of a horizon that is not naturally possible for man, because such an enlargement is beyond the resources of finite consciousness. Openness as gift involves the transformation of the subject when he is aware of himself as the gift of self by God to self. It is awareness of personal relations with God. It is the actual openness of the natural desire to the ultimate Meaning of history, mediated by the temporal, limited meaning of history.

Man is made for meaning. His pure, unrestricted desire for meaning enables him to inquire into everything, and to ask everything about everything. It implies a desire for an unlimited participation in history, in created meaning, through successive enlargements of man's actual horizon.

The enlargement of horizon following upon grace conditions man's interpretation of history, of created meaning, which he interprets according to a faith principle. History has a new meaning which results from 'adding' the supernatural; however, the condition is not mathematical. It is the intimate and complete transformation of all the historical, of the human, so as to give it, not a new material reality, but a new meaning. Christian marriage, for example, may differ little in appearances from non-Christian marriage; however, it *is* different, because its meaning is different; it has the meaning of the union of Christ and his Church (*Eph.* 5).

On the other hand, man's profane knowledge conditions his understanding of God. Religious and theological statements are socially conditioned. Such disciplines as history, biology, anthropology, psychology and sociology are making ever more important contributions to systematic theology. The historical conditioning of our knowledge of the sacred can be explained in terms of mediation. The world of everyday experience mediates theory, theory mediates criticism, and criticism mediates method. A development anywhere mediates development elsewhere, and all spheres of the profane mediate the world of the sacred.

History is what history means, and the meaning is constituted by God according to his eternal plan to restore history in Christ, in a real transformation of the human by the divine. The unity of history made divine is not effected by a process like mixing or adding together two material components; rather, the divinisation of man and history is the radical transformation of the whole by the power of meaning.

Christ translates history, the language of God, into human language. He communicates the meaning of the historical as God's *primary word*, spoken in his appearance on earth, in his life, death, resurrection, and all that pertains to his presence on earth as the sacrament of God. He is the ultimate Meaning of history communicating the meaning of history. Man's access to the primary word is through the *apostolic word*, which is God's word in a derivative sense. Christ is the primary expression of the divine Meaning, and his meaning is transmitted through the apostolic faith-interpretation of history.

Man's pure, unrestricted desire to know meaning grounds his freedom to choose, to decide whether to accept the apostolic word transmitting the meaning of Christ which God has given history. Man participates in history by the fact of his existence, by his openness to meaning as fact (no more than a principle of possible achievement); however, the extent to which he actually participates in history is ultimately determined by his use of freedom. He is free to accept the meaning which the apostolic word and the primary word of God have given history; however, the evidence of history cannot force his acceptance of this meaning, even though there is no historical evidence for rejecting it.

Freedom constitutes history by making possible the determination of history's meaning. The free, conscious decision of God actually determines the constitutive meaning of history, of all creation, of all that is not God, yet that expresses him. God determines that man should be historically free to decide, to move from the level of judgement to that of value, of ethics, of self-constitution through free choice.

The creation of history, the Incarnation, Pentecost, the triune divine indwelling in the souls of the just, are all free acts, radically extending the meaning of history, and inviting a free human response to the transformation-in-faith of man into the life of the spirit, into the death-resurrection of Christ. These acts are an invitation to a transformation made in the face of man's highest possibilities and of his recognised inability either to sustain indefinitely his development, or to avoid the irrational, meaning-less, genuinely evil factor in man's own life and that of his society and culture, of his own and other epochs. In these acts God reveals his free determination of the constitutive meaning of history within which man freely achieves his self-constitution and freely accepts or rejects the new meaning added to history in Christ. The Body of Christ is an order, a redemptive order in the social mediation of the human good. It is inserted into the historical social order to introduce grace, and *gratia sanans*, into that order. The act resulting from the freedom with which man accepts or rejects this new order is an orientation in life. Orienta-tion is the direction in which the use of liberty heads; it is the originating value in history.

History is the whole structure of the human good. This structure is based on nature, on man's needs, capability and freedom. Historical development is constituted on the formal level by meaning. Without meaning there is no human co-operation. It can be linguistic, symbolic, interpersonal. It is what is understood in the concrete situation. When one moves to the point where one considers that human activity is constituted formally by the intentional, by meaning, where meanings develop, where the understanding of human activity is the under-standing of these developing meanings, one arrives at the view-point called historical consciousness. Revelation is a new meaning added into history, and man's understanding of it also undergoes development.

History is not only a question of meaning but also of love, because the meaningful is the lovable. Man's pure, unrestricted

desire to know meaning is, therefore, a pure, unrestricted desire
to love the meaningful. Love is the proper rational emanation
following upon the apprehension of meaning. The divinely
constituted meaning of history is an expression of divine love.
The self-revelation of God in Christ expresses loving concern
about absurdity in human history.

In the Trinity the third Person, according to the Thomist
conception, is Love. He is God's Peace with his own being, his
love of his own meaning, his Consent, Joy, and Serenity. Love
is primarily that; however, in relation to history he is the divine
Concern, God's loving Will to communicate himself. The
aberrations of the human intellect are counteracted and transformed by the meaning of God's self-revelation in his Word;
the aberrations of the human will are counteracted and transformed by the Spirit of Love. God's self-revelation saves history
from meaninglessness and discord. The meaning which God has
given history should occasion man's intelligent consent to history
as it is, should produce an intelligent serenity, joy, and harmony
with history.

All knowledge of God is mediated knowledge. It is mediated
through history, the meaning of created reality. The world of
the sacred is never immediate. All development opens the way
for development in religion and theology. Even though Christians
perform the same religious acts well, those with philosophy
and theology have a better knowledge of what they are doing
and why they are doing it. This is made possible through the
mediation of another development. The co-presence of one set
of intellectual habits aids another development and makes it
more comprehensive. The knowledge of revelation is through
the mediation of the Church; theology mediates our religious
life; psychology, sociology and the other human sciences mediate
theology. Thus whatever meaning man derives from history
mediates its ultimate Meaning. In this way we can say God
speaks in history.

Man derives meaning from history through his operations.
His widely differentiated operations presuppose habits which
specify them, so that the operations occur promptly, easily, and
pleasurably with respect to any combination of differentiated
objects in the man possessing the habit. The acquired habit results
from man's capacity for development. Thus the reception of

God's self-revelation is conditioned by the level of human development. God, therefore, has more meaning for some than he has for others; he is saying more in history to some than he is saying to others, even though all belong to the same universal history.

On the other hand, the constitutive meaning of history which derives from the ultimate Meaning of history creates the exigency for man's development. Meaning demands development for its apprehension. It demands conscious, intelligent, living subjects in a subject-act-object relationship with itself. Such a relationship demands development, because activities in themselves are approximate, inefficacious, not economical, unorganised, aimless, lacking control in performance. Activity must be humanised through the development of habits. Meaning demands preparation. The narrow, prejudiced man who lives by opinion is not well prepared for faith. Faith is not a matter of opinion; it demands openness and creates openness as gift. The meaning of revelation demands openness as achievement (self-appropriation) on the part of the subject who theologises about God and all that is ordered to him.

God's meaning and self-communication are also a question of wisdom. Divine Wisdom is the ultimate Meaning to which all history is ordered; it is the ultimate horizon or context of all created meaning, within which history as a whole finally makes sense. The Divine Wisdom with one act of will, one freedom of exercise, one freedom of specification, wills all existing things (history) inasmuch as he wills one concrete world-order. The Divine Wisdom knows all existing things by knowing one concrete world-order; he knows it down to its least historical detail as a consequence of knowing it as one universal world-order. Thus he knows the component parts such as his free gifts, finite natures, their properties, exigences, and so on. Thus finite natures are what they are because of the world-order of Divine Wisdom. The constitutive meaning of history is that of a world-order; the parts have their meaning in virtue of the order into which they are structured. The world-order is what it is because of the Divine Wisdom and goodness.

The Beatific Vision is the highest wisdom possible for man. It is the ultimate enlargement of man's horizon to the ultimate context of universal meaning, when man knows God as he is known, as the effect of a grace (*elevans, lumen gloriae*), which is an openness to Meaning as a gift.

Wisdom is ultimate; its significance is basic. It tells man the right fundamental notions of history; it is acquired through the long self-correcting process of learning. Wisdom is the light whereby man grasps the universe as ordered, the necessity of that order, and the totality (history) of created being as ordered to an Absolute Meaning. Wisdom is the light whereby man comprehends that all being (history) is essentially related being, mediating the unrelated Absolute to which it is related. It is the light whereby man grasps that the meaning of all created beings (history) is ultimately derived from something beyond them ; that nothing is ultimately self-explanatory within the order of history. In this way God is the complete intelligibility that gives intelligibility to history which in itself is only partially meaningful. This partially meaningful history is ordered by its intrinsic dynamism towards an ultimate integration grasped only in faith. The only adequate manifold is the Wisdom of God.

History is the object of human wisdom inasmuch as history is the actual order of the existing universe. This wisdom grasps the meaning of order in a way that is different from prudence. The former is speculative; the latter is practical. Prudence deals with the changeable, the particulars within the order, and is limited to judgements about what we can do or say here and now. Wisdom grasps the fundamental relatedness, the necessary relatedness, the total relatedness of the existing universe that is history. The existence of God is revealed to the wise man through the limited, conditioned meaningfulness of history.

History has an objective and a subjective pole. The word which God speaks, the created universe, the dynamic world-order, mediates God's self-revelation. Within the dynamic world-order man responds. Man's activity is both a response to history, to the word which God speaks, and a constitutive part of that history, as a human instrument of God. The dynamic of inquiry reflects the objective and subjective poles of history. The word which God speaks (history) raises questions both in terms of the multi-levelled cognitional structure of the human subject characterised by the dynamism of inquiry with the exigences of the pure, detached, disinterested, unrestricted desire to know, and in terms of the historical experience of the world-order of

which man is an operative part. Man is intrinsically and extrinsi-
cally involved with God in history. He does not know God
immediately, because all knowledge of God is mediated.

History is implicitly a dialogue between God and man,
involving faith and reason, Church and world, religion and
science, manifesting the glory and revealing the truth of God
through the excellence of man (and societies). Man is structured
for inquiry within history; his life most properly consists in
seeking and finding the truth of the word God is speaking in
history. His development and perfection are rooted in the
activities of his pure desire to know operating in response to the
all-encompassing experience of history, the word which God
alone can speak. He is most authentically and consciously human
in his actual responsiveness.

The human subject reveals himself in the quality of his operations and productions. When these are intelligent, reasonable and
responsible, the individual (or society) reveals himself as an
authentic participant in the existing, dynamic, world-order of
history that is God's word and mediates his self-revelation. Only
these operations are meaningful. Only the meaningful, intelligible
and existing actually mediate the self-revelation of God, because
the dynamic world-order, the word which God speaks is a
meaningful word, an intelligible word, an existing word. The
basic presupposition is that what God is saying in history is what
constitutes history: whatever is. This alone mediates God's
self-revelation. On the other hand, what does not exist, does not
constitute history, and does not mediate the self-revelation of
God. Thus the absence of order, the absence of intelligence, the
absence of reason, the absence of responsibility (i.e. love) mediate
nothing. The extent to which man (or society) participates in
the meaningful, world-order of God's word, history, corresponds
to his efficacy in mediating God's self-revelation. Only the
meaningful mediates the meaningful. Sin, in this context, is the
culpable failure of man (or society) to mediate the sacred, to
participate meaningfully in history, the word which God is
speaking. Sin bespeaks the lack of responsibility in failing to
actualise a known possibility when this would be intelligent and
reasonable.

Because man is part of the universe, of a dynamic world-order,
his existence and development are socially conditioned. The

excellence and failures of his social context condition his possibilities for development. Society conditions his *horizon*: the totality of objects which he can deal with, master, and enjoy through the cultivation of habits. Reality is partly within and partly without man's horizon. Man does not advert to or see what is beyond it. The horizon is not absolute, because man can know and love all reality.

The broadening of man's horizon implies that his human resources for mediating the sacred are extended; that his meaningful participation in history, the word God speaks, is deepened. Our horizon is broadened when we operate on new mediated objects, and deal with new immediate objects. New experiences, symbols, conversation and reading broaden it. This is an area where the arts make an especially noteworthy contribution by enriching the imagination, providing us with something new to reflect on. The literature and poetry of Scripture, hymns, dramas, biblical scenes on stained glass windows, in carvings and paintings, have mediated the sacred for centuries. Our scope for activity is enlarged by the further development of our scientific and philosophical knowledge. Man's dependence on society, on the artistic, academic, political and economic communities for broadening his horizon is evident. What God speaks to him in history will be conditioned by society and the limits of his horizon.

What God says in history will be mediated in terms of *conversion*: the reorganisation of the subject (society), of his activities, of the world with which he is familiar. The source of this change is within the subject himself. Conversion not only means the broadening of the subject's horizon, although this is the chief task, but a change in his own interiority. Conversion implies a new and more profound responsiveness to history as the word God speaks.

*Moral conversion* effects a change from the objects of desire and fear as ultimate and absolute motives of conduct, to what ought to be absolute, to what has value and really counts, whether or not it pleases.

*Intellectual conversion* is a shift from our childhood view of reality to an ultimate reliance on rational criteria, from the real as the empirical, to the real as what is rationally affirmed. A child's prerational criteria of the real always remain as a fundamental conviction, unless revised and corrected through education, persuasion and effort.

*Religious conversion* is a shift in horizon from a natural, humanistic view to a Christian view, where the ultimate ceases to be oneself, becoming God, not naturally known, but as revealed in the Christian religion. This is a shift from egocentricity to theocentricity.

In each case of conversion what was formerly all-important ceases to be so and is replaced by a new order of things.

The *interpretation* of what God is saying in history involves *presuppositions*. The presuppositions of the interpreter's questions indicate his horizon. To paraphrase Alan Richardson, the interpreter's final judgement of the evidence of history (his response to the existing dynamic world-order, the word God speaks) will in the last resort, and after as rigorous a critical appraisal as he can make, be determined by the man he is. Nothing can abolish the personal element from the decision about what is and what is not, because judgements are made according to settled convictions about the nature of man and the world through which our historical existence and experience are interpreted. Presuppositions adumbrate the boundaries and basic thrust of that process whereby man can learn the meaning of what God is saying; they yield the range of possible interpretations.

A *universal viewpoint* escapes relativism because it is an openness to all explanations (interpretations), excluding none *a priori*, admitting none *a posteriori*, until rational evidence is forthcoming. The wider the horizon, the greater the number of possible interpretations open to the interpreter, and the greater his freedom in discovering the correct one.

The universal viewpoint does not suffice unless we take possession of our operational structures. The world of objective being and the openness of subjective spirit can be completely universal, and our conversion to the universality of object and subject can be genuine; however, without a grasp of the structure we necessarily use in guiding spirit to being, serious blunders are inevitable in our employment of the profane for the mediation of the sacred meaning of history.

A critical awareness, an appropriation and evaluation of our own powers of intelligent grasp and reasonable affirmation of the dynamic world-order of the universe of being are needed; an awareness and an appropriation of our power for harmonious accord with history, the word through which God speaks his self-revelation, are also necessary.

The dynamic world-order and its development mediate our knowledge of the sacred. It corresponds to the actualisation of the divine creative concept and plan for man in the context of a universal good in which every part possesses whatever perfection it has in virtue of its participation in the developing, universal world-order. It is through its actual relatedness and intercommunication within this world-order that the sacred is mediated.

Prior as a fact is the ontological reality of God's implicit revelation in history; subsequently, in the grasp by faith, it becomes a psychological reality of a living, developing, dynamic consciousness with the Christ-dimension given in the religious conversion. Christ's revelation enables man to become psychologically aware of the ontological presence of God constituting history. The psychological presence to self (which is both object [history] and subject [self]) mediates the ontological reality which is the presence of God to man.

Initially the question posed concerned the way of God's speech in history and man's capacity to hear it. Now we see that on the level of society there is a development of the aggregate consciousness which is implicitly related to the ontological reality of God's self-revelation in history; finally we see this revelation as the presence of God communicated to the individual by way of conversion in his personal history.

# Questioning, Presentiment, and Intuition in the Theological Thought-Process.

## HEINRICH OTT

IT is particularly necessary for theology to give an account of its own proper thought-process. For in theology there is a primacy of method: it cannot forget its method or let it remain unreflected upon, sticking to results alone. Theology needs to exhibit no experimental or statistical results which have been proven and are simply valid. The result without the way leading to it, without the method then, simply does not exist for theology. Hence, the method, the way, is to some degree implicit in each theological insight and its articulation. And only in the measure that method is so entailed can there be talk about a 'truth' of insight.

So a partial analysis of a theological thought-process is attempted briefly here. How does theological insight arise? And what does it consist in? Now these two questions are a single question precisely because, according to our initial comments, the outcome implies the way leading to it and is in a certain sense constituted by that way. Is there a specifically theological 'heuristic structure'? And what role is played in the theological thought-process by the existential moments of the existence of the theologian as an 'existing thinker', as a believer? Could it be that in theological thinking, which heads towards an understanding of the truth of faith—as the 'truth of existing before God'—such existential moments play not an accidental, but an essential and decisive role; and that it pertains to the rational clarity, to the methodological self-translucency of theology to recognise these implications? Then theology would be a moment in the existential encounter with God itself, and it would be proper to its very reality for this embeddedness, this rootedness to be made clear.

Martin Heidegger has thought out thinking in an analogous way: as rooted in the depths of an existence disclosed in mood, precisely in so far as he thinks out the 'possibility of negation as an act of the understanding (*Verstandeshandlung*),'—the 'not'— as rooted in the 'nothingness' (*Nichts*) which has been existentially experienced in the mood of anxiety.[1] At any rate we cannot treat of more than a parallel in this connection. For we want here to speak of the thinking, that is, of the understanding of *faith*.

In order to do this we have to pursue a single theological line of thought a short distance; and, in undertaking this, attend to ourselves to a certain extent, trying to understand how the steps in the process are each motivated and in what necessity or compelling need they ensue. I am going to do this on the basis of a Protestant self-understanding of theology, i.e., an understanding such that it is not faced at the outset with a scaffolding of defined 'truths of faith'.

The theological problem which we select as our theme is the *assumptio humanae naturae* by the Son of God and the *hypostatic union* which thereby comes about. What does it mean, and how can we reach and apprehend the insight that the Logos has become incarnate, has taken on 'human nature', that God has become man?

We might seek to trace the existential implications which we are supposing to be essential elements of theological thought by means of the guiding concepts of *questioning*, *presentiment* and *intuition*. In doing so we cannot sharply delimit these three concepts for events within the thought-process from one another. For together they denote (as the hypothesis with which we enter into the analysis has it) a characteristic occurrence which continually emerges in the thought-process, and gives it its direction.

In *questioning* there is an existential need to come into the clear with regard to our own existence before God and that of our fellow man, to understand more clearly and deeply where one ultimately stands. Such clearer and deeper understanding should be an aid not only to a more adequate speech about God and one's own existence, but, integrally united with this, to a more adequate living out of one's own existence before God and with one's fellows. The questioning of the theologian is thus a 'movement of existence', the performance of a need and of a desire. The theologian performs this for himself, but at the same time as a representative as it were for his believing and non-believing fellow men who need the very same clarity. This questioning does not arise from a 'pure' theoretical drive for knowledge on the part of man, but it impels to a knowledge which is practical and oriented to changing life.

In theology, then, as reflection from faith on faith, *presentiment* is grounded in the fact that it is the *believer* who commences to question. That means one to whom something has already been spoken prior to his questioning, one who has understood something already. What has been spoken to him is a complex whole. Let us call it the word of God. This complex whole is structured. It is not as if the entire structure can be viewed from above beforehand, but one aspect always points to another. Let us assume that the questioner has understood and appropriated—made it somewhat a component of his existence—the word of Jesus: 'Come to me, all who labour and are heavy laden, and I will give you rest . . .' (*Matt.* 11:28). Now the same Jesus, however, says: 'Love your enemies, do good to those who hate you, and pray for those who persecute you . . .' (*Matt.* 5:44). Let us say that the questioner has heard but not yet understood and appropriated this word. But because it is the word of the same Jesus Christ and so stands in the same context of meaning, the questioner has a presentiment that, when he has understood and appropriated this second word, he will have understood its relationship to the first, and he will, then, have seen both words in the unity which still lies hidden from him. Correspondingly, this holds true for all 'truths of faith' or all aspects of the word of God. They point to one another; and in what has been understood, what is still not understood is already virtually present to me. In this regard, it is not only dogmatic 'articles of faith' or biblical propositions in the narrower sense which go to make up the complex whole. But all of human existence is actually addressed and enlightened by the word of God. One who hears the message knows that he must relate it in all its parts to his own life. And so the existential phenomena which man experiences in himself and in his being-with-others stand actually or virtually in the light of the word of God. And therefore they too pertain to that complex whole which has to be gradually comprehended. One can understand from this description what presentiment in theological thought means: it is the dynamism which draws me along from the understood and appropriated aspects of the totality to the not yet understood and appropriated. This dynamism can work because, inasmuch as I begin to think, I am already engaged as one addressed by the totality. Since the totality of the message as addressed to me is to some degree virtually present to me even before my intelligent appropriation of its single aspects, my questioning does not head off into a vacuum. It does not go arbitrarily in any direction whatsoever. Although I ask about what I do not yet know or have not yet understood and appropriated, I do have a presentiment of the direction in which I have to question. Presentiment is the anticipation of an insight, of a solution which we do not yet possess. This anticipation is heavily freighted with feeling: I sense the sought, yet unknown, insight, as something liberating, as something satisfyingly clear, or also as something profoundly serious or even terrifying. This feeling accompanies or penetrates the exertion of my thinking; it is the 'thought-mood' which gives me ballast on the way of reflection. Thus what has been pointed out by Heidegger throws light on our notion of presentiment: 'Every questioning is a seeking. Every seeking gets its prior direction from the sought.'[2] In a later work Heidegger expresses this state of affairs more completely and at the same time defines his concept of *Besinnung*:

To strike out in a direction which a thing has already taken on its own is called in our language *sinnan*, *sinnen* (to set one's thoughts in a given direction). To put oneself in the way of the sense or meaning (*Sinn*) is the essence of *Besinnung*. This means more than merely making something conscious . . . By *Besinnung* on this conception we reach precisely that place where, without having already experienced or perceived it thematically, we have long dwelt. In *Besinnung* we proceed to a locale from which the space is first opened up which our doing or permitting measures out at any given time.[3]

Now presentiment is of course not infallible. We often search in directions where the solution does not lie. The way of thinking is an insecure adventure. We never know from the outset whether we shall arrive with a question at a useful conclusion in our own lifetime. But this fact does not disturb the significance of presentiment for thinking.

Under *intuition* I understand here the irruption signalled by the arrival of an insight, the illumination of a still unclear pattern of solution. In the actuation of intuition, then, something as it were comes forward to meet the question. On the distant horizon emerge the still vague outlines of the locale which our thinking strives to reach. (This occurrence is also not infallible: the dimly discerned pattern of solution, too, can on occasion be a *Fata Morgana*. Once again, however, the significance of thoughtful intuition is not thereby lessened.) Intuition affords the opportunity for new, more determinate questioning. Now one must approach the subject-matter more closely and get the pattern of the intuited solution more clearly into focus. Both the questioning and answering and its conceptual articulation become more precise. And in so far as they do, intuition guides the process of questioning.

The main point now is to apprehend what we have described as questioning, presentiment, and intuition not as separate activities or occurrences, but in their inter-connectedness, in the unity of a single process. There exists no 'pure (isolated) questioning', but questioning is always interwoven with presentiment. And intuition is integrated with questioning and presentiment: it becomes a determinative moment for questioning and presentiment. For they are both determined more concretely by intuition.

What has been furnished up to now is a sketch, the schema of a description of the theological thought-process. How far this description may be adapted also to extra-theological thought-processes, I leave undecided. I consider the aspects expounded here to be not yet specifically theological in their essentials. But this affects our point very little. For our concern is to understand the theological thought-process. If we happen to succeed in coming to an adequate understanding in this respect, there is no need to worry whether this understanding in the final analysis fits other realms of thought as well. To expect and demand from the very beginning that theological thought in its methodical performance be differentiated from all other types of thinking seems doctrinaire to me.

There is, however, a need to test the schema of a description of the thought-process against the reality of a distinct thought-process. Our dogmatic problem asks: what is the meaning of the sentence, 'God (in his Son, Jesus Christ) has become man, i.e., he has assumed human nature'? I believe that here the three questions: (1) What does this sentence mean? (2) How can we understand this sentence? (3) How can we sufficiently ground and affirm this sentence?—form a *single* question.

To all thinking, all questioning, all seeking, something has been pregiven. Otherwise there would be no coming to that 'prior direction (of the seeking) from the thing sought'. The pregiven is 'that which there is to think and needs to be thought'. The pregiven in the case of theology is the complex totality of the word of God as addressed and already accepted in faith, in the community of believers. The pregiven in our particular case is first of all the *Symbolum Chalcedonense*, which teaches: '. . . Dominum nostrum Jesum Christum . . . consubstantialem Patri secundum deitatem et consubstantialem nobis secundum humanitatem, 'per omnia nobis similem absque peccato' (cf. *Heb.* 4:15) . . . Unum eundemque Christum Filium Dominum unigenitum, in duabus naturis inconfuse, immutabiliter, indiviso, inseparabiliter agnoscendum . . .' This is a pregiven step in thought taken by past thinking and indeed, as such, an attempt at interpretation of a decisive aspect of the complex whole of the word of God which leaves its imprint on all other aspects. Discourse on the being of the human nature unmixed beside the divine, and yet inseparable from it in the Person of the Son of God has then been further interpreted later on by the orthodox theology of the Incarnation of the various Christian confessions as they endeavoured to clarify this discourse. This has been accomplished especially by means of the distinction of the anhypostasis of the human nature of Christ and its enhypostasis in the Person of the incarnate Logos. On this I cite Johann Heinrich Heidegger, a seventeenth-century Swiss theologian of Reformed Orthodoxy. He speaks of the 'assumptio humanae naturae in personam Filii Dei, qua Logos, Filius Dei, . . . naturam humanam propriae hypostaseoos expertem in unitatem personae suae assumpsit, ut Logou assumentis et naturae humanae assumptae una eademque sit hypostasis, extra quam ipsa nec subsistit unquam nec subsistere potest.' I would translate this: 'The assumption of the human nature into the Person of the Son of God, by which the Logos, the Son of God, . . . assumes into the unity of his Person the human nature, which has no subsistence of its own, so that there is only a single subsistence of the subsuming Logos and of the assumed nature, apart from which the latter itself never subsists nor can subsist.'

In what follows we speak of God's becoming man, or of the Son of God's becoming man. Allow me the simplification of, as it were, putting into brackets here the problem of Trinitarian theology which traditional dogmatics normally sets in the context of its treatment of the Incarnation: namely, to what degree it was precisely the Son of God, the Second Person of the Tri-unity that became man.

It does not satisfy the drive toward theological knowledge to reflect on what is pregiven and pre-thought in the tradition of the Church with its own conceptual tools, to understand and articulate it anew within the conceptual framework which that tradition itself has used. In our case, the concepts 'nature' and 'subsistence' could be decisive. But the question is whether the practically relevant insight which theological questioning is striving for may be won and articulated with the help of these concepts. The question of truth must therefore have a more primordial point of departure. Questioning may not be bound by the regulation of the language afforded by the concepts of the tradition. Questioning would reflect on what is articulated in these concepts, but not for the sake of stopping at the reflection on this articulation, at the intrinsic understanding of it via the mechanism of the concepts, but simply for the sake of ascertaining the pregiven in the first place. Questioning is not concerned with understanding the articulation performed earlier as such, and with thus clinging to its conceptual tools, but rather with thinking and articulating anew *that which is thought* in the former articulation, the intended, that which the line of thought articulated earlier was aiming at. Hence there arises in theological questioning, just because it is existentially rooted and wants the practically relevant insight, a tendency not simply to appropriate the linguistic regulations existent in the pre-thought, but to break through these and to question beyond them. There arises in theological questioning a tendency towards dissatisfaction with ready-made concepts, a sense of the inadequacy of all formulations in relation to the mystery of the God speaking to man. But this feeling of inadequacy does not lead to a doctrinaire scepticism. The transcending of given formulations and concepts does not occur in order that formulations and concepts be left completely behind, but rather that new formulations and concepts may be found. It has this orientation for the sake of the mystery itself, which has already been addressed and is thus present, and of whose life-determining and life-changing relevance one has already had a presentiment. Theological questioning is therefore the *willingness*, corresponding to the mystery of the speaking God, to let the practical relevance of this mystery become newly visible and effective. Because this willingness is there, and because in the case of theology it matches its subject-matter, theological questioning means a putting-into-question of the pre-thought. This putting-into-question, however, means no break in the continuity of the tradition. Rather, precisely in wishing to articulate it anew, it is held exactingly to the subject-matter, to the very reality which the former articulations in their turn were striving to think out and to express. The will to new articulation is also precisely the strong will to continuity of tradition.

How radically should and can the pre-thought be broken through and its meaning be newly articulated? Here I need to ask myself: what actually brings me to rely on a dogmatic concept like that of the *assumptio naturae humanae* in elaborating a theology of the Incarnation *at all*? What brings me to follow this line of approach at all? Instead of this I might have tried to explicitate the theme 'Jesus Christ' or 'God becomes man' in a much more radical new beginning—measuring it against the Chalcedonian tradition and its Orthodox unfolding. I could, for example, say: Jesus of Nazareth by his deeds and his words points so overpoweringly to God, that I, when I really encounter him, experience Jesus and God as a unity. In this consists the unity of the man Jesus with God. In this fashion I should have thought out this unity anew and articulated it anew without having recourse to the concept of an 'assumption of human nature by God'. Or I could say (with the understanding of Christ according to Rudolf Bultmann): in the claim of Jesus Christ I encounter the claim of God himself. I am confronted with a unique (ultimate, conclusively valid, eschatological) claim on my human existence, and precisely therein consists the unity of the man Jesus with God. Once again, without speaking of the assumption of the human nature, I should have newly and better understood this unity. In this way, its practical relevance which alters and modifies my life would become evident. And I know, moreover, that this is the very reality which that old idea would have been expressing.

These routes, as is well known, have been often and with many variations travelled in Protestant theology. But what is it that actually moves me now to approach the concept of the *assumptio naturae humanae* more nearly—even though I do not consider myself bound by that archaic formula and do not simply take it for granted? I cannot, as a Protestant theologian, say: the wisdom of the Church's magisterium—or more explicitly: the discipline of the ecclesiastical teaching office—causes me to engage myself from the start in a determinate direction and to exclude other directions. On the contrary, when I make my decision to strike out in a determinate direction with my asking of further questions, I have to take the responsibility for this choice upon myself; and even so I can still see myself as in accord with confirmed models of thought. When I formulate this so, I do not mean to close the door to an ecumenical discussion on the ecclesiastical teaching office. In fact it would be precisely at such a point as we meet here that serious inter-confessional talks would be most fruitful in exploring how much perhaps the wisdom of the Church, by way of an ecclesial dialogue structured in a determinate manner, meets my responsibility halfway. For the moment, at any rate, it makes sense for me simply to give an account of my way of operating as a Protestant theologian.

I make the choice of closing in on the concept of the 'assumption of human nature by God' and *not* on those radically simplifying recent interpretations of the unity of God and Jesus. This choice is like the decision I have to make on coming to a fork in the road. It is a matter of the direction (*Weg-Richtung*) of further questioning. Moreover, I have not created the fork in the road myself. It arises via history as it were 'objectively': *there exist* these various possibilities of thinking. The roads are pre-thought. Why do I decide the way I do? I do so because I have a presentiment that the way I want to go has a plus in insight and help, a plus in living truth. I have a presentiment of this without actually knowing, without actually being able to express clearly, what this plus consists in. It is a source of the greatest encouragement. Yet it is still no insight, but rather puts me in expectation of an insight. Now I may be called into debate with those who have decided otherwise. In this debate I take a stand for something, for an insight I have not yet attained, but actually only await. Nevertheless I have something to represent. Perhaps the insight takes on form for the first time in the course of the debate, which thus becomes a fruitful dialogue. Perhaps I catch sight for the first time of the plus, of which I have a presentiment, in the dispute, in the disagreement, inasmuch as I come to know the limitation of the alternative standpoint when this is held up before me and unravelled.

Now one is tempted to ask where the presentiment comes to us from. The answer would have to state: in so far as the presentiment guides me correctly, it stems from the thing itself (the 'true state of affairs'), which I *encounter* in thinking, and about which and towards which I am thinking. But it is not particularly meaningful to ask this question. Indeed, were a precise answer to it possible, then I would have already attained the insight. The presentiment would have ceased being a presentiment (the mere direction of thought). Hence, we want to stay with the phenomenon of indeterminate presentiment as it comes to the fore in the thought-process; we are simply concerned to show how presentiment 'functions'.

We have a presentiment that when we reflect upon the Incarnation, upon the appearance of God in the flesh, in history, we have to do with something more than merely speaking to mankind, something more than merely challenge, command, or invitation. The statement that God has assumed human nature seems to assert more than the statement that God speaks to us. If God speaks to us, he is by that fact near to us. But when he assumes our nature, he is still closer to us. Our further questioning under the guidance of presentiment is then the exigence for an understanding of this greater proximity.

Here I must add that in this entire process it is a matter not merely of the fact that we allow ourselves to be led by our needs, and so give ourselves over to an illusion, i.e., we represent the truth just as it would please us to have it. Of course 'need' plays an important and indeed thoroughly legitimate role. In our case, it is the spiritual need of our epoch—threatened by the dangers of inhumanity—for a new definition of humanity, a new definition of the ground-situation of man and of the standard for man growing out of this ground-situation. This is still a wide

open field. And here (so our presentiment tells us) the notion of
the assumption of human nature by God seems to bespeak
something new and decisive. Nevertheless it is not only a matter
here of our need. More importantly, there comes out of the
spiritual situation of the time a possibility of understanding, a
specific receptivity with regard to what has already been spoken
to us as the word of God. Need makes us clearsighted for distinct
aspects of the word of God. It cannot be presupposed that the
situation of theological thinking is unhistorical and that each
epoch is capable of comprehending and elucidating any given
truth of faith equally as well as every other epoch. But despite
this legitimate role of need in theological thinking as a catalyst
for the process of understanding, it is not need which is primary,
but the word addressed to us.

What is to be said, however, about the biblical grounding and
the exegetical tenability of what is in question here? This problem
can only be touched on briefly, since a more detailed treatment
is not possible in this tentative outline of the method of dogmatics.
Let us for once suppose it certain that the New Testament in
different ways says clearly enough at least this one thing: in the
man Jesus of Nazareth God himself 'put in an appearance' (*ist 'auf
dem Plan'*), to use a favourite expression of Karl Barth, which is
imprecise, pregnant, and presentiment-laden in its own right.
Let us consider this an exegetically established fact. Now what
does this 'putting in an appearance' mean? Obviously it can be
interpreted in various ways. It can be taken to mean: the voice
of God reaches us through Jesus. It could also be taken to mean
(something which does not exclude the first meaning): in Jesus
God participates in human destiny. Passages from the New
Testament authors may be adduced for both ways of viewing
the reality. Once this has been established, the discussion shifts
from pure exegesis into the realm of the dogmatical, in which
one must keep the exegetical findings clearly in view.
One would be able to say only with great difficulty: 'All the
New Testament witnesses have a well-defined theological
system in which the *assumptio naturae humanae* by God in the
Person of Jesus Christ is taught.' Just as little would one be able
to say: 'All the New Testament authors have a well-defined
theological system in which the thought of the hypostatic union
is clearly excluded.' The dogmatic discussion into which we are

compelled to enter will have to be concerned first of all with
whether one of the two interpretations, 'God speaks through
Jesus,' and 'God assumes human nature in Jesus,' may be plausibly
carried through to a provisional conclusion. If this succeeds, for
instance, with the idea of the hypostatic union, then those
perspectives of the New Testament witness which deal with the
participation of the God-man, Jesus Christ, in human destiny
(e.g., *Phil.* 2:5ff.) become guiding viewpoints for the comprehensive interpretation of that 'putting in an appearance' on the
part of God. Thus such a comprehensive interpretation is certainly
related to something biblically pregiven, which has been verified
for us by biblical exegesis. But that comprehensive interpretation
itself is not to be achieved in the field of pure exegesis, by the
ascertaining of the intentions which the biblical authors had
concerning Jesus, but through the mediation of a dogmatic
heightening of awareness alone. And this dogmatic reflection in
its turn affects exegesis, inasmuch as it lets the exegetically
ascertainable facts appear in a determinate light.

Now what has occurred here? Led by a presentiment, we have
decided for a distinctive direction of further questioning. We
have relied on a traditional idea. So it is that the idea of the
assumption of human nature by God and of the hypostatic union
becomes for us an aid to interpretation on the paths of our
further questioning. Now presentiment can scarcely be grasped
in words or in an articulate train of thought. At first it may not
be capable of being more than vaguely hinted at. But without
any doubt it impels to words and an articulate train of thought.
  The theological thought-process *in concreto* comprises then for
the most part the articulation and consequent precision of that
which one initially has only a presentiment or incipient suggestion
of. And the discipline of thinking chiefly consists in knowing the
divined and suggested as such, and in not confusing it with a
familiar and articulate insight. On the other hand, it ultimately
consists also both in knowing what at first seems to have already
been clearly articulated in its eventual need of being more deeply
questioned; and in having a premonition of what lies beyond
that ready-made articulation.
  The hint in our case was 'God's greater proximity' and 'new
definition of humanity or of the human ground-situation'. We

supposed this to be the direction in which the concept of the hypostatic union pointed us. For 'assumption of human nature' seems to mean that by this act not only God, but also the human situation (the common situation of all men, just as 'human nature' means the common nature of all men) has been qualified in a special manner.

How can this pre-divined and at first only intimated notion be more precisely determined? Here we feel that the concept of 'nature' will provide difficulties. For what does something akin to a human nature consist in? Standing in opposition for us here is the reality of 'mineness' (*Jemeinigkeit*) of which Heidegger says: '*Dasein* is therefore never to be apprehended ontologically as a mere case or instance of a genus of being (*Seiendem*) conceived of as present-at-hand . . . The addressing of *Dasein* must constantly be accompanied by the use of the personal pronoun in accordance with the character of mineness pertaining to this entity: "I am," "you are."'[4]

The mineness of the *Dasein* of all men is evident. And it is sufficient simply to *see* this. For the seeing of phenomena is a component of the truthfulness which is required of theological thinking. Consequently, were 'assumption of human nature by God' to be understood to mean that God has taken upon himself the common generic properties of man, that these then 'subsist' in him, too; then the existential phenomenon of mineness that is to be seen and recognised in its evidence and in truthfulness would be overlooked. The guiding presentiment in the course of thought already bears the imprint of such 'seeing': it has a premonition of a dead-end road and would produce a feeling of emptiness were one to pursue the traditional formula in getting one's understanding. Because it is modified by this seeing, it shies away from this path.

To be sure, the concept 'assumption of human nature' calls forth not only a feeling of *emptiness*, but also a feeling of *promise*, the sense of something liberating. It seems, indeed (I keep on saying, 'It seems . . .' with full awareness, because we are moving in the area of presentiment and not that of articulate knowledge) . . . it seems that this concept means: with God's becoming man something decisive for all men has happened, and indeed—this is the essential factor—'intrinsically', within the human situation itself, in man's very 'nature', i.e., in that which is most proper to man, that which makes him to be man.

The promise lying in the object of our presentiment proceeds therefore in the following fashion: that we, if we had understood the implications of our formula, would gain new light, a new understanding of ourselves and of our fellow men, believing or non-believing, and so a new basis on which to deal with them. For, by God's having become man, it would seem to follow that something has been changed in the existence of us *all*. Such universality lies in the concept of the 'assumption of human nature by God', inasmuch as the concept of human nature aims at what unites all men. Hence our presentiment also allows us to avoid an interpretation which merely establishes that God has become *a* man; i.e., one man among many was at the same time God. Rather—and this is where the promise of the notion lies—with God's having become man in the One, Jesus, something has happened for all—and not only 'for' all, but actually already *in* all.

Now according to what has been said before, what has happened for all and in all as well as what now arises in virtue of the hypostatic union must be described in a manner other than the following: the generic properties common to all men now subsist also in the Person of the Son of God. In another manner indeed—but how?

Here we recognise that the concept of the assumption of human nature, with its entailment of universality, itself belongs to the realm of presentiment: it only points out a direction. It looks out towards an explication and a precision still to be achieved. The presentiment steering the thought-process can be so effective in the very concepts which we use precisely because the concepts are hints of the objects of presentiment, more like arrows which point in a determinate direction than definitive boundaries of a region.

But how do we proceed from mere presentiment, which provides a direction and an expectation, to *more determinate statements*? How does one come to the lightning flash of intuition which permits one to elaborate a distinct solution. That is one of the questions to be taken up at this point. And the other is: where do the criteria for the adequacy and truth of a determinate solution lie?

Doubtless, with respect to the first question, the *imagination* of the thinker, his capacity to be perceptive and to uncover the relevant phenomena and possible points of reference, plays a not inconsiderable role. Whereas Martin Heidegger speaks of the 'experience of thinking' i.e. of the thought-process itself as an experience, one might speak here of the experience or the expertise *in* thinking, something like that of the craftsman in his hand. For once one has, guided by presentiment, engaged oneself, there emerge—to speak in images—new purviews of the landscape, new elements of the surroundings.

Let us return here to our concrete example: as soon as we allow the recognition of the mineness of human existence to deflect us from thinking of 'human nature' as a comprehensive complex of generic properties and correlatively of the assumption of such human nature by the Logos, *a new perspective* opens before us, the view onto a new landscape. At this point there becomes apparent both the possibility and the task of expressing the event at which the concept of the *assumptio humanae naturae* by Christ aims, in a manner which does justice to the personal mineness of this human 'nature', and hence in personal or existential categories. How could this event have occurred? One might say: God is—in Christ—a man, whose existence is qualified by the character of mineness. Or, as Fr Lonergan has stressed: Christ is a human subject and as such has himself suffered the pains of the cross. This definition however, must be surpassed—without of course incurring the need of putting it into question. For otherwise that plus about which we have had a presentiment would not yet have come into its own: that the Logos not only has become *a* man, but that precisely by this fact he has assumed the human 'nature' of *all* men.

A 'new element in the surroundings' comes to light in the course of our progress: the phenomenon of mineness should let the traditional concept of nature (as liable to be misunderstood in the sense of common generic properties) sink into the background, and yet on the other hand, allow the thrust towards that universality of the reality in question for us, which is implicit in the concept of nature, to be apprehended—precisely as pertaining to the plus sensed by our presentiment. Once these conditions are fulfilled, we achieve the following vantage: the divine Logos became man according to the mode of the mineness of human existence, and this must be full of significance for the mineness of all human existence. Each man must be qualified in the mineness of his own existence by the mineness of the existence of Jesus Christ. (And in this, Christ's 'subjectivity' is—perhaps, presumably—to be qualified differently from all human subjectivity.)—The 'perspective' we are speaking of here has the character of a *conclusion* ('therefore, such must be the case . . .'); it is not, however, the type of conclusion that has come to an end, but one that in its turn points the way towards something not yet determinate and which thus belongs to the realm of presentiment. Just as a concept or proposition can persevere in the area of presentiment, so also can a conclusion. By way of a conclusion there arises then, as in our case, a new perspective.

We get a glimpse of the 'new element of the surroundings' awaiting us here, when we ask ourselves the question: how can the mineness of one person become meaningful and determinative for that of another person? Where is there 'a bridge between mineness and mineness'? What can join existent entities which are never to be apprehended adequately as cases of a common genus? By asking questions like this, we run up against the phenomenon of existential *solidarity*. This phenomenon, this concept, enters our field of vision—and not simply by chance, but because we have already headed in a determinate direction, and because thereby we have come into a region in which this notion has its abode: namely, the region of the existential illumination of existence. The horizons of thought in this region are already articulated. Distinct routes have already been traversed. Much is already pre-thought. And so distinctive concepts emerge in determinate areas and come forth to meet us. Moreover, these thought-horizons are not arbitrarily formed as they are, but rather correspond in a certain 'isomorphism' to the phenomenal realms in which we exist as human beings. The notion 'solidarity' suggests itself in particular because it means that an existence as 'mine' (*jemeinige*) is 'present to' (*bei*) the other. This unique 'being-present-to' (*Sein-bei*), which we know as a phenomenon, is denoted by the concept of solidarity as both an entity and an ideal. Thus when God as Person is present to the person of the human being in such a manner that he ˮassumes the nature' of the latter, this might well be expressed by the concept of solidarity.

Nevertheless this concept does not suffice either. Here we have a presentiment of another plus: the *assumptio humanae naturae* by God can be approached somewhat or expressed approximately by the concept of solidarity. (And it is precisely in this *process of 'approximation'* that the dynamism of presentiment as approaching a still unknown and not graspable point is once again at work!) Indeed the assumption of human nature seems to imply still *more* than a solidarity between human individuals. Thus: what happens by reason of this assumption is solidarity and at the same time 'more' than solidarity. So it seems; that is to say, such is our presentiment. There is a matter of solidarity here; in other words, it is not false, but true (in the sense of 'illuminating', 'showing forth'—cf. Heidegger's notion of truth as *a-letheia*, of *aletheuein* as 'opening up', 'making manifest') to signify this reality with the term 'solidarity'. Now this does not mean that the reality in question is subsumed under the universal concept of solidarity, but rather that by the concept of the human phenomenon of solidarity it is 'approximated'.

In what, however, does the plus of which we have a presentiment consist? We are conceiving of the *assumptio humanae naturae* as 'God's being-present-to' the existence, as mine, *of all* human beings. The 'of all' here is very important: for the concept of 'nature' expresses precisely this universal aspect, namely, what pertains to all men. But this 'being-present-to' is indeed more than the 'being-present-to' between solitary human individuals; and so we shall say by way of trial, groping our way: the 'being-present-to' in this case is a 'being-in'. (Once more, we can usually grope only when a presentiment is leading us: I grope my way in a dark room along the wall to the door, because I have a presentiment that there is a door there.) The union between God and (all) men manifestly indicated in the notion of the *assumptio* cannot presumably mean merely that God has handed down a clarification of solidarity in relation to all men; nor that he fosters some sort of feeling of solidarity towards all men. Still, the concept of solidarity is useful, for it indicates the personal character of the *unio hypostatica*: that there is a question here of a relation between persons and not merely between a Person and a neutral, thing-like 'nature'. The concept of solidarity must, however, in our particular case extend so far as to entail a real givenness *in* the existence of all men (this is the direction in which

12

our ad-hoc notion of 'being-in' points). By the incarnation of the Logos and in virtue of the *unio hypostatica* something in the personal reality of all men has been changed. One has to (and this, too, is again only a presentiment-laden description) be thinking in terms of a type of *real presence of God* in the personal reality of all men.

At this point two new questions arise: the questions, 'How?' and 'Where?' How can this real presence of God be described? What is its mode? And where is it located in the existence of human beings? Or in other words, where does it make a meaningful appearance for men? Why do these two questions insinuate themselves here? Precisely because the talk about a real presence of God in the personal reality of men was an anticipation of presentiment. A new aspect of theological questioning is exhibited here; this aspect goes hand in hand with and is conditioned by the dynamism of presentiment within the thought-process. For presentiment itself heads towards concreteness and does not yet have this concreteness. And so it sets in motion the further questioning which intends the concrete.

For the purpose of answering the How-question, a new concept is suggested from within the personalist thought-horizon in which we have found ourselves: that of *waiting*. For the subject-matter hanging in suspense for us in the course of our thinking through these questions is on the one hand no mere 'indicative' which demands nothing on our part. It is indeed a *word* of God on which we base our efforts and which provides the subject-matter of the hypostatic union for our thinking in the first place. But neither can one treat of a mere 'imperative' which only makes demands of us without giving us anything. For the word of God from which our thinking departs is *Evangelium*, and that is address. Since, accordingly—and as so many theological passwords current today affirm—the real presence of God in personal human reality has at once an 'indicative' and an 'imperative' character, this presence can be expressed by the concept of waiting: God awaits. For the concept of waiting joins both: the one waiting is actually there already; but he awaits someone who still needs to come. In this way, the 'being-in' of God, his real presence within human reality, in its very existence, can be qualified as a waiting. God is there and waits—for us. He is present within human existence.

To be sure, the information provided thus far by combining the concepts of solidarity and of waiting remains in no way concrete enough. Now we have to ask, where? Where is God present in our existence? Where is this presence exhibited for us? At which point should we join ourselves to the presence of God? What is the 'locus of the presence of God' in our existence? And what does this presence of God mean for us as gift and as task, as being and as obligation? If we should be successful in saying this, then a theologically sufficient concreteness would have been attained. But we will not be able to meet these questions fully here. We can, however, ask simply what it is that urges us on to ask these further questions.

Before attempting this, however, we must turn briefly to the other problem: where does the *criterion for the truth of a theological solution* lie? Here one can begin by asserting that a theological solution must be (*a*) adequate to Scripture and (*b*) adequate to reality (related to and ever taking into consideration the reality of human existence). But this information is not enough. For the question is precisely: how may this adequacy be measured? What moves us to legitimately say yes or no to a theological solution?

Here we must notice especially that the yes or no to a theological interpretation participates in the yes and no of faith itself; i.e., in the confessional character of all Christian discourse. Therein is something obligatory with respect to the future, a type of identification of one's own future living with the content of the confession. Once this is presupposed, it seems to me that the criterion given by Fr Lonergan holds good in the most precise way in the theological thought-process: an insight is 'invulnerable' and to be affirmed in the measure that no further relevant questions can be asked which would put the insight in question.[5] Thus we have an 'operative' criterion of the adequacy of solutions, i.e., a criterion which is not imposed in the thought-process from outside (which is a complete illusion), but one which by way of an analysis of the thought-process itself illuminates it immanently. I would tend to dispute whether the point at which no further relevant questions can arise can ever actually be reached in theology, because theological thought has a historical character. But on the other hand, one can from time to time attain this point in a given situation. This means that we arrive at the point where we identify ourselves confessionally here and now with a theological interpretation according to which we can live, and according to which we can respectably succeed in organising our life or, with this interpretation as a basis, speak a word of consolation to another.

Now let us return to our where-question: what is it that actually and ultimately gives us occasion to ask this question? Here something decisive is at stake, namely: is everything that has been developed until now merely a psychology of the process? Is what we have described simply the way things go factually and on the average when we think, without having anything at all to do with the event of discovering the truth itself? Or does the dynamism of presentiment described here pertain—at least in theology—to the essence of the discovery of truth itself?

Here I must risk oversimplification by answering in a simple thesis: presentiment and the dynamism of the thought-process permeated by it have to do essentially with the discovery of truth itself, because 'there is truth'.—This proposition is to be understood as follows: there exists the true intelligibility-of-thing(s) (*Sach-Verhalt*). In theology it might perhaps be more correct to say: intelligibility-of-person(s). The truth already *is* 'somehow'. We do not invent it; rather it is, and it waits for us to know it. We do not yet know the truth—otherwise we would not be asking questions. But our not-knowing, which is the ground of our questioning, is not a *tabula rasa*. Rather we are laid claim to by the unknown truth. We already stand in an enceptive encounter with it. And this inchoate encounter with the unknown truth is the *conditio* out of which questioning grows. One can reflect on this condition. One can try to clarify it further. But one cannot properly 'question beyond it', because all questioning originates precisely here. There is thinking only where 'there is something to think'.

Hence a questioning thought is a vital encounter with truth worth questioning (*frag-würdigen Wahrheit*). Our very existence can be said to collide in questioning with the true intelligibility-of-thing(s). And articulating, grounding, discursive thinking is rooted in this vital encounter of existence with the truth, and this is just what becomes articulate. It was in this way that Heidegger founded the intellectual 'not' in the existentially experienced 'nothingness'.[6]—This vital encounter works itself out in presentiment, which propels articulating thought. In presentiment the as yet unknown truth speaks to us.

That where-question has to be put in this way because it is a question intending a more proximate concreteness and as such responds to the claim upon our thinking of the still unknown (not yet sufficiently articulated) truth of the Incarnation. At this stage, however, we shall break off the paradigmatic course of our thinking. We have tried to describe a phase of this process. The process remains incomplete. A presentiment of the further progress on our way could show up for us in a couple of sentences of Martin Buber's, which depict the mutual interlinking of divine and human reality:

Above and below are bound to one another. He who wishes to speak with men, without speaking with God, his word is unfulfilled; but he who wishes to speak with God, without speaking with men, his word is shy of the mark . . . The true address of God points to the space of lived language, where the voices of creatures go groping along, and precisely in the act of failure reach the eternal Partner.[7]

# Theological Method on the Scripture as Source

QUENTIN QUESNELL

AN ultimate and so a perpetually recurring question in theological method concerns the fundamental source of theological evidence, the starting place of theology, the basic and decisive criterion of truth to which theology and the theologian can rightly appeal. Sometimes this is seen as the question of the principles and norms for right interpretation of the Scriptures, of tradition, of dogma, as well as of contemporary phenomena. Sometimes it is merely the question of 'How do we know who is right in theology? How do we really know?' I call it here the question of the Scripture as source, partly because those are the terms in which it gained such keen attention during the excited opening session of Vatican II, and partly because that clearly puts the question directly within the area of my own special interest and work. I wish to inquire directly what answer to the question is implied or stated in Lonergan's work on theological method.

It is of course inconceivable that the book he now has in preparation will not deal directly with this topic at some point and shed considerable light upon it. But in the meantime, the book has not yet appeared. The article 'Functional Specialties in Theology', introduced as the second chapter of that book, does not really settle the question. The article specifies a first function in theology called Research, but does not indicate which, if any, objects of that research hold a privileged position. In the light of Lonergan's methodological reflections in *De Deo Trino*,[1] for instance, the 'prius scripturisticum' would seem to be simply one more historically and culturally limited set of data along with the 'prius patristicum' and the 'prius systematicum', data whose historical and cultural limitations are problems to be overcome rather than ultimate sources of answers.

Unfortunately there is no time here to go into a detailed study of these and all the other places where Lonergan touches on the Scripture as source of theology.[2] I propose for the sake of clear presentation and profitable analysis to consider no more than two of his observations relevant to the subject, and these from what may at first seem an unlikely source, *Insight*.

To take the positions of *Insight* as definitive might be a mistake. But it is never a mistake to take them seriously. I do find that later formulations often show considerable development; but they never lack remarkable consistency. Perhaps this much can be said: there are few later writings of Lonergan's in which he does not in some form or another, usually explicitly, refer his reader back to all or at least large portions of *Insight*.[3]

Further advantages and justifications for focusing our study on *Insight* are perhaps the following:

1. *Insight* is the only work so far in which Lonergan has set his reflection in the broadest possible context. Until he gives us another work of still wider scope with evidence that he has indeed envisioned new horizons, his commentators can only try to solve problems touching his thought within the broadest context they can be sure he acknowledges, especially when it is a context that few men today feel sure they have mastered.

2. Even if his forthcoming book should place his doctrine on the question at hand in some entirely new perspective or modify it seriously and intrinsically, time spent in analysing the *Insight* presentation will not be wasted. Cf. his own comments on the value that he experienced from trying to stretch up to the mind of Aquinas by studying Thomas' development from one work to the next.[4]

3. There is no reason to think the new book on which he has spent so many years will be written in any lighter a style than *Insight* itself. Time spent in unfolding the implications of any few of his heavily packed lines will be good practice for approaching whatever else he may write in the future.

## The statement of the Epilogue

The first reference I want to consider is a statement in the Epilogue. It has not earned Lonergan any friends among Scripture scholars. He writes: '. . . in a pre-eminent and unique manner, the dogmatic decision is, and the technical thesis of the dogmatic theologian can be, the true interpretation of scriptural texts, patristic teaching, and traditional utterances' (p. 740). We shall take this statement for detailed consideration in Part II of this paper. It is completely typical of many he has often made in his other works,[5] but to appreciate it properly, it will be necessary first to set it in context with the aid of another presentation from chapter XX of *Insight*. This earlier presentation will be the subject of Part I of this paper (p. 166 *infra*).

The Epilogue of *Insight*, according to the author, is written 'from the terminal viewpoint of a believer, a Catholic, and, it happens, a professor of dogmatic theology.'[6] Now one must not so stress the perfection implied by 'terminal' as to overlook the limitations implied by 'believer', 'Catholic', 'professor of dogma'. To one who shares Lonergan's personal faith-commitment, it may seem obvious that 'terminal viewpoint' and 'Catholic viewpoint' are co-extensive. To a colleague who shares Lonergan's professional commitment, it might seem equally obvious that the 'moving viewpoint' of the earlier parts of *Insight* should come to rest in the terminus of dogmatic theology.

But others who may not fully share these same commitments or who have equally compelling commitments of their own will soon observe that the twentieth chapter of *Insight* does not point specifically to Roman Catholicism, but to the need for empirically identifying for oneself the divinely provided solution to man's problem of evil.[7] That solution is described heuristically throughout the chapter. A believing Catholic would indeed conclude that this description matches that of the Church in which he was raised. To him all other forms of religion, no matter how excellent, will be not 'the full realisation of the solution' but only 'emergent trends'[8] towards it. But others will make different identifications of which is 'the full realisation' and which are 'the emergent trends'. The act of identifying, itself, as section 6 of chapter XX clarifies,[9] is always 'principally the work of God' (p. 730), and God's grace works in men in various ways. A believing Jew, a Lutheran, a Muslim, will each see his own religion as the one which in fact measures up fully to the heuristic sketch. In fact, each man's sincere belief in his own religion implies that he is doing precisely that.

Of course Lonergan wrote the description with his own faith in mind, firmly convinced that it was his own faith which fitted the heuristic description. He would have to as an intelligent 'believer and Catholic'. For he writes that the solution must be 'realised through human acts of acknowledgement and consent'[10] and that a man 'must be intelligent and reasonable in his acknowledgement of it and his acceptance of it'.[11] How can one be intelligent and reasonable in the acknowledgement of any one faith-allegiance among the many which the real world proposes as possibilities? 'A man will be intelligent and reasonable in his *acknowledgement* of the solution inasmuch as . . . he recognises that in fact there has been in human history first an emergent trend and later the full realisation of a solution that possesses all the characteristics' determined in this heuristic analysis.[12] And he will be intelligent and reasonable in the *acceptance* of the solution he has acknowledged inasmuch as he can see there is a value in so assenting because of the truthfulness of the God who has provided it.[13]

Now Lonergan would hardly expect his readers to forget all he had said earlier as they turned over page 731. Nor would he expect that those who up to page 729 had been firmly committed to a different identification of God's action in the world would be suddenly converted to Catholicism, seeing the faith commitment of their whole previous lives as unintelligent and unreasonable. Nor did Lonergan write *Insight* only for Catholics. But if he knew this would not happen at the end of chapter XX, then he must have known that his lines in the Epilogue would be read conditionally by most readers, in parentheses as it were. Any readers except Catholics would be sharply conscious that what he said 'as a believer, a Catholic, and a professor of dogmatic theology' were precisely statements made within a personal faith commitment, a personal identification (made with God's help) of which existing ongoing collaboration among the many visible in the real world actually satisfied the heuristic criteria he had laid down. Such readers, each with his own personal faith-commitment (also made with God's help), would hardly be able to read the statements of the Epilogue as statements of simply objective fact, the inescapable results of experience, understanding, and sound judgement.

But if the statements of the Epilogue are all faith-statements, nevertheless Lonergan has shown us in chapter XX what steps one would have to go through to be able to make any faith-statements intelligently and reasonably. It follows that behind the faith-statements of the Epilogue, there should be an equivalent reality described heuristically and purely rationally in chapter XX (and/or earlier in the book). Consequently, in order to find the appropriate context for the statement of the Epilogue quoted above, we should be able to turn to the description of religion in general as it is sketched in chapter XX and prepared for earlier in the book.

### PART I: THE ELEMENTS IN RELIGION IN GENERAL FULFILLED BY THE SCRIPTURES IN CHRISTIANITY

In chapter XVIII a problem is set up, and described in general terms as the problem of liberation (pp. 619–33; especially pp. 630–33). It is a consequence of the fact of moral impotence (pp. 627–30). The same impotence and its consequent problem, with special attention to their social manifestations, had been sketched in chapter VII (pp. 222–36), with some preliminary account of the needed solution (pp. 236–42). The same fact and problem take on new dimensions after chapter XIX concludes with the existence of God as the necessary answer to unavoidable questions, and so they are resumed in the sketch which opens chapter XX (pp. 687–93). The new dimensions which may be envisaged to what is now rightly and technically (p. 694) called the problem of evil are outlined there in a very general way (pp. 693–96). This is the necessary background to Lonergan's discussion of religion in the life of man.

### Some elements in the solution

He then begins (p. 696) to try to sketch that solution in some further (though still general) detail. He uses the ordinary technique with which he has developed his whole metaphysics in *Insight*, the technique of the heuristic structure.[14] One knows what one is seeking. One works out as thoroughly as possible all that is implied in the fact that one knows what one is seeking.

Here, in this case, in response to the problems described, one is seeking something with two basic characteristics: it must satisfy the intelligible unity of the actual world order; and it must solve the problem of evil.[15] The fact that the solution must satisfy the intelligible unity of the actual world order (summed up on pp. 125–28 as 'emergent probability'; on pp. 458–9 as development; cf. especially pp. 469–79 on *human* development)[16] implies that it will provide or consist in a higher integration, a pulling together and making able to function as a unity, of all the diversities of human consciousness, appetites, distractions— in general of all the many facets and aspects of human existence in the real world.

The demand for such a higher integration would be satisfied by habitual inclinations in men to live in self-sacrificing love and forgiveness, overcoming evil with good, in the conviction that the world is lovable and knowable, in the certitude that God exists and that he is providing a solution to men's problems. This can be summed up under the traditional headings of charity (pp. 698–700), hope (pp. 701–2) and faith (p. 702f.).[17] If these new human perfections are to solve the problem of evil, they must 'not arise from nature' for it is human nature that creates the problem. They must be from the God who through them is solving the problem.[18] Still, if they are to continue the intelligible order of the universe, it must also be possible for man to come to them in a basically human way.[19] That basically human way will involve the action of men upon one another.

From here on, Lonergan describes a community of men, the social phenomenon of religion, the contribution men make in community to helping one another find the faith, hope and love they need to live as men. One aspect of this will be certain truths to be believed: that there is a God, and that he is all good, wise, powerful; that man is free, responsible, and sinful. And most important of all, that God is providing a solution to man's problem of evil.[20]

These truths will be passed on in an ongoing collaboration, a new and higher collaboration of men for the attainment of truth, a collaboration which has 'God originating and preserving the collaboration' (p. 720). But this is only the cognitional aspect (p. 719). Through that collaboration and the truth it passes on to be believed, men must be brought to the hope and the love they need. How will this come about?

### The sensible, psychic elements

The most important truth to be passed on is 'that God is providing a solution'.[21] That proposition will, however, not be conveyed only in words, calling for assent to an unspecified abstract fact. It will be incorporated in a 'mystery' where 'mystery' is understood as defined in chapter XVII (pp. 546–8). That is, it will be incorporated in 'dynamic images that are partly sign' (p. 547).[22] Man needs dynamic images that point forward to the unknown which surrounds him and transcends him and which he vaguely perceives, just as he needs images in which to express to himself on a sensitive level what he has intellectually conceived. Images which are of both sorts at once are the most powerful and dynamic of all.[23].

Images of course arise in men naturally, spontaneously, in abundance. But their usefulness and importance in human living comes from the meanings men assign them or deny them (p. 532f.). Religions assign meanings to natural and spontaneous feelings, drives, and images, and so make them into signs and symbols. Each religion assigns meanings and so creates signs and symbols in its own way, according to its own distinctive intellectual interpretation of the universe (pp. 533–4): 'precisely because of its relation to the known unknown, the image can be interpreted as sign in manners that are as numerous and diverse as human ingenuity and human contrariness' (p. 534). To put it another way, there is felt within man a 'directed but indeterminate dynamism', but where that dynamism is heading 'is a question that receives countless answers' and many of these answers are religious (p. 534).

At any rate, the exploitation of dynamic images is necessary for dealing with a human being who is more than pure mind. The man described throughout *Insight* is much more than a philosophic machine. He is living, sensing, psychically complicated by awareness and flight from awareness on many different levels and in many experimental patterns.[24] A major part of his lack of integration, part of his inability to be what he feels he can be, do what he knows he should do, is that the sensible and psychic factors in his makeup do not integrate adequately with the intelligent factors.[25] The solution to his problem must take account of this and provide for it. There must be a psychic aspect to the solution to appeal to the sensible and emotional in man.[26] The solution must capture and tame each man's sensitivity, must allow and provide for the demands of his drive to intersubjectivity. Again, if man is to be brought to understanding and have his frequent failures to reflect filled in for and remedied, allowance must be made for the way a human intellect functions.

For human understanding is impossible unless a suitable flow of representations is rising up from the senses and from the imagination. To think of correcting the functioning of the understanding without providing somehow for such a suitably corrected flow from the imagination and from the senses would be folly.

To move in the other direction, transition outward from right thinking to right action, from corrected and straight thinking to corrected and straight implementation in deed, is also by way of intervening images. Between intellect and action occurs the image as psychic force to make the action possible and powerful. Between understanding and external verbal articulation, there comes again the image as sign. Both types of image are directly connected with, charged with, bearers of emotions and affections. Both are a necessary part of successful human living.

Man then needs images which are partly symbol and partly sign, dynamic images which carry psychic force. Lonergan's word for such an image, we said, is 'mystery'. A mystery, then, is linked with some distinct intellectual content, yet cannot be limited to representing one single clear idea. At the same time that it expresses a truth, it also stands for the whole fabulous human phenomenon of reaching out into, feeling oneself drawn into, orientated towards, something greater than oneself, the biggest unanswered question of them all, the 'more' that lies beyond any intellectual presentation, the 'greater' which surrounds and can ennoble life. Man grows asking questions—and beyond every question there is another question, and still another. Nor do these questions point towards mere nothingness. Questions already imply some inkling of answers. There is not simply 'the unknown'. There is the wondered-about unknown, the 'known unknown'.

The belief and the hope and even the love of which we spoke above reach out towards this known unknown, and in the concrete facilitate man's living in accord with his spontaneous orientation out of himself and beyond himself. But they do so (because they were conceived as radical—root—solutions to man's problem) on the level of knowing and willing. Mystery, with its elements of symbol and of sign, is an attempt to do the same on a sensitive level as well. And since the full solution calls for changed action, the mystery which expresses it will be of a nature to move to action. It will be so presented as to transform man's sensitive being as well as his intellectual, bring the sensitive fully into line with his intellectual being, keep it from being a hindrance and transform it into an asset by unlocking its mighty psychic dynamism and bringing it into harmony with the vast pressures of the pure desire to know, of hope, and of self-sacrificing charity.[27]

Thus on the sensitive and inter-subjective level the solution to the problem of evil will be mystery; that is, it will be a symbol (pointing to the known unknown), it will be a sign (summing up in a sensible way the essential act of faith) and it will be a psychic force. Describing that mystery Lonergan says it is 'at once symbol of the uncomprehended and sign of what is grasped and psychic force that sweeps living human bodies, linked in charity, to the joyful, courageous, whole-hearted, yet intelligently controlled performance of the tasks set by a world order in which the problem of evil is not suppressed but transcended.'[28]

Next, the mystery which is the solution as sensible must, if it is to be believed and so perform its function, be announced as true. It must be a fact, not just a suggestion to charm or entertain. If it is to be part of the solution of the problem of evil, move to action, stir men's hearts to faith and hope and love, stir the devotion and loyalty one person can in another, it must be a fact, not just a plausible tale. It cannot be read along with other redemption-myths as just one more of the same; not if it is actually to function as itself redemptive. Thus to find God's word in it, one cannot read it as one might read and compare various ancient creation-myths and observe without concern that some derive the world from the generation of the gods and others from a conflict between gods and sea-monsters. We feel no need to reconcile the two points of view, either with each other directly or in some higher synthesis expressing what they really mean. The mysteries which express the solution within the collaboration in which one shares must, on the contrary, be taken seriously. But to take something seriously is to think that it concerns reality. To take it seriously is to take it as true—if not in the literal expression, at least in the meaning (the vague or the definite, or the definite as pointing to the vague beyond) and so at least as able to be interpreted as true. For what is true is one and does not contain contradictions. That is why Lonergan says this mystery would have to be real, be fact, 'not a story but history'.[29]

So, if there is a solution it must be not just a truth but a truth embodied in a living mystery presented in some richness and fullness. It must provide man's sensitive nature with the sensible stimulation it needs. It must furnish man with the sensible data which will 'command his attention, nourish his imagination, stimulate his intelligence and will.'[30] These data must 'release his affectivity, control his aggressivity, and, as central features of the world of sense, intimate its finality, its yearning for God.'[31]

*The Scriptures as embodying these elements*

Such a mystery in our religion is, for example, the mystery of the cross.[32] Such a mystery incarnate in history is Christ the man and his suffering, death and rising.[33] Such a full embodiment of this mystery with all the sensible data demanded by man's sensitive nature is, in our religion, the sacred Scriptures. They tell the story of Christ as a story of God's love for man and some men's foolish rejection of it and the stumbling first attempts of others to live up to its implications. They provide the sensible data that man may contemplate and thoughtfully read, and so feel drawn to reach out to God. By their human subject matter and the striking events they narrate, by their varied literary style, by and in their public reading regularly in the Christian assembly they 'command his attention and nourish his imagination'. Their challenging statements about life, strikingly presented, and above all linked with an image of a compellingly beautiful person, stimulate the reader's intelligence and will to new visions of human possibility for living and new hopes of attaining them by trust and faith in the God who raises the dead and makes the things that are not as if they are. Approaching the Scriptures in a religious mood gives ample play to the religious emotive power, makes the desire for the true human life into something attractive which can be pursued as an act of love for a living person who has first loved us, and which is eminently worth all the effort, struggle, sacrifice, self-control, necessary to achieve it. Thus they 'release his affectivity, control his aggressivity'. And finally the data, the images which appear on every page of the Scriptures, the eternal symbols such as life, death, love and hate, water, bread, wine, sleep, growing plants and trees, sickness and healing, tears, songs and cries of joy—these all 'as central features of the world of sense intimate this world's finality, its yearning for God.'

Now this description will also apply to good liturgy, as well as to altars and shrines, to sacred pictures and biographies of saints, to scenes of nature contemplated in religious mood. Further instances of the principle are many. The point here is that this is the principle which explains the first and essential use of the sacred Scriptures in our religion. Moreover, if there were no Scriptures, it is almost impossible to imagine how the redemptive principle of Incarnation, cross and resurrection would be of any sensible, psychic value or moving power to any but a few chosen individuals back in the first generation of believers. It is the Scriptures (and the preaching which lives off them) which bring God-in-man to life before our eyes, which put the central Christian mystery in its central symbol vividly across; in and and through them 'Christ is portrayed crucified before your eyes.'[34]

This is the main function of the Scriptures in our faith, the role they fulfil above all others. And they fulfil it when they are being read or listened to or meditated upon as they are. That is, their natural and religious use, providing in our religion an element necessary to any full religion, is to be devoutly read.

There are other uses of Scripture, of course. They may be taken apart for study of backgrounds, motives, true and false history, geography, genealogy, archaeology, biography, philology, literature, history of religious, etc. The affirmations they contain may be excerpted, catalogued, outlined, and made the jumping-off place for reflection on the constitutive nature of God and his universe. But in comparison to the use of the Scripture for religious reading as described above, these other uses are secondary, supporting, instrumental. The Scriptures are best used for what they really are when they are *read*.

## PART II: LONERGAN AS DOGMATIC AND SPECULATIVE THEOLOGIAN

*The statement in context*

It is time to return to the statement of the Epilogue from which we began. We have already noted that it or its equivalents often reappear in many of Lonergan's treatises and theological notes.[35] Within *Insight* too the statement plays a role that is in no way incidental to the thought-plan of the whole book. For quoted fully it reads:

As historical interpretation may be based simply on a historical sense or may operate in the light of the universal viewpoint, so too the non-theological interpreter may recapture the mentality for which the books of the Old and New Testament were written or the spirit of the age in which a heresy arose and was condemned, but the theological interpreter has to operate from the firmer and broader base that includes the theologically transformed universal viewpoint; and so it is that in a pre-eminent and unique manner the dogmatic decision is, and the technical thesis of the dogmatic theologian can be, the true interpretation of Scriptural texts, patristic teaching, and traditional utterances (p. 740).

This is nothing but a fuller explanation of the third and fourth of the points at the top of the same page. They outline what he calls

the Catholic fact of
(1) an initial divine revelation
(2) the work of teachers and preachers communicating and applying the initial message to a succession of different audiences
(3) the work of the speculative theologian seeking a universal formulation of the truths of faith, and
(4) the work of the historical theologian revealing the doctrinal identity in the verbal and conceptual differences of (1), (2), and (3).

The general religious fact which corresponds to this Catholic fact had been sketched in chapter XX. It involved four kinds of collaboration in 'the solution':

man will not only accept the solution, but also will collaborate with it.
(1) Accordingly, because the solution is for all men and universally accessible, there will be the collaboration that consists in making known to others the good news of the solution and its nature.
(2) Again, because the solution is permanent, there will be the collaboration that consists in transmitting it from each generation to the next. Again, because human expression is relative to its audience, there will be the collaboration that consists in recasting the expression of the solution into the equivalent expressions of different places, times, classes, and cultures.
(3) Again, because man can arrive at a universal viewpoint, there will be the collaboration that consists in conceiving and expressing the solution in terms of the universal viewpoint.

13

(4) Finally, because the solution regards man's problem of evil, there will be the collaboration that consists in grasping and formulating the manner in which the solution is relevant and effective in each of the successive situations of individuals, classes, national groups, and of men generally (pp. 721–2).

The same four divisions are offered as a summary of what was envisioned in his analysis of interpretation in chapter XVII:

(1) initial statements addressed to particular audiences,
(2) their successive recasting for sequences of other particular audiences,
(3) the ascent to a universal viewpoint to express the initial statements in a form accessible to any sufficiently cultured audience, and
(4) the explanatory unification from the universal viewpoint of the initial statements and all their subsequent re-expressions (p. 739; summing up pp. 562–94).

This is indeed the basic problem of interpretation (using interpretation as he does, to denote not the process of coming to understand a document, but a step which understanding must precede. Interpretation is the step in which one tries to communicate to someone else the meaning one has found in a document, tries to tell another accurately what one has just read and understood).[36]

It may very well happen that any simple interpretation is correct, that it hits off for a contemporary audience the principal insight communicated by the original document. It may also happen that the interpreter knows his interpretation to be correct . . . But if interpretation is to be scientific, then the grounds for the interpretation have to be assignable . . . , there will not be a range of different interpretations due to the individual, group, and general bias of the historical sense of different experts; if interpretation is to be scientific, then it has to discover some method of conceiving and determining the habitual development of all audiences and it has to invent some technique by which its expression escapes relativity to particular and incidental audiences (pp. 563–4).

*The statement as answer to a problem*

From all this we see that the statement of the Epilogue is not necessarily intended as a bit of dogmatic imperialism. It need not be a proposal to stop normal historical research and let dogma answer all our questions. It only suggests that dogma and theology can be specialised answers to a general problem as it occurs in this specialised context, and that this specialised answer follows the general pattern of human knowing and human interpretation.

For the problem is that the Catholic faith-community, through its long history, has made use of many different formulations of what it believed. Naturally the question arises for one who looks on that community as God's working out of man's salvation: how can this diversity represent the one faith, the one solution God has provided and is providing to man's universal problems?

The question is not a minor one. Once it arises, it opens up a range of other problems: e.g., which of the varied formulations is really true? Or is there any truth involved at all? Can anyone say what Christianity is really about? What is the essential in the midst of so much diversity and change? What is, in the face of historical fact, the 'identity in difference' which Vatican I affirmed when it insisted that 'divine revelation was to be regarded, not as a human invention to be perfected by human ingenuity, but as a permanent deposit confided to the Church and by the Church to be preserved and defended'? (p. 739). The answer is not easy, as most theologians and all pastors can testify today.

Lonergan's suggested contribution to an answer is first to note that the problem need not and does not occur simply as a result of the preaching of the faith as such. Any given audience hearing the faith preached need not reflect and ask about all the other possible forms that preaching may have had earlier and elsewhere. In fact, people do reflect and ask: sophisticated, educated people in every age, and almost all people in our own historically aware generation. Thus a problem does indeed arise, but it remains, in spite of its current universality, a specialised problem. It is a question that demands an answer which will satisfy people of such a level of sophistication and awareness as to conceive the problem.

The second contribution to an answer is to point out the religious generality of the problem. (Hence the list of four kinds of collaboration from chapter XX, see pp. 173–4 above.) Though it only arises in a certain kind of culturally conditioned mind, that mind need not be Catholic. The problem is eventually inescapable for at least some members of any religious group which claims to last through time. It is true of any faith which looks back to distant origins—as most of them hasten to do. Only the utterly historically naïve or perhaps religious groups so tiny and remote as never to have been thought worth scientific historical investigation could dream that their saving message has been passed on in the same terms and thought patterns and philosophical presuppositions over many generations or even decades. Catholicism merely happens to have a history somewhat harder to overlook than most, one written large across the centre of western European civilisation.

The third element in a solution is to grasp the complete generality of the problem. (Hence the fourfold summary of interpretation from chapter XVII, see p. 174 above.) It is not peculiar to religious groups either, but belongs to any groups that seek to use the past or know the past in any way or pass it on. It is a problem for all historians, for all historically based movements, clubs, nations. It is a problem of any philosophical school which claims to preserve, elaborate, apply the thought of a great master of the past in the world today: a Kant, a Hegel, a Marx, an Aquinas; or even a master of today in a different cultural milieu: Bultmann, Heidegger in New York; Lonergan in Florida. There is a general hermeutical problem of how it is possible to seize the thought of another man and transmit it to a classroom full of students—a problem of whose solution most of us at least occasionally despair.

A fourth element in the solution is to see that it is not necessarily absurd to suppose that a solution exists—that the same truth *can* be conveyed in different formulations. For in spite of the frequency or the depth of our occasional despair, there is not one of us who does not continue to act on the supposition that such communication is possible. We not only submit our students to texts of Plato, Kant, Bultmann. We comment on these texts ourselves. We explain, we interpret. And in practice we maintain that some interpretations are better than others, more faithful to the original, for some students get, and presumably deserve, A's, others do not. How distinguish the one from the other, the better interpretation from the worse? Can men seize and pass on accurately the thoughts of the others, relate the happenings and intentions of past or distant authors, judge one another's work? Can men communicate their insights and discoveries or must all be discounted as so much varying personal prejudice? Must every interpreter begin absolutely anew? Can men never learn from one another, build on one another's work?

The possibility cannot be denied without passing judgement on other people's understanding. But that judgement already affirms the possibility in practice. And so the attempt to deny the possibility is incoherent.

Besides, the experience of communicating one same insight to different audiences (at least on a face-to-face basis) from different points of view is a common and even an everyday experience, *contra factum non valet illatio.* What is missing is not the fact—this thing happens.

What is missing is a sound explanation of the fact, which will make such communication philosophically responsible and perhaps facilitate its practice at a scientific level in the future. The explanation which Lonergan offers is in terms of what he calls 'the universal viewpoint'. Since the term occurs in the passage of the Epilogue we are considering, we had better stop to explain it.

### Excursus on the universal viewpoint

What is the explanation of scientific interpretation in terms of the universal viewpoint? It is a sketch of how communication is possible. The starting point is the grasp of what we do when we know; of why doing that is knowing; or what we know when we do it. Then comes the realisation that all men, of all times and places, do their knowing in the same way. If they have anything to communicate at all, it is because they have experienced, understood, judged, etc. Next one observes that all knowing of all men is an attempt to know being, that which is, reality. And every statement of men stands in some relation to their experience or understanding or judgement etc. about being. Every statement about the world reflects somehow a human act or a human experience by which the world is known; and every human act and experience is a pure or a combined functioning of one or other levels of human consciousness, of more or less perfect stages in the process of human knowing. If one could successfully catalogue all that enters into the process of human knowing—the steps by which it takes place, the different patterns of experience in man, the levels of consciousness, etc.—then one could have a framework in terms of which one could discuss any affirmation about anything.[37]

Another way of putting it: every statement, if it is or intends to be a statement relative to the real world, is a statement somehow about one or other or some combination of 'the metaphysical elements'.[38] And every one of the metaphysical elements stands in correlation to some element of human consciousness and knowing. But the constituent structures of human consciousness and knowing, the constituent psychological structures that make human knowing what it is, do not change. Therefore again, if they could all be grasped, listed, analysed, catalogued, they could be used as the framework in terms of which every statement could be understood and ranged in serious comparison with other statements.

Next, one must have a clear and right notion of how one man understands another man's meaning in the first place. One must realise (as most modern hermeneutics does) that the only meanings anyone can grasp are those of which one has some inkling ahead of time. If reader or listener has nothing at all in common with writer or speaker, he cannot possibly grasp his meaning. In fact, on that supposition, he could not begin to interpret him at all. One must know the language being used, one must be sure his words denote the same objects. The two must have shared some experiences. If you have never seen a *vorpl*, the other's references to the *vorpl* will not say anything to you at all. Either he then points to one or shows you a picture or he describes in terms of experiences or knowledge which the two of you do share, making so many statements about the *vorpl* in terms you do understand that you can gradually add them together to form some notion of what he means by that word too.

Now that is true in any understanding of another man's meaning. You must have some anticipation of what that meaning might possibly be. You must somehow have had the experience or the understanding or the judgement or have had enough other experiences, understandings, judgements in common with him to make it possible for him to use them to lead you through them to new experiences, understandings and judgements. If this is true in *any* understanding of what another man means, then it is the key to how communication in general is possible: for we have 1. the fact that to communicate we must have something in common from which to work out, something shared; and 2. the fact that every statement does reflect something held in common, something shared; namely, the structures of knowing, the levels of consciousness, the patterns of experience of the mind of man. The human mind's intention of being is the core of every meaning (*Insight*, p. 357ff.).

But it follows that we also have here the basis of explaining how many different people might mean the same things; and of how different expressions might point to the same reality. For the reality itself can always be expressed in terms of one or more of the metaphysical elements; and they in turn can always be transposed into corresponding categories of the human mind; and the human mind does not change.[39]

So this is the idea of the explanation in terms of the universal viewpoint. To understand and to communicate you need some anticipation of what the other might possibly be meaning. But by universal viewpoint is meant the richest possible anticipation of all possible meanings. The universal viewpoint is the grasp and application of the principle from which *Insight* began: 'Thoroughly understand what it is to understand and not only will you possess the broad lines of all there is to be understood, but also you will possess a fixed base, an invariant pattern, opening upon all further developments of understanding' (p. xxvii). Thoroughly understand what it is to understand and you possess the richest possible anticipation of all possible meanings. Thoroughly understand what it is to understand and you will possess a framework into which all actual meanings can be set and in terms of which they can be made communicable (to any sufficiently refined and trained other mind).

And this in two ways: first as a framework, a general set of classifications of meanings, an anticipation of all possible *contents* of all statements. This may be spelled out as: every statement or judgement will be a combination of experience and lack of experience; understanding and lack of understanding; of judgements and of failures to judge; and of the various orientations of the polymorphic consciousness of man (p. 567). Moreover any expression may be made on different levels or combinations of levels and be aimed at producing responses on different levels and/or combinations of levels: e.g., mere exclamation, artistically ordered experience, reflectively tested intelligent ordering—as hypothesis, as fact—and finally also including acts of will, such as wishes and commands and practical plans and decisions.[40]

But, secondly, the same principle can be used in another way.

Man develops from culture and age to culture and age, and also develops within any given culture and age. On the broadest possible canvas every human experience, understanding and judgement stands in some relation to every other one in a great interlocked series. That series is historical, factual, has actually occurred and is in fact the object of our investigation. And it is not the object of scientific investigation as so many isolated events, but precisely as series, where persons and cultures have developed or failed to develop according to the principles of emergent probability.[41] If this is granted, then it follows that a complete understanding of understanding would enable one to outline human growth towards a grasp and control of reality in such a way that another broad grid could be laid out in which all statements (all extant documents and monuments) could be arranged, and on which could be charted their relations to one another, actual and possible, theoretical and speculative, as causing one another, as reacting to one another, as groping up one alley and down another in the attempt to reach the fullness of being. If we knew everything about everything, that grid would be filled in. We do not. But our serious and scientific contributions to real advance of knowledge consist in gradually, by the regular self-corrective process of science, doing that filling in.

The very thought of such a grid suggests the second way to anticipate all possible meanings—to control and master meaning, to set up a way of talking about the relationships of meanings to one another. It is a second aspect of 'universal viewpoint'. It could be called 'universal *context*'. If this universal context is phrased in terms of the patterns of the human mind, without attempting to follow through every argument in detail, but only to anticipate the possible directions that the twists and turns of human argument could take by various combinations, mutations and permutations of the different levels of consciousness and patterns of experience, then it could be called 'basic context'.[42]

The final step to appreciating this analysis is to realise how ideal it is—how distant a goal.[43] Still it is not ideal in the sense of belonging to a never-never land. It is what sound thinkers and researchers are actually trying to do when they are most scientific. They are building up such a knowledge of man and how he experiences and knows as could provide a universal viewpoint.

They are building up such a set of relations of documents and meanings as could furnish a basic context for all meanings. They are filling in the picture of all the ways in which the meanings of one group of men can and do influence the lives of other men.

Lonergan's analysis in terms of universal viewpoint simply points out clearly what in fact is the direction and the implied goal of this activity. And even it is—as so much else in him— little more than another way of saying: the goal of science is to know everything about everything. The goal is enormous, but it is not inconceivable. And if the universe is finite, the goal is even finite. If, on the other hand, one insists that the universe, finite or otherwise, is simply an out-there, things which the scientist has to assimilate one after the other, that each individual in his own lifetime simply soaks up as much of this as he can, that each man's working horizon is simply other, then there is no community of knowledge and meaning and no science is possible. But science exists and depends on the communicability of knowledge and meanings. How? Lonergan suggests that one man's work is being done in an effort to know reality and another man's work is part of the same striving, that every man's knowing takes place in a human mind and the results of the knowing will have to be expressed in categories which are simultaneously sub-divisions of human consciousness and (isomorphically) of the real world to be known. With this analysis there is hope for communication.

Of course cognitional analysis has not been completed yet. Lonergan does not claim that he or anyone else has achieved it or that he possesses 'the universal viewpoint' or that he has fully understood what it is to understand.[44] But this is the direction in which research does spontaneously head (through the long self-correcting process of science), and in this direction it must be consciously directed. And it is from a grasp of what knowing really is that analyses of what we are doing and why it is possible must be undertaken and the apparent antinomies solved.

### Return to the statement

To return to our point: the problem to which the statement of the Epilogue was addressed was the problem of identity in difference as it appears in the doctrinal history of the Roman

Catholic Church. The answer suggested has invoked four elements:

(1) realising that looking for an answer was a specialised task within the realm of religion;

(2) realising that every religious group which took itself seriously (and the solution would have to take itself seriously) had the same problem;

(3) realising that the problem belongs to all who attempt to communicate anything on a broader than one-to-one basis;

(4) realising that such communication is not only possible but actual; and that there is an intelligible explanation of it in terms of the universal viewpoint.

### Dogmatic theology's right to exist

But if an answer is conceivable in general, if 'identity in difference' is not after all a contradiction in terms, then dogmatic decision and dogmatic theology have at least a right to exist.[45] For one can assume (as one does in identifying a given collaboration as God's advancing work) the truth and unity of one's own group's formulation of the solution; one can assume the possibility of an intelligible explanation of diverse formulations of one truth; and one can then be justified in proceeding in the concrete to suggest in any given case what that explanation might be.

This can even be a work of service and of love to many other members of the collaboration. For after all, though every intelligent member makes an act of faith by recognising God's hand at work in a given group through history,[46] he does not withhold assent to the recognition until he has finished researching the group and all its history in complete thoroughness. We should hardly live so long. He rather reasons that, if God really has provided some solution, he cannot have made it all that difficult to find. To be honest, the majority of men simply start life within some group whose general thrust towards goodness they perceive, but which they are not going to spend an entire lifetime researching before consenting to live within it according to its general principles. (If they did insist on doing so, the very notion of the solution would be frustrated in essentials—for one of the chief reasons a solution was needed was to escape the difficulty that one must make decisions and live by them before one has time or strength to think life through.)[47]

In this situation, then, some men can specialise and spend their lives in doing just that kind of complete research for the good of the many. Starting with their own act of faith in God as originating the collaboration of good men they have come to know, they will devote themselves to looking at the history of the collaboration in considerable detail. They will face the past as best they can get to know it, receiving the knowledge of the past from positive researchers and/or becoming positive researchers themselves.[48] But their function as dogmaticians will not be to do the positive research but to understand exactly how and why that research discovers faith taking such diverse forms. Their task will not be to discover how it was, but to understand why, on the supposition that one faith was being passed on unchanged, it still could take on the varied forms it did. They will try to grasp what has been going on—on the supposition that God was initiating and preserving the collaboration.[49] Where then has it been heading? Why has it taken so long to get there? Where might it be going?

Dogmatic theology in this sense does not miss the heart of religion. For understood in this way it does not attempt to substitute itself for the general preaching of the Christian message.[50] It concerns itself with the prerequisites of preaching that message intelligently to sophisticated people who can and do read history and who expect consistency in what they accept as God's solution to man's problems. Even intellectuals have souls; and should one doubt it or be content to leave them to worry about their own, still one dare not overlook the ordinary people who happen to be born into an age of some fairly universal historical awareness.

*How dogmatic theology points to true interpretation*

The dogmatic theologian begins with the supposition that Scripture and the beliefs of his own faith-group are both talking about reality. But there is only one reality.[51] Neither may express it fully, but neither is aiming at expressing anything else. Being, the true, the intelligible—these are the ultimate criteria to which both Scripture and dogma must submit.[52]

When you concretise your faith in this collaboration and so

commit your life and efforts to it as a movement towards God, then you accept the Scriptures which it accepts as true. But true means reflecting reality and moving you really towards God, the fullness of being and truth. Hence, of any alternative possibilities of interpreting Scripture, you always choose the most intelligible, the most reasonable, the one which most promotes the advance of men towards God (to the best of your understanding).

And when you concretise your faith in this collaboration and so commit your life and efforts to it as a movement towards God, then you accept the dogmatic decisions which it accepts as true. Not any and every dogmatic decision of the past or present, but those decisions which are passed on by the collaboration as 'definitive pronouncements that the Church itself cannot contradict' (p. 740). But true means reflecting reality and moving you towards God, the fullness of being and truth. Hence of any alternative possibilities for interpreting a dogma, you always choose the most intelligible, the most reasonable, the one which most promotes the advance of man towards God (to the best of your understanding).

Thus, if dogmatic theology has a function, then systematic theology has a function too. Its first function is analogous to that of dogmatics—grasping the real intelligibility of that which one subscribes to in the faith-group. But its other and special function will be to judge faith statements: not as true or false, for again that is presupposed from faith; but as more or less fully at present expressing the true. Where the current interpretation of them is seen to fall short of the true, reinterpret them in the most favourable sense; that is, in the light of the universal viewpoint. This will be preceded by the step of judging them partly in the light of Scripture (which verbally they must not contradict: for it is a faith-dictum constitutive of this group that its members will work within these limits); and partly in the light of previous tradition (some of which again you may not reject, for the community has self-constitutively decided on *it* as part of itself and so made it a faith-datum which will not be rejected but, if it ever appears to fall short, will only be reinterpreted in the most favourable sense; that is, in the light of the universal viewpoint.)

*A theologically transformed universal viewpoint*
For this, it is perhaps already clear, the universal viewpoint

explained in the preceding excursus will not be fully adequate.[53] For religion involves more than just inquiring intelligence. It involves acceptance of the dimension of the mystical pattern of experience and recognition of the experienced love of God above all things. These are in fact for each man a call to openness, a call to self-transcendence beyond even that of knowing and doing. These call man to yield to something greater than the whole created universe itself. They are a call to conversion. And so the truly universal viewpoint from which Lonergan wants to consider the history of religious thought must be the theologically transformed universal viewpoint, which includes the further dimension of accepting or not accepting a loving God actively and concretely working the good of man in spite of man; the dimension of converting or refusing to be religiously converted.

*Two kinds of dogmatic theology*
But if the theologically transformed universal viewpoint implies a norm above the mere words of Scripture or of dogma, then it follows that there are two ways of practising dogmatic theology. The first fails to look on things from the truly universal viewpoint, to place them in that broadest possible context which perpetually calls man beyond himself to face a higher reality in terms of which he must judge all things. This way rests content with what is already possessed, securely known. It results in no more than apologetics. It is conceived in terms of an opponent. There is always the other (perhaps he is one's self) who has to be convinced, beaten into submission, by whatever means. All evidence contrary to what you personally have once accepted and announced as your own beliefs is looked on as an attack to be feared and fought and repelled. This way would allow and might even demand lying, cheating, juggling the evidence.

A corresponding systematic theology would be basically content with the image as a statement of fact, and would concern itself with asking how the mysteries are possible in this sense-world all men of common sense live in. It would be busy about asking curious questions concerning the mysteries, working out their implications for a better knowledge of the metaphysical constitution of this world, deducing new supernatural truths from them as well, making suggestions for the adjustment of history, psychology, sociology and philosophy to the revealed information, etc.

The other way of practising dogmatic theology grasps what the theologically transformed universal viewpoint really is: a yielding to being and reality as to something greater than any of us, calling us beyond ourselves today to something which embraces all, something transcendent, with the power to reform and transform us and all that we know at every moment. It is the something yielded to in faith, which we have attempted, but not succeeded, in expressing in beliefs. It is something other men may at the moment be attempting to express in other beliefs, trying to reach out towards full possession of by means of other symbols and mysteries, so as to achieve through their strivings and their formulations, to the best of their knowledge and ability, the full realisation of God's solution on earth.

Grasping the universal viewpoint theologically transformed is grasping the full range of possibilities for conversion and non-conversion, and seeing at once in terms of that the terrible deficiencies in oneself and one's own group. It means realising that all religiously inclined men and movements have to be judged in terms of an act of faith which is an opening to the demands of all being and truth, to God and his universe as a possible object of love. Then one can proceed to do dogmatic theology, aware that God and one's striving for him must be expressed humanly in some concrete form, that one is not the first to have experienced God's saving action in the world, but that there has been a common striving towards him with a long history already accomplished; that to renounce that history because of all its imperfections is not necessarily to advance beyond it; that one can do an equal or perhaps greater service to present and future believers by trying to account for that history. One does this, however, not as a manifestation of group bias, not in order to defend it against 'attacks'; but as a sincere and humble attempt to understand what has been going on, what this ongoing action of God (for as such you have, to the best of your competence, identified it) in history has been; why it has not (by reason of what human failures) produced in history even yet the results one would expect of divine intervention (God knows it hasn't).

In the same spirit one would practise *systematic* theology in order to pinpoint what great reality has been all along the object of genuine striving; to capitalise on the living symbols which already exist and are for millions the link with the needed transcendent; and to explain to each new age of men how their multiple strivings after the diverse objects of changing intellectual fashions are summed up in one real and attainable beyond.

One looks, in other words, in this kind of dogmatic and systematic theology to the real universal viewpoint, true and full conversion, and so to something which still lies ahead, to be filled up by us and others.

### Two senses of the statement

If the statement of the Epilogue means merely tailoring your positive research on Scripture to meet the demands of your dogma, a plague upon it. If it means constantly reinterpreting both Scripture and dogma in the light of truth as known, good for it. Lonergan's phrasing on page 740 at first sight seems open to either of these two possibilities. Theologians with a concern for Scripture are horrified at the mere thought of the first. But they could hardly hesitate before the second.

Put another way, grasping the universal viewpoint is not merely clinging to what you have and defending it. It is grasping a principle of criticism which will operate to purify whatever you hold or think you hold (e.g. homoousion,[54] redemption[55]).

A dogmatic decision is the true sense of Scripture—if so interpreted that it truly manifests the universal viewpoint. But the mere words of any given dogmatic decision don't give you that. They give you something you accept in faith as susceptible of being taken that way—even before you are sure how to do it. Part of the work of the systematic theologian is seeing and showing how the dogmas are susceptible of such interpretation.

But since the dogmas are (believed to be) about the true and the real; and since Scripture (as true, in its specialised but admitted value as norm of expressed faith) is also (believed to be) about the true and the real—it follows that there is a true sense of Scripture and there is a true sense of every dogma and these two ultimately correspond.

Put still another way: acceptance of these formulations (dogmatic *or* scriptural) is within this group for the ends of this group. But the group has been assented to (identified) as a locus of God's action and a way to God. This identification itself and adherence to the end is the true norm of interpretation. The texts really mean—in the group, as God's word to the group

—that which truly leads to God. Narrowing, closing, backsliding, particularist interpretation all are false in the group for they are inconsistent with reality, obstacles to conversion, and the group is using them to affirm reality and achieve conversion. The search for their 'true meaning' is then identical with the search for truth, for being, for God. It is a continual call to openness and conversion. And as such those who devote their lives to the study of the Scriptures can profit from it as much as anyone else.

## CONCLUSION ON SCRIPTURE AS SOURCE

Within these patterns then, in what sense can we say that Scripture is the source of theology?

1. First and most importantly it is the source of theology in the sense that it is, within this religious tradition, a constitutive part of religious living. This community, this faith-group, passes it on from generation to generation to be read as a part of life in faith. In the reading, Scripture does what it is intended to do: provides a fleshed-out embodiment of the basic elements of the divine solution to the problem of evil. As such it operates on many levels, and much more often on the artistic, poetic, sensible, emotional, mystical than on the intellectual. To one reading within the faith-community under the simple traditional point of view that Scripture is the word of God, effects occur which are not a matter of rational reflection, speculation, or systematisation.

This use of Scripture, however, the one most essential to Christian religion, is possible only if technical experts are at hand who by their research can attain the common-sense meanings that the documents of Scripture had at the time of their creation and acceptance by the faith-community as word of God. For only men with such knowledge can—with appropriate further skills in communication—make it possible for continuing generations of Christians to read these Scriptures in such a way that they can receive their emotional impact, the full psychic force needed if the solution is to become effective in personal living. Constant 'translation' is needed,[56] and it can be done only by one who can 'recapture the mentality for which the books of the Old and New Testament were written . . .'[57] The religious use is the fundamental and the right use of the Scriptures in religion. The detailed studying of historical, geographical, genealogical, philological, archaeological minutiae by some is necessary to make active reading possible for all. There is no theological justification at all for the use of the Scriptures as a mine from which propositions are drawn which can then be— simply because so drawn, simply because 'the Bible says so'— taken by themselves separately from Scripture, used for study, analysis, catechising, the foundations of new systems, or to furnish explanatory information in astronomy, geology, history, biology, sociology, politics, philosophy or theology.

Scripture, when put to its fundamentally right use is technically a source of theology in the sense that it is a part of religion.[58] And theology is a reflection on religion.[59]

2. Among religious-minded people, of course, questions of historical interest and concern arise. What are our origins? How were things, so far back? These questions are on the level of science and theory and they are already specialised, spontaneously though they may seem to arise for men of this generation. Of course they can be answered only by unhindered positive scientific research and only by well-informed experts, progressing in knowledge according to the ordinary laws of progress in science.[60]

3. Among religious people of a certain culture, another specialised question arises: why does the teaching of our beliefs take so many different forms? Both the diversity within the Scriptures and then even more the diversity through the ages strikes one. When it does, the Scripture becomes material for the dogmatic theologian. It presents him with one more common-sense point of view once current in the Church. So do the writings of the Fathers; so do the medieval theologians; so do the Councils of the Church. He tries to understand what is the same in all this diversity.

How does he know there is something the same? This is his faith-conviction. There must be something the same since the Councils when they are defining, and the Scriptures when affirming—no matter under what bizarre metaphors—are looked on in the community as bearers of God's word, serious, meaning to be not just entertaining but talking about reality. And there is only one reality.[61]

But this cannot be reducing Scripture to conformity to the later dogmas, nor dogmas to conform to the Scriptures. It must be explaining both Scripture and definitive dogmas in the best

14

possible senses, senses conformable to the ultimate standards of truth, the theologically transformed universal viewpoint: i.e., to what can be intelligently understood and reasonably affirmed by a mind open to the possibilities of the transcendent, to the call to conversion, to the understanding and affirmation of the whole universe and all the possibilities of human development as the gift of a loving God.

This specialised use of Scripture cannot ignore historical fact. Among the things it must account for are *all* the facts as to what these things meant in their times and places . . . and this again it gets only from the technical positively researching experts.

4. Among religious-minded people, there soon arises the specialised question: what in all this is essential? When it does, some theologians must devote themselves to it systematically. In their work:

(a) they must take full account of all the data from positive historical research, simply because they want their work to have scientific validity;

(b) they must remain within the limits of the religious consciousness of the faith-community for which they work. In the present mind of the Christian faith group, that means in general that they must not violate directly what are or are thought to be affirmations of the sacred Scriptures, because this would be an offence to the religious sense and ignore the constitutive role of the Scriptures in Christian living as the word of God. Departures from the historically verifiable meaning of the Scriptures are much more easily tolerated, at least until that meaning becomes popularly known. But even departures from the text can be accepted where popular common sense, even among the most religious, has come to see that what the scriptural author affirms is false (e.g., patent historical errors, geographical, historical, biological, astronomical, etc.). In general they have to keep as close as possible to the words and, if possible, to the original sense while at the same time interpreting as favourably as possible in the light of the universal viewpoint.

Within the Catholic faith-community, by the same reasoning, they must not violate the clear wording of fixed dogmas either, for it would be a violation of the general religious consciousness of the Catholic faith group at the present time to do so. In general they must stay as close as possible to the words and, if possible, to the original sense while at the same time interpreting as favourably as possible in the light of the universal viewpoint;

(c) they must clarify the universal viewpoint—that is, they must continually and progressively by honest reflection, by openness to data from all the human sciences, by attempting to live in faith and hope and love, attempt to sharpen their grasp of the implications of the phrase: 'whatever can be intelligently understood and reasonably affirmed by a mind open to the transcendent, to the continuing call to conversion, to the understanding and affirmation of the universe and the possibilities of human development as gift of a loving God.' They must take into account, in the light of understanding and reason and freely chosen openness to conversion, the whole effort of man to transcend self, the movements through history of men towards God, and try to express this in better and better clarified and sharpened categories of the mind and conversion.[62]

5. What then is 'biblical theology'? In 1961 (*De Deo Trino*, Pars Analytica 1961, p. 10, note 6—omitted in later editions) Lonergan made it merely a subdivision of doctrinal and sacred history whose 'biblical categories' deserve no more attention than other examples of undifferentiated consciousness. Most biblical theologians would hardly be satisfied with this. They are not merely recording how things were, they are looking for God's word to the people of today. And they feel from experience that they are often able to speak to people more effectively than can the classical theologians.

This rapport with the people might of course be no more than a result of the material they work with, material written from an undifferentiated consciousness having a strong appeal for the undifferentiated consciousness of the common man. But biblical theologians commonly feel there is more to it than that. They feel their material shows the power it does because it is more directly and truly the word of God than that of the classical theologians. Is there any justification for their point of view in Lonergan's system?

First of all, some distinctions have to be made. Not all exegetes are biblical theologians nor do they want to be; not all biblical theology is good exegesis or good theology, nor do all who call themselves biblical theologians deserve the name. (The cross implied in these reservations must be borne in all sciences, even classical theology.)

The move to genuine biblical theology began, I believe, when men with some expertise in the history and culture, with some familiarity with the biblical books through constant use, some understanding of them through personal openness to conversion, and with perhaps some experience in attempting to communicate the common-sense meaning of those books to people today, came gradually to realise how much the biblical books themselves aimed at the conversion of their readers. Seeing that the books were not primarily informational but conversion-orientated, they began to wonder why seminary preparation of ministers of the gospel should give several years to learning the details of dogmatic disputes remotely connected with conversion, when the world is so far from having heard the Christian call to radical conversion and when the biblical authors show such concern with it? Could not theology be so organised that it did centre on conversion—on trust, on self-sacrificing love, on forgiveness, etc.? Since the dogmas were originally subordinate to the life, could not theology centre on the life and bring in the dogmas as later reflective developments of specialised questions which arise when one wonders why one should be faithful to this way of life?

When such men say 'biblical categories' they mean such terms and divisions of theological material as will continually lead the student of theology back to the Bible, to be read and listened to as a call to conversion and to lead him back to the realisation that he belongs to a community which reads and listens to this Bible in faith as word of God; that is, as instrument par excellence of God's call to conversion.

Does this fit Lonergan's analysis? Most of the times Lonergan mentions biblical theology he seems to be reacting to exaggerations and abuses. Besides, he speaks in a context of trying to show the need and use for dogmatic and systematic theology, the seminal questions of which will not disappear no matter how bibically orientated one becomes. Again, many of his earlier treatments of how 'the theologian' uses Scripture (cf. note 2 a) are really limited to the dogmatic or systematic theologian. 'Functional Specialties' has indicated how incomplete a consideration that is.

In practice, Lonergan shows himself in his treatises quite aware of the function of theology about which I am speaking. He tends to move heavily into Scripture, towards the end of a treatise, weaving texts together in what are almost prose poems. He tends at the same time to make his treatise climax with the practical, some aspect of the Christian solution to the problem of evil (cf. note 62).

Theoretically, the place it would fit, I would say, in his system is as a constitutive part of living religion—on which therefore theology of its nature is bound to reflect. In that place, it is even possible that biblical concerns would become organisational in theology as a whole.

Even so, a few cautions would have to be given:

(*a*) Biblical theology does not start from the bare text, any more than exegesis does.

(*b*) It does not advance by mere scientific addition of fact to fact any more than any other philosophy or theology does.

(*c*) It cannot speak in purely biblical categories, respecting fully the differences between various parts of the Bible, unless it is willing to settle for repeating the text of the Bible.

(*d*) As soon as it ceases being mere history and undertakes to speak to the people of today, biblical theology, as much as any other theology, will include and be influenced by the 'conversion or non-conversion', the 'basic orientations and attitudes' of the biblical theologian who is writing it. These attitudes and orientations must themselves be studied and justified, and the study of them will not be biblical theology.

(*e*) Biblical theology stands in constant danger of being turned into another classical theology: e.g., when it is so used as to presuppose that the Bible *as* word of God is a source of information; when suggestions are made that theology's best hope for the future is to set about exploring those biblical images which past theology has left relatively neglected; when it is forgotten that 'salvation history', 'eschatology', etc. (and even 'covenant' etc. when used to analyse books in which the word itself does not appear) are really no more biblical than 'homoousion'.

# Some Critical Thoughts on 'Functional Specialties in Theology'

## KARL RAHNER

JUDGING from the first footnote, it may perhaps be expected that in this article Lonergan gives the core of his idea on theological methods, to be presented in more detail in his forthcoming book *Method in Theology*. For according to this footnote, this article forms the second chapter of the book, while the first chapter seems only to treat scientific method in general, giving illustrations from the natural sciences and from pre-scientific cognitive operations, and the chapters which follow chapter 2 are to present the eight functional specialties in theology in detail (cf. notes 1 and 2).

Lonergan's theological methodology seems to me to be *so generic that it really fits every science*, and hence is not the methodology of theology as such, but only a very general methodology of science in general, illustrated with examples taken from theology. It could be said at most, it seems to me, that the methodology of Christian theology which Lonergan presents (and it is Christian theology that he means) represents the methodology with which every 'ideology' (used here in a neutral sense) of every society is brought to its own full self-understanding.

When it is said that Lonergan's methodology does not bring to conscious reflection what is specific in the method of Christian theology, this statement does not imply any objection to the fact that Lonergan already presupposes Christian theology actually at work and orientated to its own subject-matter. This it does presuppose, and rightly so, of course. Nor is our statement really aimed at the fact that the presupposed theological disciplines are formally or 'functionally' systematised by Lonergan in a very discerning way, and are thereby clarified in their differences and in their connections. The point of my thesis is rather that in this legitimate structuring of the one theology into its functional specialties, what is specific about Christian theology in its subject-matter, and, therefore, also in its method, actually gets lost, or does not find expression.

I think that the old thesis that the subject-matter itself prescribes the method by which it is to be known is still correct. This simple thesis, of course, does not forbid us to reflect more precisely and more radically upon a *reciprocal* relationship of dependence between the object of knowledge and the (*a priori*, transcendental, or whatever else one might call it) method that is antecedent to the object. But if theology has already considered its object *before* it reflects at all upon its own method, upon the conditions that make it possible, and upon its functional process (although Lonergan knows and presupposes this), then the method of Christian theology—if not only what it has in common with all other sciences, but also what is peculiar to it, its own specific essence, is to be given expression—cannot be described, analysed and understood in its unity and in the plurality of its specialties without beginning with what is peculiar to Christian theology, with its own subject-matter. But it is this that I miss radically in Lonergan's article.

To put this more precisely, Lonergan's theological method abstracts (*a*) from the quite peculiar and unique relationship to the concrete person, Jesus, which is proper not only to Christian faith and life, but through them to Christian theology too. Since this relationship is of a unique and peculiar kind, it follows just from this that theology has a peculiarity which other sciences simply do not have. Lonergan's methodology abstracts (*b*) from the fundamental fact that all theological statements *as theological* are related to God not as to some object or other within the field of categorical objects, but as to the incomprehensible *mystery* which can never be subsumed under the objects of the other sciences in a similar method. A theological method would have to make clear and legitimate the peculiarity of the discourse which this entails, namely, discourse precisely about God as such, as distinguished from the discourse of all the other sciences. But I can discover nothing of this in Lonergan's outline of theological method. The words 'God' and 'Jesus Christ' do indeed appear in his article, but only as designations of material objects with which the science of theology, as distinct from other sciences, is occupied, not as words from whose content the peculiarity of theological *method* as such must be determined, and which, therefore, designate something like formal objects of theology (or, in the unity of the two, *the* formal object of theology).

Thus it seems to me, on the one hand, that there is no objection to defining theological method from a general (perhaps 'Anglo-Saxon') theory of science, presupposing that this definition remains conscious of its generic or 'analogous' character. But, on the other hand, it seems to me that a more specific ('European', if you will) definition of theological method has not thereby become superfluous. It could perhaps be said that what Lonergan says, when it is somewhat more precisely applied to theology, is a modern (and better) counterpart to the *loci theologici* of Melchior Cano, and hence, in so far as it is a transposition of the classical *topoi* into functional categories, it deserves our praise, especially since Catholic teaching on theological method right up to most recent times seems hardly to have moved beyond Cano. But all of this does not seem to me to take the place of, nor to finish with, this problematic as it is treated under the heading 'hermeneutics' especially in today's Protestant theology.

Let me briefly call attention to yet another aspect of possible criticism. Lonergan, indeed, is aware of the merely dynamic unity of this kind of functional specialties in theology, which move only asymptotically towards a completed static unity of an ideal kind. But he does not seem to me to have reflected upon the historically conditioned nature of his idea of theology conceived in the light of his theory of science. It could be that a future theology, or a particular theology within a pluralism of theologies, will not find such a theory of science ideal for theology and will not want to adapt it, and will even be justified in this course at a particular time and in a particular historical situation. Perhaps this must be considered, even if one gladly concedes that in Lonergan these functional specialties in theology are so formal and so broad that very different theologies with their (more concretely conceived) methodologies can fit within his scheme.

These critical remarks are in no way intended to dispute the fact that, *sensu positivo non exclusivo*, most of what Lonergan says about the method of theology really applies to theology, or should apply. What he says also and correctly calls attention to many gaps and omissions in Catholic theology as it actually exists today.

# Lonergan's Foundational Theology: an Interpretation and a Critique

## DAVID TRACY

THIS paper will attempt an interpretation of Bernard Lonergan's crucial notion of the contemporary problem of a foundational theology. I will argue that there remains an ambiguity in Lonergan's use of the expression 'foundational' which should be clarified if the enterprise which Fr Lonergan has set for himself is to be successful. Briefly stated, I will argue that 'foundational' theology has two meanings in Lonergan's recent work, one of which has been successfully resolved through the notion of functional specialties and the second of which (viz., the critical-epistemological-metaphysical grounding of the entire theological enterprise as *theo*-logical) has not been resolved nor is it likely to be so unless some critical questions and clarifications of Lonergan's intentions at that point are introduced.

Perhaps the most difficult part of clarifying and *a fortiori* of justifying my comments on the latter aspect is the series of contexts which I believe must be understood to interpret properly Lonergan's brief comments to date on the subject.[1] For this reason I have utilised in section I of this paper the more important contexts demanding such understanding, as I have employed them in my prior interpretation of Lonergan. I regret the complexity of the procedure but, after several 'simpler' attempts, I arrived at an acceptance of the wisdom of the hermeneutic rule that whenever interpreting a major thinker on a major question, the context(s) of the discussion must be as carefully delineated as possible. The first two sections of this paper, therefore, will attempt to communicate those prior 'Lonerganian' contexts. The third section will attempt to explicitate and criticise Lonergan's own understanding of the nature of theological language in the contemporary context.

As I view Lonergan's enterprise, the 'foundational' problem

bears two principal aspects: first, the widely recognised need for theologians to differentiate and interrelate the various theological specialisations; secondly, the need to differentiate and develop the conditions of the possibility of strictly theo-logical speech—a need which the recently eclipsed radical theology debate expressed most dramatically if not most fruitfully.

Accordingly, this paper will discuss that dual aspect of the methodological problem: a first and fairly expansive section will expose and accept the resolution of the horizontal or inter-relational side of the problem as it has been developed over the years by Bernard Lonergan's notion of theology as a self-structuring unity comprised of eight functional specialisations; a second and briefer section will then assume that first eightfold context as the proper one for the discussion of the 'vertical' problem of strictly contemporary theo-logical speech or, to follow the interpretation, the second meaning of a 'foundational' theology.

And precisely that second meaning of 'foundational' theology in Lonergan's enterprise is what I should like to call to the reader's critical attention. For I find myself in an ambivalent relationship to Lonergan's method for contemporary theology. On the one hand, I consider that his notion of theology as comprised of eight functional specialties is convincing as both a differentiated and an integrated articulation of the present theological moment (as I likewise find critically convincing his argument for intelligent human consciousness as itself a self-structuring dynamic unity of four levels). On the other hand, I find his articulation of the nature of the foundational task for contemporary theology on the 'fourth level' of consciousness to be highly problematic. Yet I remain convinced that Lonergan's articulation of the eight functional specialties comprising theology is precisely the context for reformulating (in a now more differentiated fashion) the 'foundational' problem of recent radical theology. The third section of this paper, therefore, attempts an alternative formulation.

## I. LONERGAN'S CONTEXT: THE HISTORY OF THEOLOGY AS THE DEVELOPMENT OF FUNDAMENTAL 'EXIGENCIES'

Probably the most helpful way to indicate both the continuity and the difference which Lonergan's later work on the method and foundations of religion and theology involve would be to recall Lonergan's own development on the nature of cognitive meaning.[2] Indeed, only a firm grasp of Lonergan's analysis of cognitive development in the medieval and modern periods will provide his interpreters with the conditions for the possibility of understanding his later and more contemporaneously relevant work. For the methodological and transcendent exigencies to be discussed below only emerge as genuine exigencies for Lonergan in the context of his prior differentiation of the systematic and critical exigencies, both of which are developed in the 'narrower' context of the meaning of cognitive meaning especially in its most strictly scientific form. For the methodological exigence, in Lonergan's precise sense of that term, is only an exigence for the genuinely critical inquirer. And the nature of the transcendent exigence for the context in which Lonergan now speaks is an exigence and a problem only for the highly differentiated consciousness of Western man.

Indeed, Lonergan's own intellectual development is perhaps best understood in terms of the four exigencies (systematic, critical, methodical, transcendent) expressing the movement from level to level of self-transcendence. Since the principal concern of this paper, however, is the work of the 'later' Lonergan in method and on the nature of theology, the earlier steps of his career must be somewhat foreshortened. In this context, Lonergan's own intellectual development can be interpreted as one man's attempt to come to terms with the developments of the systematic, critical, methodical and transcendent exigencies in the Western theological tradition. First, then, the systematic: Lonergan's early work in Aquinas is familiar territory to the historian of Thomist hermeneutics. To recall this first work in *Gratia Operans* one may say that Lonergan's chief personal discovery was his realisation of the possibility of a strictly theoretical approach to theology. That discovery required an inquiry into the entire medieval period from Anselm's questioning spirit through Abelard's dialectics, through the medieval development of the theoretical techniques of the *quaestio* and the books of sentences up to the later medieval achievement of the *summae*. For the finest medieval achievement, the *summa*, is not just a set of unrelated questions and answers but represents rather what the Germans have named a *Begrifflichkeit*, i.e. a related set of concepts, theorems, operations and techniques which may define one's theoretic horizon. In other words, the precise meaning accorded the word 'theology' in the medieval period is a particular expression of a more general human—or at least Western—phenomenon. To state the problem in its simplest terms one may employ Piaget's vocabulary and say that the original and originating human consciousness is an undifferentiated one. However, the undifferentiated mind's attempts to meet the exigencies of its ever further questions can eventually result (as in fact it did in the Greek breakthrough to *logos*) in the differentiation of a purely intellectual pattern of experience. In short, one becomes differentiated in the measure that one's questions become precise and technical (e.g. Socrates' search for a universal definition of justice), one's demands become strictly theoretical and one's answers can be ordered into an interrelated context (e.g. Aristotle's metaphysics). In that case, the differentiated subject no longer finds himself in one 'world' but in two: the world of everyday common sense and the world of theory.

And precisely that is what the medieval theological achievement meant for Lonergan: the ability to express religious meaning theoretically through the systematic use of the categories and techniques made available by the impact of the recently-discovered Graeco-Arabic culture upon the religious traditions of Christianity. Its finest and most rigorous achievement remains Aquinas' *Summa* with their precise and systematic (i.e. theoretic) structuring of the insights of what even non-Thomists would now admit was a genuinely religious consciousness.

Yet the development of the systematic exigence in differentiated Western consciousness and the resultant displacement towards system serve to give rise to differing effects. On the one hand, they expose the possibility of freeing man from the excessive creativity of his imagination by the needed critique of a rational control of meaning via scientific definition. On the other hand, such a differentiation can and does provoke a crisis by now familiar to Western man. For besides meeting with the incomprehension of undifferentiated consciousness (as, for example, in the 'Augustinian' reaction to Aquinas' use of the Aristotelian categories), the differentiated consciousness gradually uncovers a problem all its own. The full thematic realisation of the crises provoked by that shift does not come to expression in Aquinas himself. For even if (as Metz argues in the *Christliche Antropozen-trik* and Lonergan himself argues in the *Verbum* articles) the performance of Aquinas is truly critical (i.e. with a firm grasp of psychological fact and epistemological reality), it nonetheless remains true that the thematisation of that performance in Aquinas is made in basically metaphysical, not epistemological, terms. Hence, Aquinas, however anthropocentric, is neither Descartes nor Kant but remains a medieval man for whom the systematic exigence finds expression in his Aristotelian-Neo-platonist-Thomist categories and with sure if unthematised intellectual and religious interiority.

In its thematic expression, therefore, the full force of the problem of relating the two worlds of common sense and theory was not a medieval problem. It could not be solved in medieval terms nor within the medieval context. For that reason, Lonergan turned his attention to the meaning of the post-Kantian critical exigence. To meet that exigence, *Insight* was written. The intellectual context with which *Insight* was concerned is exceed-ingly complex. But however complex these scientific, Kantian, and Hegelian origins, it will suffice for present purposes to insist upon the rise and the meaning of the critical exigence for the Lonergan of *Insight*.

In essence, then, for Lonergan the differentiated consciousness recognises the existence of a problem that is simply not present to an undifferentiated one, viz., how is one to relate these two very different languages (common sense and theory) and their resultant two very different worlds (things-in-relation-to-oneself and things-in-relation-to-one-another). In a genuinely critical attempt to face this problem, one is thrown back, with Kant and the entire modern tradition, from the world of theory into the world of the subject's own interiority. For the differentiated inquirer's attempt to relate his two languages and his two worlds forces him to investigate the possible operations grounding both. In other words, the critical inquirer is faced with three inescapable and interrelated questions: what am I doing when I'm knowing? (cognitional theory); why is doing that knowing? (epistemology) and what do I know when I do that? (metaphysics).[3] The responses of *Insight* to these questions are by now well known. For Lonergan, the possibility of the critical breakthrough is not the possibility of easy talk about intuition but only of exact speech on the appropriation of one's rational self-consciousness in its normative operations, structures and procedures. In its technical expression (self-affirmation as a virtually unconditioned) that self-appropriation resembles the world of theory. But in its own fundamental moment it expresses a quite distinct exigence. For it is the critical exigence alone which forces the subject to that level of heightened awareness present in the purely intellectual pattern of experience that can make him critically aware of his operations in their normative structures and procedures. Among other factors, that exigence recognises that the classical control of meaning via theory must now yield place to the critical control of meaning via a thematic grasp of intellect in its normative structures, operations and procedures.

And if that critical exigence reaches the level of self-affirmation, it reveals to the critical subject the need and the possibility of yet another exigence, the methodical one. For what is method in the critical meaning of that word? May it not be defined as the normative (as critical) pattern of recurrent and related operations yielding progressive and cumulative results? And is not any science worthy of the name principally committed not to its results but to its methods? A critical science, moreover (i.e. philosophy) may attempt what is known as transcendental method. One way of expressing Lonergan's employment of transcendental method is to recall the fact that unlike other methods which exploit the opportunity of particular fields, transcendental method (in *Insight*) aims at meeting the exigencies and exploiting the opportunities of the human mind itself.

Nor is that reality as obscure as the name may at first glance seem to indicate. As a matter of fact, in one sense, for Lonergan, everyone knows and observes transcendental method. We observe it inasmuch as we are attentive, intelligent, reasonable and responsible—in short, inasmuch as we are true to the self-transcending demands of our intelligence. In another sense, of course, it is quite difficult to be at home in transcendental method. For it is not necessarily accomplished by reading books (including *Insight*) nor by listening to lectures (including Socrates') nor by analysing language (including scientific). Rather it is achieved in its primal and originating moment only by a personal heightening of one's own consciousness and, in its second and correlative moment, by a thematisation of that consciousness. It is, in its essence, something which no man can do for another but each must be willing to do for himself. *Insight*, in other words, does not impose a Lonerganian system but invites the reader to achieve his own self-appropriation. That achievement, moreover, is a gradual one: for in accordance with the moving viewpoint of *Insight* itself, in the earlier section ('Insight as Activity') the reader (through a set of exercises provided by mathematical, scientific and common-sense examples) is led to experience the basic operations of rational consciousness as experience, understanding and judgement. Gradually too he begins to understand the unity and structural interrelatedness of his experienced experience, understanding and judgement. And finally—in the central moment of self-affirmation—the reader is enabled to affirm his understanding of his experienced experience, understanding and judgement. In the fourth stage of such personal intentional self-transcendence, he may further resolve to conform to the normative component in his operations by forcing his action to follow his knowledge.

In summary, Lonergan's own intellectual development—up to the present insistence upon the importance of the new context of historical consciousness—reveals the possibilities and the fruits of his previous commitment to the systematic and critical exigencies. For unless the systematic exigence is clearly differentiated (as in the original Greek accomplishment, as in the medieval achievement of Aquinas, as in the scientific and critical revolutions of modern consciousness), the imperatives of the critical exigence will not even be experienced. And unless a truly critical exigence is allowed full range and the thematisation of its resultant interiority completed, the full meaning of that turn to methodology in Lonergan's precise sense cannot be understood.

II: METHOD AS FOUNDATION—THEOLOGY AS A SELF-
STRUCTURING UNITY OF EIGHT FUNCTIONAL SPECIALTIES

Within the dual horizon of a prior differentiation of the systematic and critical exigencies and of the new theological context of historical consciousness with its multi-levelled dimensions of meaning, the properly methodical exigence, in Lonergan's sense, becomes the foundational theological problematic.

To this question Lonergan has, with increasing frequency, devoted his major attention from 1959 to the present.[4] Indeed, the question of method in the human sciences, philosophy and theology is, for many of their practitioners, the principal question on the present horizon. As the gains of the phenomenological movement have made especially clear, the method employed is the key to all the products of any discipline. But only those who have worked through the systematic and critical exigencies have an adequate notion of the nature of the methodological problem as foundational in Lonergan's first use of the term. For others it tends to become a secondary or even a relatively unimportant problem. It sounds to them (as Gadamer reminds us) as if one were seeking for some new rules (usually logical) that could be be followed blindly by any 'hewer of wood and drawer of water'. Indeed, to many it sounds disturbingly like the last gasp of a dying classical culture. Now, if the contemporary search for method were in fact a search for 'new' logical rules whence one might deduce one's conclusions, then that distrust would be well-earned. Yet the fact is that the contemporary search for method, by and large, is nothing of the sort.

In Lonergan's case, to be more specific, the methodological search is neither for new rules nor for a new 'system' but for a basic pattern whence all rules can be derived. That pattern will include the logic of the classical period but must add the contemporary scientific interest in inquiry, observation, discovery, experiment, synthesis and verification. It further demands a context wherein the multi-dimensional levels of meaning (and not only scientific meaning) may find an intrinsic place in the analysis. It might be helpful to note that Lonergan is not (even in *Insight*) simply analysing in an Aristotelian manner a consciously successful science (viz., physics) and then judging all other disciplines as scientific or not by their degree of similarity to physics. Indeed, he has shown that he is not unaware of the gains of the *Geisteswisschenschaften* controversy nor of the methodological complexities involved for anyone who recognises the multi-dimensional horizon of historical consciousness.[5] Rather Lonergan's own development (in *Insight*) has been to derive a preliminary notion of method from the successful empirical sciences (classical and statistical heuristic methods) and to proceed from there to cognitional theory. There he attempts to thematise the invariant properties of a method that may be called transcendental in the precise sense of self-affirmation and the consequent notions of being, objectivity, reality. From this thematisation he moves forward to try to determine the function of transcendental method in its relations to the particular methods of the various sciences. Within that context, therefore, method may be defined as a normative pattern of related and recurrent operations yielding cumulative and progressive results. This notion of a basic pattern is obviously the fundamental problem. And its nature must be to become a method in the generic sense given above while still maintaining its transcendental character. For basic method cannot be confined categorically to any generic or specific type of result or to limited fields but instead is central to all fields where the basic transcendentals (be intelligent, be reasonable, be responsible, develop and, if necessary, change) are operative. In short, a basic method would apply to all fields where the human mind in its invariant structure, procedures and operations is operative including, therefore, theology.

To conceive theology in terms of Lonergan's notion of method, therefore, is not to ask a second-level question but a properly foundational one. To put this aspect of the foundational theological problematic in its strictest terms: can the theologian determine a basic pattern for all the patterns of related and recurrent operations involved in the theological task? Can he determine a fundamental theological method which will allow all practitioners to collaborate systematically with one another? Can he ground that pattern in a transcendental method which is not open to fundamental revision?[6]

In the present theological situation, therefore, Lonergan argues that there exist two fundamental types of specialisation: field specialisation and subject specialisation. Field specialisation divides the data to be examined: the Scriptures, the Fathers, the Councils, the medieval, renaissance, reformation, enlightenment, modern, or contemporary periods. Within each of these there are further specialisations: e.g. Scriptures—Old Testament, inter-testamental period, New Testament; Old Testament—laws, prophets, writings, etc., etc. All these specialisations increase their scope as the enormous amount of archaeological and textual materials accumulate into ever more probably accurate critical editions. Subject specialisation, on the other hand, performs a distinct task: it divides and studies the results to be taught in the different departments, subjects and courses. Thus it is that every

15

complete theological curriculum must include Semitic languages, Hebrew history, religions of the Ancient Near East, New Testament theologies, the theologies of the apostolic Fathers, the theology of the Councils and so on. When one recognises both types of specialisation as legitimate and indeed necessary, there gradually emerges a recognition of the need, herein labelled methodologically foundational, to find a way to differentiate the stages in the single process from data to results. Such a need is fulfilled for Lonergan by his development of what he names 'functional specialisation', i.e. a specialisation which deals directly with neither data nor results but seeks to distinguish the *stages in the process* from data to results. Each stage, moreover, operates functionally towards the next for at each stage there is a different pattern of related and recurrent operations applied to the results of the preceding stage. Each successive stage presupposes the results of the preceding one and complements them by moving them that much closer to the final goal. To clarify this discussion, a table is given below of the eight-fold functional specialties which define, for Lonergan, the theological task:

*Table showing two phases of theology combined with four levels of consciousness*

| Structure of Consciousness | Mediating Theology | Mediated Theology | |
|---|---|---|---|
| deliberation | (4) dialectic | foundations | (5) |
| judgement | (3) history | doctrines | (6) |
| understanding | (2) interpretation | systematics | (7) |
| experience | (1) research | communications | (8) |

Indeed, on a properly theoretical and methodical level, one might say that *a priori* conditions for the possibility of the eight-fold functional specialties can be established. In the first place theology operates in two phases. There are various ways by which one might express the two phases. Three of them will be symbolised here: in biblical categories one listens to the word in the first phase and bears witness to it in the second; in medieval categories, one can describe the movement as that from the *lectio* (reading) to the *quaestio* (technical questions raised by and to the readings); in more contemporary categories, one would describe the historically conscious man as, first, encountering the past and then taking his stand towards the future. The first phase, then (research-interpretation-history-dialectic) is an attempt to encounter the Judaeo Christian past in its multi-dimensional, genetic-dialectic development, while the second phase (from one's articulation of one's foundations through doctrines, systematics and communications) is one's own attempt to speak to the present and the impending future from within a basic theological horizon.

In the second place, the four levels prior to each phase are correlative to the four functional and invariant levels of consciousness uncovered and thematised by transcendental method. Those four levels of consciousness, as analysed in *Insight*, pursue four distinct but interrelated goals. For in either the spontaneous inquiry of common sense or the methodical labour of science, the inquirer always moves through four levels: he tries to establish the data (experience); he then tries to understand them (understanding); he next attempts to establish the facts (judgement); and finally, he makes his decision on what is to be done about his knowledge (decision—action). Common sense, as Lonergan defines it, pursues all four without sharply distinguishing among them. Scientific inquiry, on the contrary, consciously uses all four levels first in pursuit of the first goal (what are the data?); then in pursuit of the second; then of the third; and then of the fourth. As the scientist moves to the second, third and fourth levels, moreover, he must allow each level to presuppose the results of the former and complement them by pursuing the activity proper to that level. Once again, but now more exactly, one is involved in *Insight's* moving viewpoint to ever higher viewpoints.

Accordingly, if the relationship of these eight functional specialties to the fourfold levels of the structure of Lonergan's transcendental method is basically clear, a further clarity may be brought to bear on the discussion by elaborating the more exact meaning of each speciality in the common theological enterprise. The aim of the present discussion, moreover, will not be exhaustive but suggestive, not explanatory but descriptive.

*First, research:* the textual critic, for example, will determine with as high a degree of scientific probability as possible just what the relevant data of the Christian message and the Christian tradition are. In short, he will strive to establish (by all the scientific means available to him) critical editions of all relevant Christian texts.

*Second, interpretation:* the interpreter will first presuppose the relevant data established by the textual critic: he will next recognise that the data in question are not simply 'givens' (as in the empirical sciences) but involve and indeed are constituted by 'meanings'. He will then attempt to establish as accurately as possible and by means of all the scientific tools available to him (parallel texts, form criticism, redaction criticism, etc.) the precise meaning of the texts under discussion.

*Third, history:* the historian will first presuppose the meaning established by the interpreter. On his own, he will then complement the latter's work by using the best available historical criteria to establish just what as a matter of fact actually happened in particular events and just what was the basic movement going forward through all the varied interpretations used to communicate that event or series of events. In other words, there remains a ground of historical factuality which may not be interpreted away by even the most brilliant exegesis. That ground is uncovered by the critical judgements of the authentic historian as he attempts to determine as accurately as possible (e.g. the Warren Commission Report, or Trevor-Roper on *The Last Days of Hitler*) the ascertainable facts (i.e. the reality) of the event which provoked so many various interpretations. To return to a more theological context, anyone familiar with the intricacies involved in historical discussion of the meaning and/or factual status of the infancy narratives in the gospels or the far more important resurrection narratives will be fully familiar with the importance of the distinction employed here. It would be well to reconsider, however, how crucial is Lonergan's differentiation of the meaning element on the level of understanding-interpretation from the matter-of-fact, 'true meaning' element on the level of judgement-history. For Lonergan, it is that precise sense of critical differentiation which allows the theologian's work to be as critically as it is historically grounded. Without such a differentiation, he argues, the theologian's need for critical historical work and, within the limits this provides, for the historical events of the Christian tradition itself, can collapse under the heavy burden of a thousand interpretations.

Indeed, the still further differentiation of this level of judgement-history from the fourth level of decision becomes even more crucial in contemporary theology, as the *Historie-Geschichte* debate more than suggests. For as that debate developed, one witnessed a somewhat distressing scene: on the one hand, the seeming inability of several Roman Catholic and Anglican biblical and doctrinal scholars to rise to the decision-level of Bultmann's discussion of history as *Geschichte*; on the other hand, the spectacle of the incapacity of many existentialist theologians to appreciate either the discomfort of their 'salvation-history' or doctrinal colleagues or the possible epistemological ambiguities of their own decision-emphasis position. In purely theological terms, therefore, the epistemological-ontological status one accords the role of judgement is crucial. It is especially crucial for a religious tradition (viz., the Judaeo-Christian) which has historically insisted that its religious stance is grounded in certain historical facts.

*Fourth, dialectic:* Lonergan's notion of dialectic is a relatively simple, empirical one here, viz., the concrete unfolding of opposed but related principles modified by the actual unfolding. The notion, he argues, is needed since the theologian's work does not cease after he has established as accurately as possible the data, the interpretations and the historical facts and perspectives. For as every student of theology knows only too well, debates rage on every one of the prior three levels. There are, in the first place, different selections of data: is Scripture alone the data relevant to Christian inquiry? Or does there exist a tradition which must also be studied? If the second, then what is that tradition and what is its relationship to the Scriptures? Are they really one? Or distinct and separate? Or do there also exist other, less immediately Christian data which are or should be intrinsic to Christian theological inquiry?

In the second place, there are many different interpretations of the same data. To name only the most obvious, there exist a classical Lutheran, a Calvinist, an Anabaptist, an Anglican, a Roman Catholic, an Orthodox interpretation of the same New Testament data. Each of these interpretation's histories, in its turn, contains a whole history of past and present differing interpretations of the same data and an entire series of prophetic witnesses to the Christian fact. In such a context, the only way that the historically conscious contemporary theologian can remain faithful to the demands of his discipline is to operate within a genuinely dialectical context in the sense determined above.

As I understand Lonergan, then, the functional specialty 'dialectic' is a scientific way of dealing with the moral and religious event called 'conversion' from which alone, he argues, theology may authentically speak.[7] At that level, the theologian has the opportunity to encounter the religious situation as it is now and as it has been in a past mediated to him by his dialectical involvement with the authentic religious traditions.

It is precisely here, however, that the ambiguity mentioned earlier emerges. Since that ambiguity will be examined in the next section, here we might simply ask this question: is the 'religious' 'conversion' mediated here dogmatically or critically? The intellectual 'conversion' is clearly meant to be mediated critically (viz., by the self-affirmation of *Insight*). But what of religious conversion? Is it mediated by dialectical reflection upon the results of earlier historical theology—thereby *assuming* (as a dogmatic affirmation) the truth-value of the data (presumably religious) interpreted and critically investigated by the historian? Or is it, too, to be *critically* mediated, thus transcendentally justifying the use of religious—in fact of a specific religious— God-language? If the former alone be the case then Lonergan's enterprise may be dialectically *foundational* for a *collaborative methodological* theological enterprise for all those theologians (of whatever tradition) who accept an authoritative (and, in that sense, dogmatic) grounding for all genuine theological work. But it will not be for those (viz., in the Liberal, Modernist or neo-Liberal traditions) who demand a *critical* dialectical mediation of religious and theological meaning and language. The ambiguity is intensified in Lonergan's case, I submit, by the fact that *Insight* is precisely an attempt for a critical mediation of at least intellectual conversion and would seem, therefore, to *imply* a Liberal (in the sense of *critically* mediated) stance for religious conversion as well.

But, to return to the first sense of dialectics (viz., as methodologically collaborative) one may continue the discussion of the functional specialties. For Lonergan, at the level of decision-dialectic-conversion, therefore, the theological task proper to 'hearing', to 'lection', to 'encountering' the Christian past is realised. The next major need is to attempt to thematise.

*Fifth, foundations:* for Lonergan, the role of foundations as a theological specialty is to objectify the conversion into a basic horizon. As the category 'conversion' is central to the level of dialectic, so 'horizon' is to the level of foundations. The category 'horizon', as Lonergan employs it, is defined as a maximum field of vision from a determinate standpoint with objective and subjective poles, each one of which is determined by and determines the other. A basic horizon, moreover, possesses a basic subjective pole (intellectual, moral, religious and Christian conversions)[8] and an objective pole (as the thematisation of those conversions). Foundational theology, then, attempts to articulate the basic horizon from within which a theologian operates.

But we should note how the same ambiguity emerges for the category 'horizon' in foundations as for 'conversion' in dialectics, viz., is the basic horizon mediated in a thematic manner critically or dogmatically? One should further note that even if Lonergan's recent relative silence on 'Christian conversion as mediated in a thematic way' in favour of the thematisation of 'religious' conversion be employed the same problem is still present, viz., does it suffice for a foundational theology to thematise the dialectical conclusions of the dialectical, historical, hermeneutic and research results of empirical studies of religious traditions or does not the truth-value of any or all religious claims have to be critically defended? If the former alone be the task, then one has provided a collaborative foundational methodology for all those who share the assumptions of the truth-value of the religious (and *a fortiori* of the *theological*) but one has not *critically* grounded the *entire* enterprise—which is precisely what one would be led to expect as needed by the implicit logic (and actual nineteenth- and twentieth-century developments) of the fourth level of existential consciousness. It remains unclear to this interpreter, then, just where Lonergan is going or will go on this question of his understanding of 'foundational theology' but, as the next section will argue, his earlier and his more recent thought (in *Insight* and on religion) would seem to imply that he should not accept an authoritarian solution but rather attempt a critical one. For the present purposes, however, it should be sufficient to indicate that the relationship of foundations to dialectic is that of thematisation to conversion-meaning.

*Sixth, doctrines:* one should note, first of all, that for Lonergan doctrine becomes a properly *theological* question only after the work of the first five theological specialties has already been accomplished. One must have developed from data through interpretation, history, dialectics and foundations before the basic horizon is established whence one may understand that movement towards doctrine and system involved in the Christian community's development from what Lonergan has named the *quoad nos* of the Scriptures to the *quoad se* of the Councils. Secondly, the several Christian doctrines each demand analysis by the properly qualified textual critics, exegetes, historians, dialecticians, and 'foundational' theologians. On the foundational level, moreover, the presence of a thematised intellectual conversion is essential for understanding the nature of the doctrines precisely because its absence would not lead one to respect the movement of the *quoad se* as needed. Thirdly, the placement of the specialty 'doctrines' on the third level of consciousness is also, I believe, of considerable interest.[9] For just as with the 'facts' of history, doctrines are placed by Lonergan not on the level of experience or understanding or decisions but of judgement. In other words, doctrines *affirm* incompletely but truly (i.e. really) certain essential features of the Christian belief. Within the foundational horizon proper to the Christian theologian, doctrines can provide the minimal judgements and affirmations proper to the Christian's belief. And even granted the limitations and present inadequacies of the classical categories of the conciliar, patristic and medieval periods, it still remains true that the Greek movement to *theoria* (in present categories, the movement to and from intellectual conversion) allowed the Christian community then (as it might now) to clarify certain affirmations of its basic beliefs. The transposition, for example, from the nature-person categories of Chalcedon to the person-as-presence-in-the-world categories of a Rahner or a Schillebeeckx is a transposition which occurs only within a basic continuity with those affirmations which Christians (beginning with the New Testament 'Jesus is Lord') have traditionally made. Once again, therefore, the importance of Lonergan's critical analysis of the distinct nature of judgement for his handling of the related problems of history and doctrines cannot be overemphasised.

*Seventh, systematics:* the nature of systematics has already been articulated in the earlier discussion of Lonergan's interpretation of the medieval achievement. For there it was argued that the exact nature of the medieval achievement was its articulation of a strictly technical language and of rigorously theoretical techniques aimed at clarifying and explaining the scriptural and doctrinal beliefs of the Christian community. In short, it is imperative for the theologian at the systematic level of discussion to search out some technical language that might express as clearly as possible the intrinsically mysterious nature of the realities he affirms as believer. And even if the classical categories of an Aquinas or a Calvin are no longer adequate to that systematic task, this does not methodologically exempt the contemporary theologian (*if* he has resolved the *foundational* problematic) from the effort to achieve in the new scientific context what they achieved in theirs.

*Eighth, communications:* at this final level, the hotly debated problem named 'relevance' emerges. Indeed here the disciplines variously named catechetics or religious education or pastoral or ministerial theology must find their contemporary transformation. Certain central factors intrinsic to that transformation may be noted in this brief discussion. In the first place, the question of communication emerges as a properly theological question only after each of the first seven functional specialties has played its proper role. For no more than can intuitionist theories save the epistemological day, can imaginative leaps from 'Jesus' to the fabled man-in-the-street (or at the barricades) save theology as a critical discipline. In short, simplest solutions solve nothing in the long run for they only require the eventual re-emergence of the original and originating problem. In the second place, vague calls for a revised 'pastoral' theology will not suffice. Instead the theologians must learn to collaborate with the methods and the results of contemporary theoreticians in the fields of communications theory, comparative literature, political theory, psychology, sociology, cultural anthropology and the rest of the whole range of recently developed and developing human sciences. Otherwise even very good theology may yet continue to crash against the charge of irrelevance from non-theologians (or even from other theologians—as in Cox's sociological critique of Bultmann or Metz's political-historical critique of Rahner). In the third place, while there can be no pretence that any one theologian can master the methods of all seven of the preceding specialties, much less can he become an expert in all the various sciences which the level of communications includes. But he can learn (as Cox or Metz or Callahan show) to collaborate with human scientists, first in a genuinely theoretical way (by learning the science in its accepted procedures and results), and only then with theological applications.[10]

Such, as I understand it, is Lonergan's notion of functional specialties. It remains necessary, however, to discuss more explicitly the relationship of this to a successful contemporary foundation for theology.

### III: CONTEMPORARY THEOLOGICAL FOUNDATIONS: RELIGIOUS AND THEOLOGICAL MEANING AS GROUNDED CRITICALLY OR DOGMATICALLY

To reformulate the discussion thus far: there would seem to be two notions of 'foundational' theology operative in Lonergan's thought. The first, or more properly methodological one, is an attempt to differentiate and integrate the various theological disciplines by grounding those differentiations and subsequent integration in the differentiations (experience, understanding, judgement, decision) and integration (the self-structuring intentionality of the inquirer) of human consciousness itself. That problem is resolved for Lonergan by his development of the foundational notion of the theological enterprise as an intrinsically collaborative self-structuring unity comprised of eight *functional* specialties—and the latter differentiated and integrated precisely as *functional* in relationship to the 'invariant' structure of human consciousness (experience, understanding, judgement, decision). I would maintain that this understanding of theology does permit the methodological collaboration of the several disciplines and as such is a major contribution—and, in that precise methodological sense, a foundational one—to the entire theological community.[11] It does not, however, provide critical grounds for the enterprise itself—more precisely, for the truth-value of the claims to ultimacy of religious and explicitly theological language.

I realise that Lonergan need not perform this latter task if he wishes to declare the entire theological enterprise to be *grounded* in the authoritative claims of the Christian tradition. Certainly he was able to work out his own rigorously impressive (but pre-methodological) foundations for his Trinitarian and Christological theologies in precisely that way (i.e. by a defence of the generic demand for the dogmatic element in religious claims and the specific claims of the 'dogmatic realism' of the Roman Catholic doctrinal tradition).[12] If he chose, he could continue to develop those theological questions (and others) as systematic positions in his exact sense of the term and as grounded in the dogmatic principle of Roman Catholicism emerging from dialectics and thematised as *the* dogmatic realistic horizon in 'foundations'.[13]

But several Lonerganian themes would seem to indicate that this particular traditional resolution (in a far more sophisticated methodologically collaborative context, to be sure) should not be employed. I shall examine two such themes on the basis of the discussion of section I of this paper: First, if my earlier interpretation of the intrinsic connections between Lonergan's contexts for the history of theology (viz. the medieval, modern and contemporary) and the exigencies of human consciousness (viz. the systematic, critical and methodological respectively) be correct, then does not the explicitly contemporary methodological context (in Lonergan's sense) demand a *critical* grounding? In short, to resolve the explicitly contemporary theological problematic by means of an *ordering* (via functional specialties) of the various disciplines comprising the theological task should demand a critical resolution of the conditions for the possibility of the entire enterprise. Moreover, precisely that problematic (and *not* merely the problematic of dialectics and thematisation of the non-critically grounded results of research-interpretation and history) should emerge on the historically conscious fourth level of *Ex-sistenz* as *the* problematic of the entire discipline.[14] Otherwise (i.e. except in the case of *Insight's* critical thematisation of the nature of intellectual conversion) one is left with a thematisation of religious conversion methodologically faithful to the results of empirical and dialectical studies but not itself critically justified. But how, then, is 'foundations' clearly differentiated from 'systematics' since both would have to assume—on dogmatic not critical grounds—the dogmatic principle (and the resultant doctrinal traditions) as grounding them? The argument, then, is not that there is *no* difference between Lonergan's notion of systematics and, say, Aquinas' (the former is more historically *and* methodologically self-conscious) or, for that matter, between Lonergan's present notion of systematics and his former systematic theologies.[15] Rather the argument is that there remains no critical difference between Lonergan's present notion of foundations and his present notion of systematics except, possibly, that the latter would treat more specific questions and the former would treat more general (and in that precise sense more 'foundational') ones, e.g. Christian God-language. But—and this is the essential difficulty—both would assume their task to be developed not critically but dogmatically. This argument does *not* demand, I believe, that the dogmatic principle (to repeat, precisely as the articulation of the truth-value of religious claims) be rejected on a foundational level (i.e. a 'pure' Modernist position) but it does demand that it be critically justified.

Yet Lonergan, to my knowledge at least, seems relatively unconcerned in an explicit fashion with this crucial (indeed foundational) aspect of the problem. And yet it becomes increasingly difficult to understand why the logic of his own position would not force that to become *the* explicit foundational question for his theology. For if the methodological exigence presupposes the critical does not the contemporary methodological theological enterprise have as its central question the conditions of its own possibility? And Lonergan's own careful formulation of the relationships of the exigencies would seem to indicate, at the very least, a more careful and more adequate context for raising that foundational question than either the relatively undifferentiated 'Is God dead?' posing of the question or even the *relatively* contextually unsophisticated 'Does not the contemporary experience of secularity ultimately erode all claims to the truth of religious meanings and language?' For it is precisely Lonergan's rigorous formulation of the transcendental implications of the scientific ideals and methods peculiar to modernity and his post-*Insight* involvement in the problematic of historical consciousness that provide (i.e. as intellectual conversion thematised and as the fourth level explicitated as historically conscious) a highly sophisticated context for raising the question 'What, then, are the conditions for the possibility of religious and explicitly theological meanings?' as distinct from the question 'What is the most adequate thematisation of the religious conversion-meaning dialectically mediated from the results of the historically-conscious empirical study of religious traditions?'[16]

I would maintain, therefore, that the God-language employed by Lonergan's earlier systematic theology (viz. *Ipsum Intelligere* for general God-language or the analogy of intelligible emanations for explicitly Christian Trinitarian God-language)[17] would not necessarily be rendered erroneous but would be rendered *uncritically* grounded for contemporary theological foundations. In short, if one wished to employ it one would be compelled to defend it critically as would not be the case in traditional systematic theology.

And a similar but admittedly quite distinct problem would emerge for the God-language developed in chapter XIX of *Insight*.[18] First we might notice two related contextual problems: the chapter is articulated within the context of a scientific intelligibility open at once to a critical 'proportionate' metaphysics and a critical meaning of mystery. It is further articulated in the context of the question of ethical value. But neither the discussion of mystery nor the discussion of ethical value are developed as such for an explicitation of religious value. This may not prove to be the case in Lonergan's post-*Insight* volume, *Method In Theology*, where one finds listed in the chapter headings reformulated notions both of symbol (following a critique of Cassirer) and of moral values prior to a discussion of religious value. My presumption is, then, that Lonergan does recognise and will develop a notion of religious conversion within the context of the intellectual conversion of insight (including that of symbol)[19] and of moral conversion. The indications of the nature of his critical explicitation of religious value that have appeared in print thus far, however (viz. on 'being-in-love' as originating principle and on 'ultimate concern') are suggestive to be sure but not critically justified (nor, unless I misread him, are they claimed to be so justified). And within that context (viz. religious values as claiming truth about ultimate reality), the question of an explicitly God-language (and, *a fortiori*, of an explicitly Christian God-language) would have to be critically justified.

In the meantime, however, there remains the argument of chapter XIX of *Insight*. Yet one must note, contextually, that the argument for the existence of God would seem to emerge from an incompletely developed context, one which has not critically justified the truth-claim of religious meaning. One could reply to this contextual difficulty, I realise, that it is *merely* a contextual task, i.e. that desirable as such critical explicitation of religious meaning may be for a discussion of God-language, it is not necessary precisely because the religious meaning is an existential condition of the possibility of successfully responding to the question of the existence of God but not necessarily a transcendental condition of possibility. But this response would, I believe, be inadequate: for, in Lonergan's post-*Insight* development the phenomemon of historical consciousness is precisely what has given rise to the clearer differentiation of the fourth level of 'existential' consciousness and is precisely where the question of religion and of God is raised for contemporary man (and, therefore, for the contemporary theologian).[20]

Indeed these apprehensions about the nature of chapter XIX are increased, I submit, when one reads Lonergan's own interpretation of the relationship of that chapter's argument to traditional natural theology.[21] For he clearly states that the argument is a reformulation of the traditional argument with two critical differences. The first difference is clear and, I agree, critical: viz., a reformulation of causality from a critical and not immediately metaphysical viewpoint ('If being is completely *intelligible* . . .'). But the implications of the second difference are somewhat more difficult to understand, viz., that the argument is dependent upon the prior critical explicitation of the precise philosophical 'position' (as contrasted with all counter-positions). But what is implied here? Is the critical inquirer sufficient for the demonstration? Need he not already be moral? (And if so what is the *critical* meaning and justification of such moral 'conversion'?) Need he not already be religious? (And if so what is the *critical* meaning and justification of such religious 'conversion'?) Or does intellectual 'conversion' and its resultant philosophical 'position' already determine him as 'moral' and as 'religious' and, therefore, as affirming the existence of God? If that be the case then must one not develop the critical justification of these prior two steps as essential to the explicit argumentation? And, further, if moral and religious conversion do require prior explicitation to the question of God, how could the discussion of evil *logically* follow rather than precede the solution to the question of God. Lonergan's argument for that logical progression, I believe, is clear enough, viz., that evil becomes a *problem* only in the context of the existence of a good God.[22] But that does not seem probative. For just as error is a problem for one critically justifying the truth-claim of 'intellectual conversion', similarly evil is a *problem* for one trying to critically justify the truth-claims of moral and religious 'conversions' and *a fortiori* of one trying to justify critically the ultimate groundedness of both in 'God'.

Allow me to clarify the nature of this criticism: I do not deny *a priori* that the 'argument' in chapter XIX could be critically re-expressed in the critical context of the historically conscious, intellectually, morally and religiously converted men (as *a priori* I do not deny that one of the more immediately metaphysical traditional arguments could be) but until such explicitations are made, I submit, one is not discussing contemporary man and the problem of God but rather one is discussing a crucial aspect of contemporary man's contemporaneity (viz., intellectual 'conversion' and its metaphysical implications) and then reinterpreting the traditional argument from contingency in terms of that intelligibility. In short, until such explicitations are made, chapter XIX is not related intrinsically to the first eighteen chapters of *Insight* in the exact manner that each of those eighteen chapters is related to the previous ones. For in terms of the heuristic structure of *Insight*, each chapter presupposes the previous chapter and complements it by developing explicitly the further questions that cannot be resolved on the basis of the former viewpoint. Yet chapter XIX, if my analysis be correct, does not raise all the further relevant questions (viz., it does not explicitate moral and religious conversions) and does not, therefore, fulfil Lonergan's own criteria for the 'virtually unconditioned' nature of judgement.[23] Hence, its 'higher viewpoint' is not really a genuine one of the previous eighteen chapters but a transposition into a quite distinct enterprise—namely, a reformulation of the traditional Thomist argument from contingency for the existence of God in the context of Lonergan's reformulated notion of causality and the philosophical implications of the 'position' on intellectual conversion.

I have tried to argue the case for this critique of Lonergan's notion of foundations from within the implications of Lonergan's own position.[24] I have suggested, in effect, that the principal role of dialectics and foundations is not merely to thematise authoritatively accepted religious and theological meanings but to develop the means to validate that acceptance (in which case, for example, the dogmatic principle would become self-authenticating) which is precisely the point at issue. I have argued this case on the basis of the relationship between the systematic-critical and methodological exigencies for Lonergan's various formulations of theological language, in order to suggest that neither his former Thomist nor his *Insight* reformulation of the Thomistic position resolves the critical difficulties of precisely the foundational problematic which his explicitation of the fourth level and of the specialties 'dialectics' and 'foundations' would seem to imply[25]—even if he does not so explicitate it as the peculiarity of the contemporary (as distinct from both the medieval and the modern) problematic for theology.

Finally, if this suggested reformulation of the question is admitted, certain factors in Lonergan's methodological formulations to date might find a more foundationally integrated reformulation as well. Among such factors are the following:[26] *Firstly*, the relationship between the finitude of the scientific inquirer who has explicitated self-affirmation and the finitude-historicity (as existential consciousness of the theological inquirer as human scientist critically investigating the nature of his historicity).[27] In short, Lonergan's fourth-level analysis will be characterised not by a merely cultural change from classical to historical consciousness (a change of ideals and categories more proper to reformulating traditional systematics) but by the radically historical-temporal nature of the theologian himself as finitely-temporally-historically transformed by intellectual, moral and more-than-finite religious values. Indeed to ask that question, in that context, of the conditions of the possibility of religious meaning for the finite historical inquirer would be one way of formulating the foundational problematic for contemporary theology. Moreover, it would be a formulation of the question, I believe, faithful to Lonergan's own insistence on the 'incarnate' inquirer and on his own latter disavowel of any faculty theories for intellect and will in favour of a critical emphasis on dialectically

mediating the pre-thematic, pre-conceptual, originating 'world'.
*Secondly*, that formulation of the question, I suggest, could and
should lead to Lonergan's reformulation of his *transcendental*
position on the relationship between the 'life-world' and the
'scientific' world.[28] And involved in that relationship would be
Lonergan's own explicitation of (*a*) the critical relationship of the
'feelings' in the 'experience' of the 'critical' inquirer in his attempt
to understand, judge and, yet more importantly, decide; and
(*b*) the relationship of his theory of meaning to language, or if
one prefers, the critical relationship of Lonergan's transcendental
turn to the linguistic turn.[29] This would seem especially important
for articulating the relationship of Lonergan's theory of the
meaning of 'symbolic' meaning and language not merely to
Cassirer's neo-Kantian formulation but to more properly
phenomenological formulations (precisely as themselves emerging
in the context of the analysis of the relationship of the *language*—
of the *symbols* in the contemporary life-world—to the contemporary scientific world of language-meaning) and their
reformulated relationship as the proper context for a transcendental analysis of the pre-thematic, originating religious
meaning-language.

*Thirdly*, and finally, that reformulation, I believe, would allow
Lonergan to attempt to explicitate as his fourth level 'foundations'
the hermeneutic circle which I believe his position wishes to
maintain.[30] But one should note that precisely such a critical
reformulation might allow for a critical not dogmatic affirmation
of the traditional (and contemporary) hermeneutic circle of the
theologian, viz., 'Fides quaerens intellectum; intellectus quaerens
fidem'—or, to formulate it in Ricoeur's more explicitly contemporary fashion 'The symbol gives rise to *thought* and *thought*
is always *informed* by symbol'.[31]

*Fourthly*, precisely such a critical reformulation of the question of
dialectics-foundations for contemporary theology would also
open Lonergan's foundational *thematisation* to critical dialogue
with the call for the post-classical conceptualities for thematisa-
tions of God-language most forcefully argued for by the process
theologians.[32]

*Conclusion*

Perhaps a summary of the major points of this paper would
seem in order here. I have felt free to presuppose an understanding

16

of Lonergan's technical language and categories and I have tried to argue my case from within that language. Thus I have in the first place employed (and implicitly accepted) Lonergan's formulation of one way of interpreting the history of theology—viz., in the light of the four exigencies: systematic-critical-methodological-transcendent (section I).

I have also employed (and explicitly accepted) Lonergan's formulation of the concrete, empirical possibilities for methodological collaboration in contemporary theology via an interpretation of contemporary theology as a self-structuring unity of eight functional specialties (section II).

I have criticised the role accorded to 'dialectics' and 'foundations' as 'functional specialties' in Lonergan and have suggested that the implications of Lonergan's critical position (from *Insight* on) would lead an interpreter to expect a critical formulation of moral, religious and Christian 'conversions' and of the Christian God-language as horizon resultant therefrom. It would not lead me to expect either a dogmatic articulation of those 'foundations' or a more sophisticated (but still dogmatic) empirical methodological foundation from the results of historical studies or a reformulation of traditional Thomist God-language from the 'position' of 'intellectual' conversion alone.

Finally, I have—all too briefly, I realise—suggested an alternative formulation of 'foundations' and further suggested the critical questions that emerge for such an alternative formulation.[33] But since that alternative is easily recognised as (and admitted to be) more strictly 'phenomenological' than Lonerganian 'empirical-transcendental' I have not elaborated upon it here except to suggest that if the prior critique be correct then here is one major area where the *critical* collaboration which the 'Lonergan Congress' called for might occur between at least two major contemporary positions, namely, the transcendental and the phenomenological.

# BERNARD LONERGAN RESPONDS

I HAVE been asked to respond and, obviously, I must. Not all papers, however, call for the same type of response. There are those that admit no more than an expression of my admiration and my gratitude. Bishop Butler has taken the heuristic structure, set forth in chapter XX of *Insight*, and filled it out in the light of his first-hand knowledge of the Second Vatican Council. Quentin Quesnell is an impressive New Testament scholar;[1] but he is also at home in the intricacies of a theory of interpretation, and he is concerned to vindicate both biblical and dogmatic theology. Frederick Crowe envisages a similar problem from an opposite angle; patiently and gently he cuts through much loose thinking to come up with a point I find highly illuminating, namely, that the mind revealed by a text may not be something coherent and tightly knit but may prove to be a conglomerate of items of great variety with representatives of every shade of difference from fleeting impressions up to well-formed and clearly formulated convictions. Heinrich Ott has given us a delicately nuanced yet firmly fleshed account of the manner in which his theological reflection unfolds, while Alois Grillmeier has drawn on the history of law, specifically of imported legal systems, to illustrate the problems that confront ecumenism as a result of centuries of diverging traditions. To such work there manifestly is no finishing touch I could add.

In a number of papers, however, questions are raised regarding my views on the method of theology. On that topic I have a book in process. Some ten chapters have been completed of which one on 'Functional Specialties in Theology' has been published.[2] While I cannot make available here the 350 pages of typescript that have not been published, some answer I feel should be given to such questions as the following: Does theology begin from truths or from data? Is it to be conceived on the analogy of natural science? What is meant by religious conversion? Must not theological method contain a specifically theological principle? Is it dogmatic or critical? Is the method envisaged theologically neutral? Is it specifically theological?

First, then, Fr Crowe has noted that formerly I placed the starting-point of theology in truths while now I place it in data. This raises a complex issue that cannot be treated fully at once. But I would note that behind the shift there is a greatly enlarged notion of theology: if one accepts the notion of functional specialties, then there pertain to theology investigations that otherwise have to be conceived as auxiliary disciplines, e.g., textual criticism of scriptural, patristic, medieval manuscripts. A further point is that, as long as one remains within the Aristotelian orbit, one conceives theology in terms of its material and formal objects and, indeed, of its *formale quod* and *formale quo*.[3] On the other hand, when one adopts a strictly methodological viewpoint, the emphasis shifts from objects to operations and operators. In terms of functional specialties theology is an eightfold set of interdependent normative patterns of recurrent and related operations with progressive and cumulative results. Where formerly a discipline was specifically theological because it dealt with revealed truths, now it is authentically theological because the theologian has been converted intellectually, morally, and religiously.

Next, does the shift from truths to data imply, as Professor Gilkey believes, that I am conceiving theology on the analogy of natural science? By no means! P and Q are analogous if they are partly the same and partly different. To conceive Q on the analogy of P is to have only a partial knowledge of Q. Hence, the scholastic attempt to conceive of theology on the analogy of the science set forth in Aristotle's *Posterior Analytics* was most unsatisfactory, and my concern with method is precisely to remedy the defects inherent in any approach by way of analogy.

However, to avoid analogy is not an easy matter. Over and above familiarity with the history of theology and with its current problems, there are two main steps. The first is an exploration of mathematics, natural science, common sense, and philosophy to uncover the basic and invariant structure of all human cognitional activity and so to reach a transcendental method, i.e., a method that is the condition of the possibility (not of the actuality) of all the special methods proper to each of the special fields of human inquiry. Such a method will be relevant to theology, for theologians always have had minds and always have used them. It will not be, however, the whole of theological method, for to it there must be added the specifically theological principle that differentiates theology from other fields.

Professor Gilkey also has philosophic and theological objections against the method I have proposed. The theological objection will have to wait until I have mentioned Fr Curran's paper on conversion. The philosophic objection is that there is a profound discrepancy between the very modern notion of intelligibility in the third chapter of *Insight* and, on the other hand, the retrograde, Greek notion that emerges in chapter XIX, in which a tolerance for mere matters of fact is attributed to obscurantism. Now I grant that my third chapter presents an ideal of science quite different from that presented in Aristotle's *Posterior Analytics*. I deny that it offers any grounds for a Kantian or positivist assertion that the only valid human knowledge is knowledge of this world. And, while the term 'intelligible' is used in different senses in *Insight*, the primary meaning is always the same: the intelligible is the content of an act of understanding. Understanding, of course, occurs in many ways. There is the understanding that occurs in mathematics, the understanding that occurs in natural science, the understanding that occurs in the exercise of common sense, the mathematical, scientific, and common-sense understanding that is sough in the first eight chapters of *Insight*, the philosophic type of understanding that emerges in chapter XI when an act of understanding is reached that is not open to revision, the understanding developed in the process of encircle-ment and confinement that yields a metaphysics of proportionate being, and there is the final demand for understanding that in chapter XIX joins Professor Gilkey in rejecting the contingency, relativism, and transience of the contemporary secularist outlook.[4]

Fr Curran has taken Christian conversion as his topic. Later I shall have something to say on the distinction and the relations of intellectual, moral, and religious conversion. For the moment I am concerned with religious conversion. What I mean by it I have set forth in Thomist categories in a series of articles on

*Gratia operans.*[5] In those categories, by religious conversion I understand the gift of habitual grace as operative. It may be prepared by actual graces as operative, and it is to be perfected by still further actual graces as operative; but it is the central event. While the Thomist notion is basically metaphysical—an absolutely supernatural entitative habit radicated in the essence of the soul with the operative habits of faith, hope, and charity resulting in the potencies of the soul—still this notion was evolved to satisfy scriptural and patristic doctrines and to resolve religious problems. Specifically, it had to do with the contrasts between nature and grace, reason and faith, human affection and agape, a good name on earth and merit in God's eyes, moral impotence and a capacity to love God above all.

Now both the transcendental and the methodological turn require that the realities of the subject be primary and basic while metaphysical concepts become secondary and derivative. Accordingly, instead of speaking of habitual grace, I speak of conversion, of a transformation of the subject that is radical, dynamic and, in principle, permanent. That such a transformation occurs and what are its properties can be worked out from the Scriptures, patristic writings, ascetical and mystical writers, and one's own experience of the spiritual life; and one can reach such results with the same assurance as one can establish from the same sources the existence of habitual grace.

To religious conversion, then, I would ascribe as a minimum two notes: first, it is a change in one's antecedent willingness; one becomes antecedently willing to do the good that previously one was unwilling to do; secondly, the free and full acceptance of this change constitutes the existential decision that contemporary moral theologians name one's fundamental option, one's basic religious commitment. While this decision may lead to a change of ecclesiastical allegiance, it need do no more than make one a better member of the religion or non-religion one has inherited. Again, as a change in the subject, it can be detected within the data of consciousness; but this does not mean that the data are labelled 'religious conversion' or 'fundamental option'; nor does it mean that one is freed from temptations or from aridity in prayer or that one is not inclined to have a poor opinion of oneself. Finally, the fact of conversion appears much more in its effects than in itself; and when it becomes noticeable in itself, then, in Fr Rahner's phrase, it is with a content but without an object. *Nihil amatum nisi praecognitum* is true of human love, but it is not true of God's love that floods our hearts through the holy Spirit given to us [6]

Enough has been said for it now to be possible to meet Professor Gilkey's demand for a specific theological principle. That principle is religious conversion, but it must be explained (1) in what sense conversion is a principle, (2) how this principle produces its effects, (3) what is its point of insertion, (4) how it is objectified, and (5) why such a principle should be invoked instead of divine revelation, the inspiration of Scripture, the authority of the Church, the agreement of patristic and theological writers, the *sensus fidelium*.

First, then, a principle is what is first in an ordered set, *primum in aliquo ordine*. If the ordered set consists in propositions, then a principle in the set will be the premises from which the rest of the propositions may be deduced. If the ordered set consists not in propositions but in real causes and real effects, then the principle consists in the causes. Now the theological principle is religious conversion itself. It is not knowledge of religious conversion, awareness of religious conversion, interpretation of the psychological phenomena of conversion, propositions concerning conversion. It is simply the reality of the transformation named conversion, and it is that reality whether or not its subject has the foggiest notion of what it is or whether it has occurred.

Secondly, how does the principle produce its effects? It does so spontaneously. Conversion results in a transvaluation of values, in a new efficacy in one's response to values, in a new openness to belief, in a new outlook upon mankind and upon the universe. Specifically, it does not import into theological method any special rules for research into religious matters, the interpretation of religious documents, the history of religious events and movements. On the contrary, especially in the first four functional specialties—research, interpretation, history, dialectic—the same methodical precepts are to be acceptable to believers and agnostics alike.

Thirdly, though believers and agnostics follow the same methods, they will not attain the same results. For in interpreting texts and in resolving historical problems, one's results are a function, not only of the data and the procedures, but also of the whole previous development of one's understanding. To aim at eliminating that previous development would result in a second childhood. All that can be done is to purge it of its biases, to remove its blind spots, to enlarge its horizons. Nor is that to be achieved by some simple master-stroke, but only by unremitting efforts to be attentive, to advert to one's failures to understand and to strive to overcome them, to be more exact in one's judgements, to be ever more responsive to values and, above all, to be ever able to learn from what others have learned.

Such is the general character of the interpretative and historical work. Carl Becker had no doubt that the historian's investigation and judgement were under the influence of the dominant ideas in the climate of opinion of his day.[7] H. I. Marrou was willing to distinguish the historian from the history he writes but he denied that the history can be independent of the concrete man that the historian is.[8] While Becker and Marrou were struggling against a positivism that had captured historical thought at the end of the nineteenth century, H. G. Gadamer traces similar thought back to the Enlightenment and to Cartesian methodic doubt. The task, for him, is not the elimination of all assumptions but the elimination of mistaken assumptions. The Enlightenment assumed that assumptions were to be eliminated. In fact, they are not the personal judgements of the individual but rather the historicity of his cultural being. It is only through that historical heritage that he can become equipped to understand his past history and, the greater that heritage, the greater the development it demands of him if he is to understand it aright.[9]

What holds generally for interpretation and history, also holds for the interpretation of religious documents and for accounts of religious history. The point was already made by St Paul. 'A man who is unspiritual refuses what belongs to the Spirit of God; it is folly to him; he cannot grasp it, because it needs to be judged in the light of the Spirit. A man gifted with the Spirit can judge the worth of everything, but is not himself subject to judgement by his fellow-men' (1 *Cor.* 2; 14 f.).

Fourthly, how is the theological principle, conversion, objectified? Its spontaneous objectification is called by St Paul the harvest of the Spirit: love, joy, peace, patience, kindness, goodness, fidelity, gentleness, and self-control (*Gal.* 5:22). In mediating theology, in research, interpretation, history, dialectic, the discernment of the spiritual man brings to light what others disregard. Dialectic brings to light oppositions in appreciative and evaluative interpretation and history, in the history of movements, in determining the meaning of texts, and in the special research performed in the prosecution of the foregoing tasks. Foundations takes sides: it selects as its stand some coherent set out of the array of opposing positions; and, in so far as it is guided by authentic conversion, its selection will be an implicit objectification of what conversion is. The explicit objectification, however, occurs in doctrines, in systematics, and in communications in accord with the several purposes of these specialties.[10]

Fifthly, why is the theological principle placed in religious conversion and not in divine revelation, the inspiration of Scripture, the authority of the Church, the consensus of patristic and theological writers, the *sensus fidelium*, or the like?

The reason for the shift is functional specialisation. If there are eight functional specialties, if they are ordered, not chronologically for they are interdependent, but by presupposition and complementation, if foundations is fifth in the order and doctrines are sixth, then manifestly the foundations do not consist in some of the doctrines. But the existence of a divine revelation, the inspiration of Scripture, the authority of the Church, the significance of the patristic and theological teaching are all doctrines. Therefore, none of them pertain to foundations.

Now this does not imply that divine revelation, inspired Scripture, ecclesiastical pronouncements, patristic and theological writings are not sources for theology. They remain sources, but they are considered in a series of different manners. In the first instance, they are data for general and special research. In the second instance, each item is acknowledged to possess a meaning, and this meaning is determined by an exegete. In the third instance, the many items of meaning come together in an ongoing process, history. In the fourth instance, the history is acknowledged to manifest the values and disvalues brought about by persons, and the conflicts brought to light are catalogued and compared. In the fifth instance, a decision is taken with respect to the conflicts. Only in the sixth instance, do we come to the truths contained in the sources.

Next, if the foregoing tasks are to be performed properly, there are three main requirements. The first is that one's idea of interpretation and of critical history must not be distorted either by the abundant supply of mistaken and misleading theories of knowledge or by the widespread and abominable practice of those that are convinced that an academic discipline must be this or that because of the analogy of some other academic discipline. The second is that one must find a methodical way of handling the problem of divergent value-judgements. The third is the insertion of a theological principle. Just how all this is to be done, I have explained in some 200 pages of unpublished typescript. More cannot be said now.

The next question is Fr Tracy's and, as well, it bears on a point made by Professor Davis. Is, then, the functional specialty, foundations, dogmatic or critical?

From what has already been said, it is clear that foundations does not consist in the enumeration and affirmation of some or all dogmas, for dogmas are doctrines, and doctrines are the concern of the sixth specialty, doctrines. On the other hand, since foundations founds doctrines, systematics, and communications, it follows that foundations will lead to the acceptance of doctrines and so of dogmas.

The question may mean, however, is foundations merely assumed or asserted and in that case dogmatic or, on the other hand, does foundations itself rest on earlier grounds that are critically evaluated?

Foundations, then, consists in a decision that selects one horizon and rejects others. The horizons in question are determined by the conflicts revealed in dialectic. The choice of one and the rejection of the others are operations on the fourth level of intentional consciousness, the level of deliberation, evaluation, and decision, the level on which consciousness becomes conscience. Operations on this level are critically motivated when the deliberation has been sufficiently comprehensive and when the values chosen and the disvalues rejected really are values and disvalues respectively. But the sufficiently comprehensive deliberation is secured through the functional specialties of research, interpretation, history, and dialectic. The value-judgements are correct when they occur in a duly enlightened and truly virtuous man and leave him with a good conscience. Due enlightenment and true virtue are the goals towards which intellectual and moral conversion move. Conscience, finally, is the key, and its use by humble men does not encourage dogmatism in the pejorative sense of that word.

Is this critical? On views I consider counter-positions it is not critical. On views I consider positions it is critical. On the counter-positions the object is out there now, the subject is in here now, the two are irreducible, objectivity is a matter of taking a good look, and value-judgements are always merely subjective. On the positions, objects are what are intended in questions and known by answers, subjects do the questioning and answering, objectivity is the fruit of authentic subjectivity, and subjectivity is authentic when it is self-transcending. Such self-transcendence is twofold: there is the cognitive self-transcendence that reaches a virtually unconditioned to pronounce on facts, possibilities, probabilities; there is the moral self-transcendence in which one becomes a principle of benevolence and beneficence by acknowledging and choosing what truly is good, really is worth while; and the criterion that one has done so is one's good conscience provided one is duly enlightened on the issues and truly virtuous.

Such is the general scheme, but the method implements it. The implementation is a prolongation of the procedures in my book, *Insight*, where positions and counter-positions were distinguished on knowledge, objectivity, and reality, and readers were invited and helped to attain a self-appropriation that would enable them to opt unhesitatingly for the positions and against the counter-positions. But in theology there has to be faced the further problem of value-judgements. To evade that problem would eviscerate theology. To assert one's own values as the true ones would simply be dogmatism. There exists, however, a third way. One can allow all-comers to participate in research, interpretation, history, and dialectic. One can encourage positions and counter-positions to come to light concretely and to manifest to all their suppositions and their consequences. One can expect some to mistake counter-positions for positions and, inversely, positions for counter-positions. One can hope that such mistakes will not be universal, that the positions will be duly represented, that they will reveal themselves as positions to men of good will. It is by this third way that the method would ground foundations, objectively, in the situation revealed by dialectic and, on the side of subjective development, in intellectual, moral, and religious conversion.

The second last question to be considered was raised by Professor Lindbeck, Is the method theologically neutral? He concludes that it is. I should agree that it is, first, because theological sources initially have the status of data; secondly, because the methodologist leaves the theologians to determine which sources are relevant and how privileged each one is and, thirdly, because in general the methodologist leaves all theological questions to the theologians.

There is, however, a necessary exception. For the method to be a method in theology it must implement a specifically theological principle, and the principle selected has been religious conversion. About such conversion the methodologist has to make some theological statements, but his purpose is not to influence results to be obtained by the method but simply to explain how the method can be expected to reach any theological results whatever. Indeed, it is not the methodologist's views on conversion, any more than those of Aquinas or Luther or Calvin or some introspective psychologist, but conversion itself in its spontaneous consequences that exerts an influence on the results of research, interpretation, history, and dialectic.

In the second phase of mediated theology, however, there are to be set up not only general categories regarding man and his world but also specifically theological categories. These radiate out from the initial theological category of conversion to the community of the converted, to its traditions, to its origins, to its destiny, to its God. Such categories, be it noted, as presented in foundations are regarded simply as models. They are not descriptions of reality or hypotheses about reality but simply explanatory sets of interconnected terms that it will be useful to have available when the time comes in doctrines, systematics, communications to describe realities or to form hypotheses about them.

When it comes to doctrines, one can at present expect divergences to become manifest. But the method does possess a strong measure of theological neutrality. It provides an operative framework within which different communions can do much in common, acknowledge differences, work backwards to their roots, define issues with clarity and, where they still disagree, regard each other with genuine mutual respect.

While then I think the method possesses considerable theological neutrality, it is not methodically neutral and it is not philosophically neutral. It cannot be methodically neutral, for if one proposes a method, one means what one says and not something else. It is not philosophically neutral for it evaporates into thin air when rather firm positions on cognitional and moral operations, on their objectivity, and on the corresponding reality either are not grasped or are abandoned.

This absence of methodical and philosophical neutrality may delay acceptance of the method. But a too rapid acceptance would risk being superficial, and a superficial acceptance would betray the method with superficial performance. What is to be hoped for is the open-eyed and fully deliberate acceptance that brings forth solid fruits and thereby initiates a movement.

The final question is Fr Rahner's who has asked whether the account of method in the article on functional specialties is specifically theological. Clearly functional specialties as such are not specifically theological. Indeed, the eight specialties we have listed would be relevant to any human studies that investigated a cultural past to guide its future. Again, since the sources to be subjected to research are not specified, they could be the sacred books and traditions of any religion. Finally, while there is a theological principle assigned, still it is not placed in authoritative pronouncements but in the religious conversion that turns men to transcendent mystery; and while I believe such a turn always to be God's gift of grace, still it becomes specifically a Christian conversion when the gift of the Spirit within us is intersubjective with the revelation of the Father in Christ Jesus.

Three observations are, perhaps, in order. The incompleteness of the chapter on functional specialties only shows that one is not trying to say in one chapter what one hopes to convey in a dozen. Secondly, in our day of ecumenism, of openness with non-Christian religions, of dialogue with atheists, there is not a little advantage in a theological method that with slight adjustments can be adapted to related yet quite different investigations. Thirdly, to advert now to some points raised by Fr Curran, I should urge that religious conversion, moral conversion, and intellectual conversion are three quite different things. In an order of exposition I would prefer to explain first intellectual, then moral, then religious conversion. In the order of occurrence I would expect religious commonly but not necessarily to precede moral and both religious and moral to precede intellectual. Intellectual conversion, I think, is very rare.

To conclude, writing this paper has helped me clarify my own thinking and so it may be of use to others. I fear, however, that the answers I have given will at crucial points only raise further and more complicated questions. But to attempt to anticipate them here would only raise still further issues, and so I must be content if I somehow manage to meet most points in the rounded whole of my overdue book.

May I take this occasion to thank the organisers of the meeting at St Leo's, to thank all that participated, and in particular to thank those that contributed to the present volume.

# Notes

## Lonergan and Ecclesiology

[1]*Collection*, 216–7.     [2]*Insight*, 748.     [3]*Insight*, 696.
[4]Art. 3, *Dei Verbum*, The Documents of Vatican II, ed. W. M. Abbott, S.J., London and Dublin 1967, 112.
[5]Art. 9, *Lumen Gentium*, op. cit., 24.     [6]Art. 16, ibid., 35.     [7]*Insight*, 697.
[8]*Insight*, 696.     [9]*Ibid.*, 697.     [10]*Ibid.*, 719.     [11]*Ibid.*, 720.     [12]*Ibid.*, 721.
[13]*Ibid.*, 723.     [14]*Ibid.*, 729.     [15]*Ibid.*, 723.     [16]*Ibid.*, 723f.
[17]*The Subject*, Aquinas Lecture for 1968, Milwaukee, 10.
[18]*Insight*, 51.     [19]*Ibid.*, 52.     [20]*Ibid.*, 266f.     [21]*Ibid.*, 724.
[22]*Ibid.*, 577–94.     [23]*Collection*, 240ff.
[24]Art. 4, *Gaudium et Spes*, op. cit., 202.     [25]*Collection*, 241–5.
[26]*Ibid.*, 242.     [27]Art. 5, *Dei Verbum*, op. cit., 113.     [28]*Collection*, 242–3.
[29]*Th.N.C.*, 39.     [30]*Collection*, 252ff.     [31]*Ibid.*, 256.     [32]*Ibid.*, 259.
[33]*Ibid.*, 267.     [34]*Th.N.C.*, 44f.
[35]'Institution versus Carismata', *Theology of Renewal*, vol. 2, ed. L. K. Shook, New York 1968, 46.

## Dogma versus the Self-Correcting Process of Learning

[1]'History and Dogma', *Letter on Apologetics and History and Dogma* (E. tr. A. Dru and I. Trethowan), London 1965, 222.
[2]*Ibid.*, 224.     [3]*Ibid.*
[4]*The Historian and the Believer: The Morality of Historical Knowledge and Christian Belief*, New York 1966, 119.
[5]*Ibid.*, 164.     [6]*Op. cit.*, 275–6.     [7]*Ibid.*, 274.     [8]*Op. cit.*, 252.
[9]Cf. *Func. Sp.*, 485–504. 'Judgement [is open] to acknowledgement of new and more adequate perspectives, of more nuanced pronouncements, of more detailed information' (p. 500).
[10]*D.D.T.* II, 20.     [11]See *Func. Sp.*, *loc. cit.*
[12]Cf. *D.D.T.* II, 59: 'Iam vero cum intellectus sit voluntatem movere atque dirigere . . .'
[13]*Fut. Chr.*, 7.
[14]See *Func. Sp.*, for example, p. 491: 'Doctrines express judgements of fact and judgements of value. They are concerned, then, with the affirmations and negations not only of dogmatic theology but also of moral, ascetical, mystical, pastoral, and any similar branch.'
[15]See vol. II, 23–24.
[16]See *The Subject*, Milwaukee 1968, 2–8. It is in this paper too that Lonergan criticises the old faculty psychology; see pp. 19–20.
[17]*Ibid.*, 4. See p. 14 on the absolute objectivity of judgement.
[18]See pp. 164–78 in *The Presence and Absence of God*, ed. Christopher F. Mooney, New York 1969; my quotation is from p. 172.
[19]See *Th. M.F.*, 452–61; quotation from p. 455.

235

[20]*Insight*, 378. Distinguish the absolute character of judgement from 'the comprehensive coherence that is the ideal of understanding' (p. 344).

[21]*D.D.T.* II, 20.     [22]*Insight*, 713.     [23]*Ibid.*, 714.

[24]*Ibid.*, 174. Those who wish to investigate the notion further may consult the index of *Insight*. It should be noted that sometimes the term 'self-correcting process' is applied more precisely to common sense, in which case it is the common-sense parallel to the advance of science; this seems to be more or less the regular usage in *Insight* and it becomes explicit in 'Natural Knowledge of God': 'Common sense meets such questions by . . . the self-correcting process of learning. Natural science meets them by the process of direct and indirect verification' (p. 62 of article referred to in note 34 *infra*). However, the term is also applied to science in *Insight*, p. 303. Note also that during the learning process 'one's own judgement is in abeyance' (*ibid.*, p. 286).

[25]*Insight*, 540. The question is complex: there are revisions forced by further data, and there are those due to the advent of new investigators; in regard to the latter we can escape relativism by passing from a descriptive to an explanatory viewpoint.

[26]This difference I first heard expressed by Lonergan himself in his 1962 institute on the method of theology, but I believe it is widely recognised; Ritschl, we are told by Philip Hefner, was bothered by the problem of continuity, which is the Catholic principle, and discontinuity, which is the Protestant principle, see *Faith and the Vitalities of History*, New York 1966, 32.

[27]See *D.V.I.*, 9–11.

[28]This point too I owe to Lonergan; see the *reportatio* of his course, *De intellectu et methodo*, Gregorian University, 1959, 44–5 (also *Insight*, p. 716).

[29]See John Henry Cardinal Newman, *An Essay in Aid of a Grammar of Assent*, London 1930, 377. The passage is worth quoting at greater length: 'Of the two, I would rather have to maintain that we ought to begin with believing everything that is offered to our acceptance, than that it is our duty to doubt of everything. The former, indeed, seems the true way of learning. In that case, we soon discover and discard what is contradictory to itself; and error having always some portion of truth in it, and the truth having a reality which error has not, we may expect, that when there is an honest purpose and fair talents, we shall somehow make our way forward, the error falling off from the mind, and the truth developing and occupying it.' Newman had formed this mentality some time before he wrote the *Grammar*; see pp. 94–5 of that work where he quotes one of his earlier writings.

[30]See *D.D.T.* I, 10–11, 13, 112; there are also indications of this idea in vol. II, e.g., pp. 25, 28–9, 60 (it should be remembered that the long introduction to vol. II was largely worked out before that of vol. I). There is a section, 'De usu fontium . . . ,' in Lonergan's course of lectures, *De methodo theologiae* (see the *reportatio* made by his students, 1962, pp. 56–7). It is extremely useful on the question of that limited general truth a theologian asks of Scripture, and on the way he may attain it with certainty despite the repeated revisions of exegesis.

[30a]Notice that when I call this formula 'catholic' I am affirming that it leaves behind the particularities of the Greek mind as well as those of the Hebrew.

Nicea was not a capitulation to Greek philosophy but a victory over it; see
*D.D.T.* I, 5–112 (summary on p. 112).

[31]See Karl Rahner. 'Current Problems in Christology,' *Theological Investi-
gations*, I, Baltimore 1961, 149–200. Notice the title of the German original·
'Chalkedon—Ende oder Anfang?' (*Das Konzil von Chalkedon* . . . , III, ed. A.
Grillmeier and H. Bacht,Würzburg 1954).

[32]See *Func. Sp.*, 490.

[33]Richard E. Palmer, *Hermeneutics. Interpretation Theory in Schleiermacher,
Dilthey, Heidegger, and Gadamer*, Evanston 1969, 133. Notice, p. 132, that
Heidegger's world is not objective over against a subject (as Lonergan's is, at
least in the phrase quoted) and, p. 133, that it is unobtrusive—the structural
whole and the place of elements within it appear at the moment of breakdown.

[34]See 'Natural Knowledge of God', *Proceedings of the Twenty-Third Annual
Convention of The Catholic Theological Society of America*, Washington, D.C.
1968, 54–69; see especially 59–60. The first instance of this use of 'promotion'
that I have noticed is in 'Cognitional Structure', *Collection*, p. 229; but there
it is not used of the transition from understanding to judgement. The latest
instance is in *Func. Sp.*, p. 500.

There was recently an instructive example of the confusion that can be
caused by such a misapprehension as I have described of the 'truths' we hold.
When the decision was made to exclude various 'saints' from the Roman
calendar, those who thought these figures pertained to the truth of their faith
were badly shaken. Others, however, who regarded St George (say) as part of
the furniture of the religious mind, but not at all as someone whose existence
had been promoted to the level of truth, were quite unruffled; for them St
George, like Tobias, Santa Claus, the Holy Grail, and so forth, still pertains
to the furniture of the Catholic mind, but he is more clearly located now in
the conglomerate.

[35]I cannot go into the judgemental process in detail here. I must simply
refer those not familiar with Lonergan to his *Insight*, especially chapters 9–11.
For some account of the dialectical process that goes on as the Church learns
a new truth, I may refer to my paper, 'The Conscience of the Theologian
with Reference to *Humanae Vitae*', to appear in *Conscience: Its Freedom and
Limitations*, Fordham University Press (proceedings of the Seventh Biennial
Institute in Pastoral Psychology).

[36]G. L. Prestige, *God in Patristic Thought*, London 1952, 213.

[37]The question of the virtually conditioned and its use in simple statements
of this sort came up at the congress, so I must explain that I do not mean that
'knowing' the fact that it is raining is equivalent to 'taking a look'—though
my written words may have suggested that. The full story, it seems to me, is
that looking out of the window is a final step in reaching the virtually
unconditioned, and the judgement in this case seems simple only because there
are a great many conditions that exist in a habitually fulfilled state in my mind.
For one thing, the words 'raining', 'out', etc., have a meaning that is part of
my habitual knowledge; however, they became part of my habitual knowledge
only in a laborious process in which other conditions of various kinds were
fulfilled. Again, knowing the difference between sleeping and waking is one
of the conditions of rational judgement; that too is now habitual with me, but

once it was not; I had to learn it, and in the process of learning had to reach a virtually unconditioned in which various conditions of a quite different kind from those presently relevant were fulfilled.

[38]'Natural Knowledge of God,' *op. cit.*, 61. See also 'Belief: Today's Issue', *Messenger* (Toronto), June 1968, 9.

[39]Or, I might better say that there is a difference between the use of 'is' in a question or supposition and the positing of 'is' in a statement, but the existential intention is present in each case ('existential'—i.e., in the neo-Thomist use of the word).

[40]Thomas Aquinas, *Summa theologiae*, I, q. 13, a. 11.

[41]See *D.V.I.*, 332.

[42]*Op. cit.*, 246, 275, etc. But notice, p. 284, that Blondel too acknowledges a finite element in the human knowledge of Jesus.

[43]The following question was also put to me at the congress: Do you exclude *a priori* at least some propositions that would falsify dogma, e.g., that Jesus was a fraud? Must you not hold that historical investigation cannot produce evidence for such a proposition? And then do you not determine history by dogma?

To this I would answer that there are propositions which in principle are not falsifiable—e.g., the fundamental validity of cognitional process in general, which has to be assumed in the very attempt to falsify it. Next, there seems to be a somewhat similar situation in faith. The adherence of faith is a first in its own order; all further pursuit of truth about Christ supposes such an adherence as its basis. That Christ is a fraud would therefore be excluded by faith somewhat as the falsifiability of cognitional process in general is excluded by one who tries to understand the process and judge upon it.

But now it seems to me we must go deeper. To deny the fundamental validity of cognitional process is not only to issue in internal contradiction but also and more importantly to reject cognitional process and its validity as a *value*. Similarly, to open the question whether Jesus was a fraud is not only an internal contradiction for the believer but a rejection of the value that has been revealed to him. The believer accepts that value and does regard it as impregnable by history, but I wonder if the historians do not accept parallel values of their own which they attach to the past and assume in the very exercise of their vocation. In any case, if they escape internal contradiction in regard to Christ by not believing, we cannot say they forever escape the more fundamental confrontation with values whose rejection is far more serious than internal contradiction.

### Christian Conversion in the Writings of Bernard Lonergan

[1]See *Th.N.C.*, 44–5.

[2]See David W. Tracy, *The Achievement of Bernard Lonergan*, New York 1970, 19–20.

[3]See *Th.N.C.*, 44.

[4]See Bernard Häring, C.SS.R., *The Law of Christ* I, Westminster, Md. 1961, 385–481; *id.*, 'Conversion', in *Pastoral Treatment of Sin*, ed. Philippe Delhaye, New York 1968, 87–186.

[5]See Yves Congar, 'The Idea of Conversion', *Thought*, 33 (1958), 5–20: a modified and enlarged version appeared in *Parole et Mission*, 11 (1960), 493–523. This later version is reprinted in Congar, *Sacerdoce et Laïcat*, Paris 1962, 23–49.

[6]*Th.N.C.*, 44.

[7]See Lonergan, 'The Transition from a Classicist World View to Historical Mindedness', in *Law for Liberty*, ed. James E. Biechler, Baltimore 1967, 126–33.

[8]See B. Guldner, 'Conversion', *The Catholic Encyclopedia* IV, 347–8.

[9]*New Catholic Encyclopedia* IV, 286–94, includes under 'Conversion' a four-part article: 'Conversion, I (In the Bible)', 'Conversion, II (Psychology of)', 'Conversion, III (Theology of)', 'Conversion, IV (Obligation of)'. Other entries are: 'Conversion to Life of Grace' and 'Convert Apostolate'.

[10]See *Pacem in Terris*, art. 7.

[11]See Paul Ramsey, 'Pacem in Terris', in *The Just War*, New York 1968, 70–90.

[12]See Charles E. Curran, *A New Look at Christian Morality*, Notre Dame, Ind. 1968, 170–73; 232–3.

[13]See Häring, *The Law of Christ* I, 339–64.

[14]See Häring, *Pastoral Treatment of Sin*, 91–2.

[15]Billy Graham, 'Conversion—A Personal Revolution', *The Ecumenical Review*, 19 (1967), 271.

[16]See Reinhold Niebuhr in *Love and Justice*, ed. D. B. Robertson, Cleveland and New York 1967, 154–8.

[17]Gibson Winter, *The New Creation as Metropolis*, New York 1963, 75–6.

[18]See Graham, 'Conversion—A Personal Revolution', *op. cit.*, 280–84; Emilio Castro, 'Conversion and Social Transformation', in *Christian Social Ethics in a Changing World*, ed. John C. Bennett, New York, 1966, 348–66.

[19]*Th.N.C.*, 46.   [20]*Ibid.*, 44.

[21]See *Insight*, 687–730; *D.V.I.*, 521–734.

[22]*D.V.I.*, 676. The following paragraphs in the text summarise Lonergan's explanation of the law of the cross.

[23]See Dietrich Bonhoeffer, *Ethics*, ed. Eberhard Bethge, New York 1962, 3–8.

[24]*Ibid.*, 24.   [25]*D.V.I.*, 622–31.

[26]See 'Openness and Religious Experience', *Collection*, 198–201.

[27]*Ibid.*, 200.   [28]See *Insight*, 696–703; 718–30.   [29]*D.V.I.*, 526, 578.

[30]See Johannes B. Metz, 'Foreword', in Karl Rahner, *Spirit in the World*, New York 1968, xviii.

[31]See Tracy, *op. cit.*, 19; chapter vii, 163–81.

[32]*Fut. Chr.*, 5–10; see also a lecture, *Faith and Beliefs*, delivered by Lonergan at different places in 1969 and 1970.

[33]See Carolus Boyer, *Tractatus de Gratia Divina*, 3rd edn. Rome 1952, 48–63.

[34]See *Collection*, 198–201.   [35]See *Fut. Chr.*, 9–10.   [36]*Insight*, 632.

## Lonergan and the Teaching Church

[1]New York and London 1967.   [2]*Collection*, 248.

[3]'A New Dogma', 13.   [4]*Collection*, 76.   [5]*D.D.T.* I, p. 17, n. 4.

[6]*Insight*, 723.   [7]*D.D.T.* II, 21.   [8]*Collection*, 134.   [9]*Collection*, 135.

¹⁰The chapter, 'Functional Specialties in Theology', from *Method in Theology* offers the possibility of a less narrow interpretation of doctrines, systematics and their relationship. Of itself, however, the chapter is an insufficient basis for me to suppose any substantial change in Lonergan's views.

¹¹*Collection*, 133.     ¹²*Collection*, 135.     ¹³Cf. *Collection*, 133.

¹⁴Francis Oakley, *Council Over Pope? Towards a Provisional Ecclesiology*, New York 1969, 178.

¹⁵*Th.N.C.*, 42.     ¹⁶*Ibid.*, 42.     ¹⁷*D.D.T.* II, 51–2.

¹⁸Edward MacKinnon, S.J., 'The Transcendental Turn: Necessary but not Sufficient', *Continuum*, 6 (1968), 225.

¹⁹*Proceedings of the American Catholic Philosophical Association for 1967*, 258.

²⁰*Func. Sp.*, 503.     ²¹*Th. N.C.*, 46.     ²²*Collection*, 266.

²³*Collection*, 266.     ²⁴See *D.D.T.* II, 51–2.

²⁵*Belief: Today's Issue*, 11.     ²⁶ 'The Challenge to Protestant Thought', *Continuum* 6 (1968), 239.

## Empirical Science and Theological Knowing

¹George Santayana, *Scepticism and Animal Faith*, New York 1929, 4.

²The only exception is perhaps Michael Polanyi, who also ranks at the summit of modern interpreters of contemporary modes of knowing.

³See *Insight*, 76–7.     ⁴*Ibid.*, 78–9.

⁵See 'Dimensions of Meaning', *Collection*, 257–8. One cannot help wondering on what principles Lonergan would convince either John Dewey or A. J. Ayer of his sincerity in seeking to eradicate all 'myth' from our thought—for they would define most of his theological language—and ours too—as modern illustrations of the myths *they* were seeking to expunge from our midst.

⁶The first statement of this appears probably in David Hume's *Dialogues on Natural Religion*; it is repeated in Kant's criticism of the classical proofs of God, and has been republished in modern form in the naturalistic principle of the continuity of analysis (i.e., all assertions about things must be continuous with scientific analysis, and so of the same form, cf., Y. Krikorian, *Naturalism and the Human Spirit*, New York 1944). Finally, it is elegantly phrased by Whitehead in his own basic definition of intelligible explanation, what he calls the naturalistic principle of explanation, or the ontological principle: 'Only actual entities [entities that are part of the given system of finite things] can provide legitimate explanations for anything.' Cf. A. N. Whitehead, *Process and Reality*, New York 1929, especially 27–8, 36–7; and *Science and the Modern World*, New York 1925, chapter XI, especially 249–50. The same confinement of intelligible questioning, and so intelligible explanatory answers, reappears in linguistic philosophy wherever it is assumed (1) that only contingent statements can be assertive, and (2) that all contingent assertions are empirical in form.

⁷Lonergan seems to realise this point—though, as we shall see, he roundly denies it at two crucial points—when he surmises that the reason Greek philosophy sought a 'level of necessity' beyond the contingent world was because it had a different (and presumably wrong) understanding of scientific method as productive of eternal and necessary truths rather than hypothetical

and contingent truths. Cf. 'Dimensions of Meaning', *Collection*, 260. However, it is interesting that in that passage he only draws the conclusion that modern philosophy has penetrated into the concrete and contingent, and *not* that it is now confined by the same logic to that same realm.

⁸Cf. *Th. N.C.*, 37–8.   ⁹*Insight*, 636.   ¹⁰*Ibid.*, 652.   ¹¹*Ibid.*, 654.

¹²'Metaphysics as Horizon', *Collection*, 214.   ¹³See *Th. N.C.*, 34–9.

¹⁴Lonergan gives different definitions of being in the course of his argument in *Insight*: (*a*) 'The pure desire to know,' and (*b*) 'Whatever is to be grasped intelligibly and affirmed rationally' (p.642), which lead to the definition of being as (*c*) 'the content of an unrestricted act of understanding' (p. 643). But then (*d*) comes the move from *content* or *object* to *act* or *intelligent subject*: 'The primary component of being is the unrestricted act of understanding'—a move the grounds for which I could not find (pp. 643–4, 646).

¹⁵Cf. especially *Insight*, 320–22. Cf. also 'Cognitional Structures', *Collection*, 226–7: 'Objects are present by being attended to, but subjects are present as subjects, not by being attended to, but by attending. As the parade of objects marches by, spectators do not have to slip into the parade to become present to themselves' (p. 226).

¹⁶This presentation of the problems of modern theology as Lonergan sees them and Lonergan's proposal for a secure theological method are drawn (1) from his paper 'Theology in its New Context', and (2) from 'Functional Specialities in Theology'.

¹⁷See *Func. Sp.*, 486, 495, 500.   ¹⁸*Ibid.*, 491.   ¹⁹*Ibid.*, 490–91.
²⁰*Ibid.*, 494.   ²¹*Ibid.*

²²Lonergan explicitly affirms a dependence of the first stage (of research, interpretation, history and dialectics) on the second stage, dominated by conversion, *ibid.*, 501–2. The dependence outlined, however, seems to be one of *understanding* only, or, as he puts it, 'one has to understand the doctrine (stage 6) in order to write the history of it (stages 3 and 4)'. This level of dependence—while undoubted—is not that to which we here refer, namely a dependence entailing the horizon in which theology as inquiry (from stages 1 through 6) becomes possible, and thus one in which the whole conception of 'stages' as here presented is overthrown.

²³*Ibid.*, 490; see also *Th. N.C.*, 44 ff.

²⁴Augustine, 'Concerning the Teacher'; cf. also 'On Free Will', Book II, paragraphs 20 to 49; 'Of True Religion', paragraphs 53 to 57. The latter two works can be found in *Augustine: Earlier Writings* VI, E. tr. John H. S. Burleigh, Philadelphia 1953, 147–66 and 251–4.

²⁵Many of these same points are made by Michael Polanyi in his important book *Personal Knowledge*, New York 1964. For a more adequate defence of this interpretation of knowing, and of its relation to Lonergan's thought, cf. this writer's *Religion and the Scientific Future*, New York 1970, chapter II.

²⁶Cf. *Insight*, 348–50. Cf. also Polanyi, *op. cit.*, chapter VI, 'Intellectual Passions'.

²⁷Cf. for the discussion that follows in the text, *Insight*, 279–89, 319–22, 342–7.

²⁸Cf. for the discussion that follows in the text, *ibid.*, chapter XI, 329–47.

[29]See the definition of the *object* of theology: 'God and all things as ordered to him, and Christ, Head and members,' *Func. Sp.*, 10.

[30]A more complete and comprehensible discussion of this view of theological method has appeared in this writer's *Naming the Whirlwind: the Renewal of God Language*, Indianapolis 1969, Part II, chapter VI.

[31]See Lonergan's description of conversion as personal, involved, transformative and yet communal and historical, 'when passed on by the individual to other individuals', *Th. N.C.*, 43–4, and *Func. Sp.*, 490–91.

[32]Cf. Paul Ricoeur, *The Symbolism of Evil*, E. tr. Emerson Buchanan, New York 1967, 161–71, 348–57, in which he argues that fundamental religious symbols are given for our reflection rather than arising out of it. The same basic point is, of course, central to Paul Tillich's understanding of theology: theology is reflection on those symbols of the historic community through which the power of Being, and especially that of the New Being, is communicated to us. See Paul Tillich, *Theology of Culture*, New York 1959, chapter V, 'The Nature of Religious Language'; and his *Dynamics of Faith*, New York 1957, chapter III, 'Symbols of Faith'.

## The Reception of Church Councils

[1]Cf. *Councils and the Ecumenical Movement* (*Konzile und die Ökumenische Bewegung, Studien des Ökumenischen Rates*, 5) Geneva 1968, with the preface by Dr L. Vischer, who recalls New-Delhi 1961, Montreal 1963, Aarhus 1964, Oxford 1965, Badgastein (Austria) 1966, Bristol 1967. One should also refer to the symposium on 'The Reception of Chalcedon' in Geneva 1969, with the participation of several Catholic theologians: Fr Walter Burghardt, S.J., Brother M. J. van Parys (Chevetogne), Fr A. Grillmeier, S.J.

For the idea of 'reception' see Livius Stan, 'Über die Rezeption der Beschlüsse der ökumenischen Konzile seitens der Kirche,' in *Konzile und Ökumenische Bewegung*, 72–80; Werner Küppers, 'Rezeption, Prolegomena zu einer systematischen Überlegung,' *ibid.*, 81–104.

[2]Cf. Ferdinand Elsener, 'Rezeption', *Staatslexikon* VI, Freiburg in Bresgau 1961, 893–7.

[3]Cf. Hans Dombois, *Das Recht der Gnade.* Ökumenisches Kirchenrecht I, Witten 1961, 815–36: 'Grundvorgänge und Grundbegriffe des Kirchenrechts, 1 *traditio* und *receptio*'.

[4]Franz Wieacker has written most informatively about reception from the viewpoint of the jurist in his *Privat-Rechtsgeschichte der Neuzeit*, Göttingen 1967, which has an excellent bibliography. Cf. Georg Dahm, 'Zur Rezeption des römisch-italienischen Rechts', *Historische Zeitschrift* 167 (1943), 229–58; Paul Koschaker, *Europa und das Römische Recht*, Munich and Berlin 1958; H. Coing, 'Römisches Recht in Deutschland', *Ius Romanum Medii Aevi* VI, Milan 1964, 6.

[5]See F. Elsener (note 2 above), *loc. cit.*, 895.

[6]See F. Wieacker, *op cit.*, 116.    [7]*Ibid.*, p. 114, note 45.

[8]*Ibid.*    [9]*Ibid.*, 127.    [10]*Ibid.*, 132.

[11]*Ibid.*, 132; see also G. Dahm, *op. cit.*, *Historische Zeitschrift* 167 (1943), 240–52.

[12]F. Wieacker, *op. cit.*, p. 126, note 3.     [13]*Ibid.*, 126.

[14] *Ibid.*, 126–7.     [15]*Ibid.*, 130.

[16]*Ibid.*, 131; see also G. Dahm, *op. cit.*, *Historische Zeitschrift* 167 (1943), 242–3.

[17]F. Wieacker, *op. cit.*, 69.     [18]*Ibid.*, 143 ff.     [19]*Func. Sp.*, 40.

[20]See *Collection*, 252–67.     [21]*Ibid.*, 255–6.     [22]*Ibid.*, 264–6.

[23]See *Func. Sp.*, 488–91.

[24]Cf. my article on the subject, 'Konzil und Rezeption, Methodische Bemerkungen zu einem Thema der ökumenischen Diskussion der Gegenwart', *Theologie und Philosophie* XLV, 3 (1970), 321–52.

## Protestant Problems with Lonergan on Development of Dogma

[1]See *Func. Sp.*, 487–8.

[2]*Die Bekenntnisschriften der evangelisch-lutherischen Kirche*, Göttingen 1959; E. T.: T. G. Tappert (ed.), *The Book of Concord*, Philadelphia 1959. A good example of what I am calling a 'catholic' reading of the Reformation by a Lutheran scholar is J. Pelikan, *Obedient Rebels*, New York 1964.

[3]See Lonergan's treatment of Dewart's *The Future of Belief* in 'The Dehellenization of Dogma', *Theological Studies*, 28 (1967), 336–51.

[4]'Introduction to the Old Testament', *Works of Martin Luther* VI, Philadelphia 1932, 368.

[5]For a fuller, though somewhat different treatment of these criteria see my essay, 'The Problem of Doctrinal Development and Contemporary Protestant Theology', *Concilium*, XXI: *Man as Man and Believer*, New York 1966, 133–49.

[6]*Collection*, 68–83.

[7]This characterisation of Lonergan's proposal is arrived at chiefly on the basis of his essays, 'Theology and Understanding', and 'Christ as Subject: A Reply', both in *Collection*, pp. 121–41 and 164–97, together with spot-checking of passages in *De Deo Trino* and *De Constitutione Christi ontologica et psychologica*, Rome 1961. I was also helped by Edward M. MacKinnon, 'Understanding According to Bernard J. F. Lonergan', *The Thomist*, 28 (1964), especially pp. 363–72 and 488–501, and his 'Cognitional Analysis and the Philosophy of Science', as well as by R. L. Richard's essay, 'Contribution to a Theory of Doctrinal Development'. The latter two items are in F. E. Crowe (ed.), *Spirit as Inquiry: Studies in Honor of Bernard Lonergan, Continuum* (1964).

[8]There is, to be sure, a weak sense of 'cumulation' which is possible even in what I am here designating as a 'Protestant' view of development. The Church's reading of the scriptural testimony is aided by seeing how it has been interpreted in other periods from different perspectives. This, however, does not allow for the kind of 'organic' growth illustrated, e.g., in the Marian development from virginity, through perpetual virginity and immaculate conception to the Assumption.

[9]MacKinnon, 'Cognitional Analysis and the Philosophy of Science', *op. cit.*, 65.

[10]This, of course, does not deny that legitimate theological (though not dogmatisable) consequences might be derived from such hypotheses. An example of this might be the development of Thomistic Trinitarian theory

proposed by F. E. Crowe, 'Pull of the Future and Link with the Past: On the Need for Theological Method,' *Continuum*, 7 (1969), 30–49.

[11]E.g., *Th. M. F.*

[12]Richard, "Doctrinal Development', *op. cit.*, 223.

[13]*Ibid.*, 216.

[14]I owe this term to A. Anselm, 'Doctrinal Development and Dialectic', *Continuum*, 6 (1968), 3–23 *passim*.

[15]It is considerations of this kind which make a Protestant theologian reluctant to apply the term 'inerrant' to any dogma even when he considers it theologically impossible for that dogma to be mistaken in the sense that it did not rightly exclude what it excluded (e.g., Arianism by Nicea).

[16]'The Dehellenization of Dogma', *op. cit.*, 344.

[17]*Ibid.*, 346.

[18]*Ibid.*, 347. The passage I have paraphrased, reads as follows: 'Does Dewart's Christian . . . in the part about Jesus Christ . . . observe two sections, a first containing divine predicates, and a second containing human predicates? Next, to put the question put by Cyril to Nestorius, does he accept the two series of predicates as attributes of *one and the same* Jesus Christ? If he does, he acknowledges what is meant by one hypostasis . . . Again, does he acknowledge in the one and the same Jesus Christ both divine attributes and human attributes? If he acknowledges both, he accepts what is meant by the two natures.'

[19]*Ibid.*, 345.     [20]*Ibid.*

[21]I have in mind here the invasion of spirituality by Trinitarianism described by J. Jungmann, *Pastoral Liturgy*, New York 1962, 1–63, especially the formulation on p. 34.

## History as the Word of God

[1]See P. McShane, S.J., 'Bible, Meaning, Metaphysics', *The Month*, 39 (1968), 26.

[2]See *Collection*, 223.

[3]See F. Crowe, S. J., 'The Development of Doctrine', *The American Ecclesiastical Review* CLIX (1968), 243.

[4]*Ibid.*

[5]See F. Crowe, S.J., 'Development of Doctrine and the Ecumenical Problem', *Theological Studies*, 23 (1962), 40.

[6]See P. McShane, *art. cit.*, 21.

[7]See James Connolly, *Human History and the Word of God*, New York 1965, 159–74.

[8]See F. Crowe, 'Development of Doctrine and the Ecumenical Problem', 40–42.

[9]See *Collection*, 86.     [10]*Ibid.*, 85.

[11]F. Crowe, 'The Development of Doctrine', 243.

[12]See *Collection*, 249.     [13]*Ibid.*

## Questioning, Presentiment, and Intuition in the Theological Thought-Process

[1]Cf. *Was ist Metaphysik?* 5. Auflage, Frankfurt am Main 1949, 26.

*Notes*

²*Sein und Zeit, Jahrbuch für Philosophie und phänomenologische, Forschung VIII*, Halle 1927, ¶2.

³'Wissenschaft und Besinnung', *Vorträge und Aufsätze*, Pfüllingen 1944, 68.

⁴*Sein und Zeit*, ¶ 9.    ⁵Cf. *Insight*, 284.

⁶See note 1 above; see also the second chapter 'Der persönliche Gott', of my book *Wirklichkeit und Glaube* II: *Der personale Glaube*, Zürich-Göttingen, 1969.

⁷M. Buber, 'Zwiesprache', *Werke 1*, Munich 1962, 188f.

### Theological Method on the Scripture as Source

¹*D.D.T. II*: Pars Systematica, 43–53.

²a. There are statements about how to use Scripture in theology in 'The Assumption in Theology', *Collection*, pp. 70, 72, 73–5, 81, 83. In *De Constitutione Christi Ontologica et Psychologica* (Rome 1961³) pp. 42–4, 49–53, 57f., the *verum divinitus revelatum* is discussed as a starting place for theological reflection, but the term as used there does not refer directly to Scripture, but to points 'proclaimed in Catholic dogma and commonly accepted among theologians' (p. 57f.). *Divinarum Personarum* (Rome, 1959²) also used 'verum divinitus revelatum' for standard dogmatic propositions, whether or not they are found stated in Scripture: cf. pp. 8, 17–19, 44, 48, 53f. In *De Deo Trino*, Pars Analytica, 'divinitus revelata' again is used for more than Scripture—see pp. 5, 9, 10 (note 6), 11f., 112, 158f., 194, 250, 300f. Cf. 'Theology and Understanding', *Collection*, pp. 128, 131, 134f. for more apparent emphasis on dogmatic norms of interpretation.

There are methodological comments on the use of Scripture in *D.V.I.* in Thesis 1, pp. 2, 3, 17f., 21, 23–28, 37, 54; in later theses, cf. Thesis 11, pp. 314, 316f.; Thesis 12, pp. 389, 394f., 410f., 445–7, 558, 562f., 589; in *D.D.T.* I: Pars Dogmatica cf. (besides material already handled in Pars Analytica) pp. 6–8, 10, 12–15, 19ff., 22f., 25–6, 140–1, 153, 228ff., 235; in *D.D.T.* II: Pars Systematica cf. (besides material already handled in *Divinarum Personarum* 1959) pp. 8, 21f., 32, 46, 53. Cf. also his 'De Argumento Theologico ex Sacra Scriptura', pp. 1–4; 'De Methodo Theologiae', pp. 48–60; 'De Intellectu et Methodo', pp. 54, 64–8; 'Theology in its New Context', pp. 37–41; 'Canon Law Seminar', pp. 2, 6, 7, 9 (in MS.; Bibliography 111); 'The Absence of God in Modern Thought', pp. 11f., 14 (in Bibliography 120).

b. The amount of actual quotation from Scripture in Lonergan's published writings is surprisingly small until one reflects seriously on the implications of functional specialisation. There are no quotes from sacred Scripture in *De Constitutione Christi Ontologica et Psychologica*, in the *Gratia Operans* articles, the *Verbum* articles, in the smaller treatises and notes *De Ente Supernaturali*, 'De Notione Sacrificii', 'De scientia et voluntate Dei', 'Analysis fidei', 'De ratione convenientiae . . .' (with its entire sketch of Incarnation, redemption, theology of history, etc.). A few incidental citations of Scripture occur in 'Finality, Love and Marriage' (*Collection*, pp. 16–53), and 'The Assumption in Theology' has a few quotes.

In *Divinarum Personarum*, the first quote from Scripture occurs on p. 175. More follow on pp. 184, 201, 216f., 223–38. In *D.D.T.*, Pars Analytica the first 'argument from the Scriptures' appears on pp. 123–8. More follow on pp. 202–4, 250–61, 284ff. *D.V.I.* uses Scripture heavily in Thesis 1 but after that only in scattered instances (pp. 293, 317, 384–7, 390, 394f., 410ff., 416f., 424f.) until heavy use appears again in Theses 15 and 17.

[3]See *De Constitutione Christi*, 6, 10; *D.D.T.* I, 18; *D.D.T.* II, 5; 'De Methodo Theologiae', 24; 'De Intellectu et Methodo', 1.

[4]*Insight*, 747f.

[5]Cf. the references in the first part (a) of note 2 above. Most of them concern directly the relation of the magisterium and/or the dogmatic-systematic theologian to the use of Scripture.

[6]*Insight*, 732.    [7]*Ibid.*, 729f.    [8]*Ibid.*, 698; 720.    [9]*Ibid.*, 729f.

[10]*Ibid.*, 697.    [11]*Ibid.*, 721.    [12]*Loc. cit.*    [13]*Loc. cit.*

[14]*Ibid.*, 392; cf. 577f.    [15]*Ibid.*, 696.

[16]The section on human development closes with the reflection that '. . . within this metaphysical context it has been found possible, I believe, to offer a single integrated view that finds its point of departure in classical method yet embraces biology, the psychology of behaviour and depth psychology, existentialist reflection upon man, and fundamental elements in the theory of individual and social history, of morals and asceticism, of education and religion' (*ibid.*, 479).

[17]They are new and higher habitual orderings of man's knowing, willing, and acting, but they are more God's work than man's own. Man sees the need of them, wants them, consents to them, but they are not merely the products of his own knowing, willing and acting. The products of his own knowing, willing and acting constituted the problem; they cannot of themselves constitute the solution. These elements of the solution must come from elsewhere —they 'do not arise from nature' (p. 697). They are in some sense 'supernatural' (p. 697).

[18]*Insight*, 697; 687; 720.    [19]*Ibid.*, 696f.; 719.    [20]*Ibid.*, 721.

[21]*Ibid.*, 719–21.

[22]Symbol: an image as 'linked simply with the paradoxical known unknown'; Sign: an image as 'linked with some interpretation that offers to indicate the import of the image' (*Insight*, 533).

[23]On the name 'mysteries' which Lonergan gives to these, cf. his comment: '. . . if that is an ambiguous name, if to some it recalls Eleusis and Samothrace and to others the centuries in which the sayings and deeds of Jesus were the object of preaching and of reverent contemplation, still that very ambiguity is extremely relevant to our topic' (*Insight*, 547). Cf. note 33 below.

[24]Cf. especially chapters VI and VII.    [25]*Ibid.*, 467–79.

[26]This need was prepared for earlier; cf. *Insight*, 181–203; 242–4; 467–79.

[27]*Ibid.*, 723.    [28]*Loc. cit.*    [29]*Ibid.*, 724.    [30]*Loc. cit.*    [31]*Loc. cit.*

[32]Cf. *Insight*, 724: '. . . a world order in which the problem of evil is not suppressed but transcended.' And cf. Lonergan's explicit spelling out of this in the 'law of the cross', in Thesis 17, *D.V.I.*, especially pp. 571–6: 'mortis transformatio'; 'peccatorum stipendia tam socialia quam individualia sustineant, et sustinentes in occasionem maioris virtutis cum Christo transmutent. Hoc enim est quod apostolus praecepit: Noli vinci a malo, sed vince in bono malum (*Rom* 12; 21)' (p. 575f.). Cf. also 'Canon Law Seminar' (Bibliography 111), p. 9f.

³³Cf. 'De ratione convenientiae', p. 8f., especially: 'Latius dicitur idem nomen (mysterium) cum in recitatione coronae marianae vel in exercitiis spiritualibus meditamur super mysteria vitae D.N.J.C. Jam vero mysteria eiusmodi late dicta in primis per repraesentationes sensibiles innotescunt, deinde ea significant quae iam intellectu perspeximus, tertio ad pleniorem intelligentiam invitant, quarto affectus, emotiones, sentimenta commovent, erudiunt, confortant. Quae omnia quanti sint momenti ex eo elucet quod sicut omne quod ratione decernimus et voluntate eligimus eo promptius et facilius in actiones externas procedit quo magis parata est pars sensibilis ad imagines et affectus convenientes evocandos' (p. 8).

³⁴*Gal.* 3:1.    ³⁵Cf. note 2 above.    ³⁶See *Insight*, 562f.

³⁷*Ibid.*, 564ff.    ³⁸*Ibid.*, chapter XV, especially pp. 431-7; 483-7.

³⁹The unchangeable pattern of operations of the human mind is a necessary presupposition. The supposition has nothing to do with possibilities of evolution or devolution but with grasping the problem of communication as it presents itself. The minds with which in fact we are concerned to communicate are minds which have affirmed something because they have understood something and judged it to be true and to be worth trying to communicate. As for other minds which are not trying to communicate with us or which are trying to communicate that about which they have understood nothing and have no position as to whether it is so or not, such minds are not the ones with which we are here concerned in the problem of communication.

⁴⁰See *Insight*, 569.    ⁴¹*Ibid.*, 698; 209-11; 121-8.

⁴²The role of context as well as content is described in *Insight*, p. 580f.; 578; 568-73. More prominently, and using the term 'basic context' it appears in the notes 'Hermeneutics' (Bibliography, 90), p. 14f.

⁴³This is completely typical of Lonergan's technique: envision as clearly as possible the goals for which one is implicitly striving; prune from one's explicit conception of these goals all which is unrealistic, contradictory, impossible; point in the direction of concrete fulfilment; accept the reality of human failure; and face the fact of the minimal progress towards the goal made up to the present. Thus his various 'methods' are rarely recipes: 'do this, do that, then finish up as follows.' Knowledge of what concrete steps to take will arise by trial and error in working with the concrete materials of the given science—here, of exegesis (lower-blade work: cf. *Insight*, p. 577f.).

It is important to notice how severely and soberly Lonergan limits the results attainable by the scientific hermeneutics he describes: pp. 569-71 indicate some of the non-intellectual components of human predication which cannot be scientifically reproduced; pp. 579ff. make it clear he is explaining only the upper blade of method; pp. 590-4 list many more elements which must be left untouched as the 'residue' of scientific hermeneutics: earlier abandoned or transcended positions of the author, unknown influences upon him, the imperfection of the tools of expression he had available, the automatisms which appear in actual expression, the millions of combinations of accidents that have brought just these documents in just these conditions into our hands, etc. etc. *A fortiori* and in marked contrast to what is often presented as 'the Catholic position on hermeneutics'—the fuller sense, *sensus plenior*—

Lonergan's method rules out from the beginning any attempt to solve problems by reading the mind of God.

⁴⁴Cf. e.g., *Insight*, 483, 691, etc.

⁴⁵Here and in what follows, 'dogmatic theology' will be used in the technical sense established in *D.D.T.* I, pp. 8–14. There it is carefully distinguished from systematic and from positive theology: 'Positive . . . places only the questions which arise from the evidence, wants only the intelligibility which can be seen in the evidence, and corrects and increases its understanding only by means of new evidence or by more careful examination of the evidence it has . . . It does not pass over the uncertain, the obscure, the exceptional in order to concentrate on the certain, the clear and the ordinary. Rather it gives greater attention to those points which show need of clarification. Its end is that the sense, the mind, the teaching of any author being studied should some day be brought to light in all its parts, according to all its aspects—some day, not right now. And if, as the skill of investigators grows and enough time passes by and if almost innumerable studies should be made so that finally all the authors of some one past age would come to be known thoroughly, then indeed the particular spirit and almost the living image of that culture would seem to be reconstituted before our eyes. But the positive theologian wants that kind of overall view of the whole thing only if it arises from an intimate knowledge of all the individual facts' pp. 8f. (Translation mine.) On pp. 10ff. every one of the points just given is denied of the *dogmatic* theologian. The dogmatic theologian says: 'Right *now* faith is most certain; the objects of faith have already been defined by the Church; the definitions have already been drawn from the sources with the assistance of the holy Spirit. But what has already been done can hardly be said to be possible only in some very remote future' p. 13. (Translation mine.) He seeks what is 'commune, definitum, cohaerens, certum' (p. 14). He wants to practise 'theology's most noble task'; namely that of showing 'how the doctrine defined by the Church is contained in the sources in that same sense in which it is defined' (p. 14; cf. *Humani Generis*, DB 2314; DS 3886; cf. note 2a above). It is the right to exist of dogmatic theology, taken in this precise sense, that needs explanation.

⁴⁶See *Insight*, 721.      ⁴⁷*Ibid.*, 693; 697; 623f.; 627–33.

⁴⁸Cf. note 44 above. And compare further developments in the article 'Functional Specialties in Theology'.

⁴⁹Cf. what he writes in *D.D.T.* II about theology not judging '*an* sit' but only '*quid* sit'; aiming at understanding of the faith, not at assent (p. 12) and 'secundum se neque vera est neque falsa' (p. 19).

⁵⁰Cf. *Func. Sp.*, 492, 499.

⁵¹This insight is at the heart of much of *De Deo Trino* I: Pars Dogmatica. It is explained in the section 'Doctrinae trinitariae evolutio' (pp. 104–112) under such page headings as 'Verum Dei verbum', 'Verbum Dei et dogma', 'Processus dialecticus'. It explains the otherwise difficult expression Lonergan favours: 'Verbum Dei qua verum' or 'Scriptura qua verum dicens', and especially the seemingly strange suggestion (*D.D.T.* I, p. 22): '. . . dogma arises from the revealed and handed on word of God in so far as that word is considered *as true*; therefore, in so far as one prescinds from all the other treasures contained in the word of God' ('. . . eatenus ex verbo Dei revelato

et tradito oritur dogma, quatenus ipsum verbum *qua verum* consideratur, quatenus ergo a caeteris omnibus divitiis in verbo Dei contentis praescinditur').

These statements would not be suggesting that the dogmatician objectively possesses some criterion others do not for separating true affirmations of Scripture from those which are not true; or for distinguishing which affirmations of Scripture are seriously intended and which are not. Nor need they deny that images, poetry, rhythm, sound etc. may, at least on occasion be the vehicles of the truth of the Scriptures and so thoroughly its vehicles that no proposition can possibly be abstracted from them which will express that truth apart from them. All that these statements need mean is that what our religion is about is the real world; what we believe, we believe as really so; what our Scriptures affirm, we take seriously and, if they seem to affirm contradictions, impossibilities, it must be because they have not been rightly understood or because they are speaking symbolically or of something different from what they seem, etc. The point is what he calls 'realismus dogmaticus' (*ibid.*, pp. 105ff.): the fact that because one accepts dogma, or because one accepts the Scriptures as the word of God, one finds oneself committed to the existence of a real world and the possibility of affirming something true about it. That commitment, added to the natural power of the inquiring open human mind, can make all the difference. (cf. also *Insight*, pp. 701, 721; *The Subject*, pp. 31–3). In *D.D.T.* I it becomes the starting place of the dialectic process which kept the believing community dissatisfied with every possible formulation for the Father-Son relationship that was proposed until in consubstantiality (as Lonergan explains it—cf. note 54 below), a sense that did not contain an implicit contradiction and was not a counterposition, was worked out.

⁵²'. . . the dynamism constitutive of our consciousness may be expressed in the imperatives: be intelligent, be reasonable, be responsible; and the imperatives are unrestricted—they regard every inquiry, every judgement, every decision and choice. Nor is the relevance of the imperative restricted to the world of human experience, to the *mundus aspectabilis*; we are open to God.' 'Existenz and Aggiornamento', *Collection*, p. 249.

Again, on the constant need to reflect on the authenticity or lack of authenticity of the religious tradition to which one belongs: '. . . devaluation, distortion, corruption may occur only in scattered individuals. But it may occur on a more massive scale, and then the words are repeated but the meaning is gone. The chair is still the chair of Moses, but it is occupied by the Scribes and Pharisees. The theology is still scholastic, but the scholasticism is decadent. The religious order still reads out the rules and studies the constitutions, but one doubts whether the home fires are still burning. The sacred name of science is still invoked, but one can ask with Edmund Husserl whether any significant scientific ideal remains, whether it has not been replaced by the conventions of a clique. Then the unauthenticity of individuals generates the unauthenticity of traditions. Then if the subject takes the tradition, as it exists, for his standard, he can do no more than authentically realise unauthenticity., 'Existenz and Aggiornamento', *Collection*, p. 246f.

And on the need to make one's own judgement in regard to the entire past as a central moment in theology: 'Research, then, interpretation, history, and dialectic reveal the religious situation. They mediate an encounter with persons witnessing to Christ. They challenge to a decision: in what manner or measure am I to carry the burden of continuity or to risk the initiative of change?' *Func. Sp.*, p. 494.

[53]Cf. the theologically transformed universal viewpoint in the description of *Insight*, pp. 680–2, and especially p. 739: '. . . it receives further determinations from our final chapters on transcendent knowledge. For general transcendent knowledge [—knowledge of the existence of God] is concerned with the ultimate condition of the possibility of the positions, and special transcendent knowledge [—knowledge that God is providing a solution to man's problem of evil, and what that solution is] is concerned with the *de facto* condition of the possibility of man's fidelity to the positions.'

The article 'Hermeneutics' explicitly adds that the range of interpretations must include 'conversion and its opposite' (cf. p. 13f., p. 7f.). For conversion and its opposite are the foundations of the basic orientations and attitudes which philosophy and theology try to express scientifically. Every text and every interpretation of every text are somehow expressions of basic orientations and attitudes which rest on conversion or refusal to convert. Conversion and its opposite are the foundations of the basic meaning of all texts, whether of authors, of interpreters, or of philosophers or theologians or methodologists.

I am also adding determinations suggested by 'Existenz and Aggiornamento' p. 248f.; 'Theology in its New Context', p. 44; and the lecture 'The Future of Christianity'.

[54]This purification extends even to defined dogmas. They are true only when they are correctly understood. Clearly, for instance, Christ is not truly God and man if by 'God' you mean a ghost and by 'man' a three-toed sloth. But even understanding by the individual terms of the proposition exactly what everyone else explicitly and consciously understands by them is not enough. 'Correctly understood' means affirming that which is so, and affirming it correctly and for all time, and the affirming is about 'ultimate truth'. This is the real intention of the framers of dogma; and so, although one party among the defining bishops may have taken a word in one sense and another party in another sense, still both intended to be making a statement about ultimate reality which would serve the Church for all time. They may not have attained the clarity or the distinctness they would have liked, but all parties knew what they wanted: they wanted the truth, and they were ready to submit any particular sense of their own to the truth in case a different sense from their own should be clearly defined.

Similarly, the truth is what the community accepted the dogmas as, when it made its act of faith after the Council. Of course it wanted to know what the defining Fathers had meant—but it accepted the definitions as true even before it knew for sure what they had had in mind: 'Whatever the Catholic Church believes and teaches', as the catechism Act of Faith puts it. And if they later hear differing interpretations of the decrees from Fathers who were present at the Council, they know both sides of a contradiction cannot be true; but something is true or nothing was defined. They do not settle the matter by an impossible historical reconstruction of exactly what was in the mind of each of the Fathers at the moment of voting for the definition, but by some technique of 'authentic interpretation'—either by an agreed upon official organ or by the simple fact of which among the differing possibilities of interpretation comes to prevail in the schools and then in the living Church. Or they conclude that, in spite of the words, nothing definite was defined in this matter—a surprisingly frequent conclusion in the fine print of the scholia or footnotes of scholastic manuals.

But similarly, when a defined dogma seems to contradict what a community later comes to know for sure on other grounds, the conclusion is again that nothing was defined or that the dogma has not been rightly understood, or something similar. For the true interpretation of a dogma within a community which assents to the dogma as an affirmation about reality, is the one which conforms with reality. Consequently a dogma 'correctly understood' is always one understood in a way coherent with the categories of being and of the mind, an understanding in the light of the theologically transformed universal viewpoint.

Lonergan practises this kind of purification, usually without pointing to the fact that he is doing so. (Whether it should be called 'reinterpretation' or not depends on how certain one can be of the exact sense the framers had in mind. Their intention was certainly to express the real. But did they actually think in counterpositions, or were they merely limited by the language available in their time? Who can say? Lonergan develops often the theme of how the original, creative genius is limited by the expressions available in his culture; so that a new idea often cannot find adequate expression in word until a generation or two has gone by in which it has had time to build a culture of its own by means of a living—though struggling—community).

For instance, Lonergan praises the excellence of Nicea's definition of the Father-Son relation. 'Consubstantial', he explains, is a technical term standing for the fact that 'the same things are predicated of the Son as of the Father, except that He is Father.' (*D.D.T.* I, pp. 75–87.) In this sense, the term 'consubstantial' implies no counterpositions, nor is it bogged down in images, nor does it attempt to reduce divine reality to categories of this world (cf. *Insight*, p. 734). It makes a true affirmation and nothing more.

This definition of consubstantial is moreover found in the writings of Athanasius defending Nicea, so there are grounds for taking it (even historically) as the real intention of the authors. But what a student learning his dogmatic theology from Lonergan's *De Deo Trino* might never notice is that Athanasius in writing about the Council also used many other explanations of what consubstantial meant, among them many of the classic images from the time before the Council. And more important still, in later theology as actually practised across the Church, Lonergan's refined, true sense of consubstantial has not played the prominent role one would expect of so precious a pearl. Most textbooks and treatises, books and articles, scientific as well as popular, tend to explain consubstantial without ever adverting explicitly to *this* meaning. Their explanations even as late as the twentieth century, involve counter-positions, impossible images, and possible but useless questions. Cf. for example *Sacrae Theologiae Summa* II (BAC Madrid 1952), 273f., 276 (¶ 345–55); cf. also the articles in the *Dictionnaire de Théologie Catholique*, 'Consubstantiel' (III, 1604–15); XV, 1654–7; 'Nicée'; 'Arianisme', I, 1795–6 includes long quote, for instance, from Athanasius, 'De Decretis' (P. G. XXV, 452) with no reference to this definition.

[55]Lonergan practises the same sort of purification in regard to the redemption (cf. *D.V.I.*, Theses 15 to 17; 'De ratione convenientiae'; 'Canon Law Seminar' and the references to *Insight* there). In brief, what he does is show that the various scriptural and traditional images used for Christ's salvific actions all find their 'intelligibilitas' in the 'lex crucis', which is therefore the 'essentia' of redemption. But the 'lex crucis' is nothing else than the Christian statement of how to transform evil which is heuristically anticipated by reason in chapter XX of *Insight*.

The old words and images were incoherent, often contradictory, projected bizarre notions of God and speculation on the mechanics of supernatural influence in this world. In Lonergan the words and images remain but they receive a meaning coherent with the universal viewpoint.

Again, is this reinterpretation or is this what (historically) the first Christians, the authors of the Scriptures, etc. actually thought of when they first used these images? A believer will say, they meant what God wanted to be a message for the ages—but that could only be what is true, what conforms to reality. Consequently, Lonergan has uncovered (at least so far as we can judge with present knowledge) their real meaning, even though they themselves would almost certainly not have been able to express it. A non-believer will see in the traditional words only many quaint images and peculiar world-views from another age; and in Lonergan a demythologising, rationalising reinterpretation which has chosen to put philosophy above religion and faith.

[56]The article 'Functional Specialties in Theology', conceiving all of theology as a dynamic unity (p. 497) with the parts 'intrinsically related to one another' as 'successive parts of one and the same process' (p. 486), maintains that theology's 'earlier parts are incomplete without the later' (p. 486), 'the later presuppose the earlier and complement them' (*ibid.,*). 'Functional specialisation distinguishes and separates successive stages in the process from data to results' (*ibid.*). The final stage is communications (p. 492). Research, dogmatic, systematic understanding are all *intermediate* stages. Such communication would, in one of its important aspects, coincide with 'the common-sense communication of common-sense meaning' discussed in the article 'Hermeneutics'. In the light of Part I of the present paper, one can see that Lonergan allows for its importance in religion; the fact that it plays no role in his discussion of 'dogmatic theology' is simply because dogmatic theology, as carefully defined and distinguished by him, has its own special problems in confrontation with Scripture and they are simply different problems: unity in diversity, the *prius scripturisticum* etc.

[57]*Insight*, 740.

[58]This may happen with little awareness or very great awareness of the conclusions reached in the various specialised branches of theology. How much will vary in individual cases and cultures. There will always be some influence, because not all people can hold back their specialised questions for ever, and once some begin to ask them, the rest are not likely to remain in completely naïve ignorance much longer.

At least the definitive dogmatic decisions of the Church and (hopefully) the most successful work of the speculative theologian will make themselves felt. For the reading, as reading in this community, must not violate definitively agreed upon norms within this community—in so far as these norms themselves are intelligently understood and reasonably affirmed. The definitive dogmatic decisions (in Catholicism) settle what the community definitively agrees upon. The systematic theologian looks after both: tries to sum up what is definitively agreed upon and tries to show how it may be intelligently understood and reasonably affirmed by a mind open to the possibilities of conversion, of the transcendent.

⁵⁹Cf. *Func. Sp.*, 496–8; 'Belief, Today's Issue', 12; 'De Methodo Theologiae', 15; *Th. M.F.* (MS. Bibliography, 122) 5; 'Absence of God in Modern Culture' (MS. 3, Bibliography, 120); etc.

⁶⁰The workers themselves, however, will not withdraw from the community to do their research. They continue to be believers and continue intelligently aware as scientists of the progress being made in other specialised branches of the interlocking structure which is theology. Cf. *D.D.T.* I—p. 8, note 5, commenting on the honest and independent research which is the proper method of the positive theologian: 'Do not confuse proper method with integral method. Proper method includes those things which make positive theology something distinct to be practised by itself. But the *integral* method of positive theology has to add besides those points that are common to dogmatic, systematic and positive theology—such things, namely, as that they proceed by the light of faith and with the teaching Church as leader and that they mutually enrich one another. So what we said above about the proper method of positive theology should not be taken in some exclusive sense. It is just that the points which pertain to the integral method are not unknown nor obscure, and hardly have to be repeated here where we are asking not about integration but about the prior differentiation'—*ne confundas propriam methodum cum methodo integra. Ad methodum propriam ea tantummodo pertinent quae theologiam positivam faciant et distinctam et seorsim exercendam. Sed eiusdem partis positivae methodus integra ea insuper addit quae partibus dogmaticae, systematicae, et positivae sint communia, ut scilicet luce fidei et Magisterio duce procedant mutuoque sibi opitulentur. Quae ergo supra de methodo propria dicuntur, sensu exclusivo minime sunt intelligenda. Quae autem integram methodum respiciant, neque ignota neque obscura sunt neque hic repetenda ubi non de integratione sed de priori differentiatione agitur.*

⁶¹Cf. note 51 above.

⁶²For example, Lonergan works out in *D.D.T.* I the real meaning of homoousion: 'Those things which are affirmed of the Father are affirmed of the Son, excepting that he is Father.' This is the 'content' of the Christian belief that Jesus is Son of God, this and no more. In *D.D.T.* II, using the psychological analogy to clarify (but not to explain or to add to this faith-affirmation) he comes finally to the true meaning of the scriptural statements that Jesus and the Spirit are sent to us, dwell with us, do certain things among us. Mythology disappears and true affirmation remains: the faith-affirmation that such and such transforming effects occur among men *as from God.* In *De Constitutione Christi* and *De Verbo Incarnato* the traditional as well as the scriptural statements are present about Christ's divinity, his special gifts of nature and of grace, etc.

18

But they are not used to ground theses conveying added information about him or how he came to be, or about the constitution of the universe which received him. The statements are kept to the essentials of the faith affirmation, attempts to 'explain' them are shown to be still-born; and finally the affirmations themselves are shown to be the necessary and adequate presuppositions (by way of the four causes—cf. Thesis 17, Praenotamen I, pp. 515–18, especially p. 518) of the Christian mystery of the redemption: that is, they are shown to be implications of our faith that the concrete solution that we believe in to the problem of evil is from God as God's gift.

The Christian mystery, the 'essence of the redemption', is the 'law of the cross'. It answers point for point to man's need for a solution to his problem of evil; and gives the true meaning of the figured statements of Scripture that Christ's death was a redemption, a sacrifice, a conquest, a vicarious satisfaction, an intercession, etc. etc. (cf. also Theses 15–16.)

Lonergan's thought on these things is perhaps most clearly revealed in the Scholion to Thesis 17: *De Causa Peccati*. The thesis itself had argued: Scripture teaches that death is the penalty of sin, but the devil together with Adam had been the origin of both the sin and the penalty (*Gen.* 2: 15—3: 19); by the envy of the devil death entered into the world (*Wis.* 2:24) etc. . . Scholion II on the cause of sin explains the surd of sin in metaphysical terms. But the explanation is very difficult, and so he closes it with a paragraph which begins as follows: 'I seem to hear someone or other saying that these points are too abstruse. Well, those who cannot understand arguments can be trained with the aid of stories. Let them therefore listen to the Scriptures teaching that sin and sin's penalties took its origin from the serpent (*Gen.* 3:1ff.) that by the envy of the devil death entered into the world (*Wis.* 2:24) . . . etc.' And he adds a little later: 'Of course it is true that one who reduces sin and the penalty of sin back to the serpent has not as yet arrived at the ultimate reason why. For it can be asked further why a good God created the serpent. However, there seem to be a good many who become mentally exhausted long before they arrive at the ultimate reason why. And for their sake it is a good thing to omit deeper matters and simply narrate things that are clearer. . .' (p. 543).

### Lonergan's Foundational Theology: an Interpretation and a Critique

[1]I have felt free to keep the footnotes to a bare minimum for this paper in the hope that readers will be familiar with the relevant sources in Lonergan's work and in the confidence that extensive verification for my interpretations can be found in my book, *The Achievement of Bernard Lonergan*, New York 1970. Indeed, the first two sections of the present paper represent slightly revised summaries of chapters 9 and 10 of that work.

[2]Lonergan's interpretations of the medieval period are to be found principally in his doctoral dissertation *Gratia Operans: A Study of the Speculative Development in the Writings of St Thomas of Aquin*, Rome 1940; cf. also, *Theological Studies*, 2 (1941), 289–324; 3 (1942), 69–88; 375–402; 533–78 and his *Verbum: Word and Idea in Aquinas*, London 1968; his interpretation of modern cognitive meaning is, of course, to be found in *Insight*.

[3]This formulation is Lonergan's own as it will appear in his *Method In Theology* in the section on transcendental method.

[4]The principal sources revealing this concern are *De intellectu et methodo*, Rome 1959; *De methodo theologiae*, Rome 1962, and the forthcoming *Method In Theology*.

[5]Cf. *Collection*, 240–51; 252–67; and *Th. N.C.*, 34–46.

[6]The formulation on method as 'basic pattern . . .' is Lonergan's own. The latter two interpretative questions are my own. For examples and textual verification of this section cf. chapter 10, *The Achievement of Bernard Lonergan*, *op. cit.*

[7]For the clearest published expression of this to date, cf. *Th. N.C.*

[8]On 'horizon', *inter alia*, cf. 'Metaphysics As Horizon', *Collection*, 202–20. For Lonergan's indication of the problematic posed by the relationship of 'religious conversion' and 'Christian conversion', cf. his talk for the American Academy of Religion (1969), *Faith and Beliefs*.

[9]I suggest that here is where Newman's influence upon Lonergan is most pronounced although Lonergan's formulation of judgement as a 'virtually unconditioned' is far more technical than Newman's 'illative sense'. Both, however, are committed to defend the 'doctrinal principle' as judgemental.

[10]For an example of Lonergan's own insistence on this possibility, cf. his article 'The Example of Gibson Winter', *Social Compass* (1970).

[11]That is, precisely in so far as it may allow a differentiated and disciplined (i.e. *functional*) manner of collaboration among the several participants in the theological task and of theologians with other disciplines.

[12]Cf. especially Lonergan's lecture *The Origins of Christian Realism*, Toronto 1961, and the introductory sections of his treatise *De Deo Trino I: Pars Dogmatica*.

[13]I do not wish to imply that Lonergan has taken or will take this position. Indeed, the argument implies that he could not without further work in 'dialectics' and 'foundations'.

[14]In other words, at least two presuppositions of a Christian foundational theology would need such critical defence: (1) the theistic thematisation of religious experience (given the explicit and implicit atheism of much of modernity and the 'atheistic' stance of some Eastern religions—both of which factors would presumably emerge in studies conducted on the level of 'dialectics') would demand explicitation; and (2) the Christological claim to uniqueness as the thematisation of Christian religious experience would demand justification (or, at the very least, a 'universalist' reinterpretation) within the context of a dialectical study of other religions. That Lonergan himself is not opposed to this need would seem to be implied by such recent lectures as *The Future of Christianity* at Holy Cross College, 1969 and *Faith and Beliefs*, *op. cit.* However it remains unclear to me whether the theistic and Christological presuppositions of a foundational theology will be thematised in Lonergan's own 'foundational theology' in *Method In Theology*.

[15]For example, Lonergan would now demand that any attempt at a Christology be a collaborative one as distinct from his own former work in *De Verbo Incarnato* (Rome 1960), which, to be sure, did attempt to

'collaborate' by employing the findings of Grillmeier, Lyonnet *et al* but not in a functionally collaborative manner.

[16]Lonergan's formulation can do so, to repeat, precisely by raising *the* question of the radical theology debate (viz. transcendence) only as a precisely formulated question emerging from the context already differentiated by the systematic, critical and methodological exigencies.

[17]On *Ipsum Intellegire* cf. especially *Verbum*, 183–91; on intelligible emanations cf. *D.D.T.* II: Pars Systematica, 70–74; 261–90.

[18]*Insight*, 634–86.

[19]More exactly, that there will be a more refined and expanded notion of symbol in *Method In Theology* than was the case in *Insight*.

[20]I have expanded on this interpretation of the radicality of historical consciousness for contemporary theology in a paper 'Why Orthodoxy in a Historically Conscious Age', for the American Catholic Theological Society (Detroit 1970)—to be published in 1970 proceedings.

[21]To be found in his unfortunately unpublished lecture on his 'natural theology' at the University of Chicago Divinity School, 1967.

[22]*Insight*, 688–93.

[23]Since at least two conditions (the adequate thematisation of 'moral' and 'religious' conversions) are not yet fulfilled, a 'virtually unconditioned' is not yet achieved.

[24]Not, of course, to imply that only such a critique can hold true but to recall that if the critique is from within a position it bears stronger weight.

[25]That is to say, it is precisely within the context of the thematisation of the prior three exigencies that the radical question of contemporary transcendence can and should be raised as the problematic of a contemporary foundational theology.

[26]It is important to emphasise that the factors cited are not meant to be exhaustive, e.g. the social dimensions of Lonergan's transcendental position would also require at least expanded treatment and possibly reformulation.

[27]In Lonergan's terms, finitude-historicity would demand explicitation of moral and religious conversion and not merely intellectual conversion. In my own terms, the adequate explicitation of 'religious conversion' would demand the critical justification of the theistic and Christological presuppositions of a Christian foundational theology in a more adequate manner than Lonergan has thus far provided.

[28]These expressions are not Lonergan's but more proper to phenomenology. In Lonergan's case, *Method In Theology* treats the questions involved in 'life-world' analysis (e.g. feeling, praxis, symbol) far more adequately than *Insight's* treatment of 'common sense' cf. especially chapters VI and VII). An adequate interpretation or critique of Lonergan's formulation would, of course, have to await the publication of *Method In Theology*.

[29]This problematic aspect of Lonergan's thought has been especially noted by Edward MacKinnon; see for example, 'The Transcendental Turn: Necessary But Not Sufficient', *Continuum* 6 (1968), 225–31.

[30]That is, in so far as Lonergan's position even if it does not explicitate 'Christian conversion' still remains within the traditional Christian theological circle 'fides quaerens intellectum; intellectus quaerens fidem'.

<sup>31</sup>Cf. Paul Ricoeur, *La Symbolique du Mal*, Paris 1960, 323–32.

<sup>32</sup>Cf. Schubert Ogden, *The Reality of God*, London 1965, 1–70.

<sup>33</sup>Each of these questions would admittedly demand extensive and critical interpretation and justification—a task which is, needless to say, not attempted here. Indeed even if their suggestiveness alone is adequately communicated, for the moment that may suffice. It is a relatively easy task to locate possible difficulties in a position as ambitious and masterful as Lonergan's. It is quite another task to advance a fully developed alternative position.

### Bernard Lonergan responds

<sup>1</sup>See his *The Mind of Mark*, Analecta Biblica, 38, Rome 1969.

<sup>2</sup>See *Gregorianum* 50 (1969), 485–505.

<sup>3</sup>See Yves Congar, *A History of Theology*, Garden City N.Y. 1968, 230 ff.

<sup>4</sup>Cf. L. Gilkey, *Naming the Whirlwind*, Indianapolis 1969, 40 ff.

<sup>5</sup>See *Theological Studies*, 2 (1941), 289–324; 3 (1942), 69–88; 375–402; 533–578. An edition in book form entitled *Grace and Freedom* has been prepared by J. Patout Burns, S.J.

<sup>6</sup>Cf. *Rom.* 5:5; K. Rahner, *The Dynamic Element in the Church*, London 1964, 132 ff.; O. Rabut, *L'expérience religieuse fondamentale*, Tournai 1969, especially p. 168. W. Johnston, *The Mysticism of the Cloud of Unknowing*, Tournai 1967.

<sup>7</sup>See *Detachment and the Writing of History*, Essays and Letters of Carl L. Becker, edited by Phil L. Snyder, Ithaca N.Y. 1958, especially p. 25. Also Charlotte Watkins Smith, *Carl Becker: On History & the Climate of Opinion*, Ithaca N.Y. 1956.

<sup>8</sup>See H. I. Marrou, *The Meaning of History*, Baltimore and Dublin 1966. See also his 'Comment comprendre le métier d'historien,' in *L'histoire et ses méthodes*, Encyclopédie de la Pléiade, XI, Paris 1961, 1465–1540.

<sup>9</sup>See H. G. Gadamer, *Wahrheit und Methode*, Tübingen 1960, 254 f., 260 f. The whole section, 250–90, is relevant.

<sup>10</sup>May I note here that the specialty, foundations, provides not the total foundation of theology, for that includes method in theology, but simply the foundation for doctrines, systematics, communications, inasmuch as these make explicit a personal or collective stand on disputed issues.